Survive the Savage Sea

Short Tales from Our Ocean Heritage

Robert Parsons

Also by Robert Parsons

Lost at Sea, Vol. I

Lost at Sea, Vol. II

Wake of the Schooners

Toll of the Sea

Vignettes of a Small Town
(Grand Bank, Newfoundland)

Survive the Savage Sea

Short Tales from Our Ocean Heritage

Robert Parsons

St. John's, Newfoundland
1998

We acknowledge the support of The Canada Council for the Arts for our publishing program.

We acknowledge the financial support of The Department of Canadian Heritage for our publishing program

Cover: David Peckford

∞ Printed on acid-free paper

First printing June 1998
Second printing July 1999
Third printing November 2000

Published by
CREATIVE BOOK PUBLISHING
a division of 10366 Newfoundland Limited
a Robinson-Blackmore Printing & Publishing associated company
P.O. Box 8660, St. John's, Newfoundland A1B 3T7

Printed in Canada by:
ROBINSON-BLACKMORE PRINTING & PUBLISHING

Canadian Cataloguing in Publication Data

Parsons, Robert Charles, 1944 –

Survive the savage sea

Includes bibliographical references and index

ISBN 1-895387-96-5

1. Shipwrecks — Newfoundland. I. Title.

FC2170.S5P372 1998 971.8 C98-950117-5
G525.P374 1998

Dedication

To Otto Kelland, a friend

and

Matthew 21:22 KJV

Table of Contents

Foreword -- xi

Acknowledgements -- xv

Chapter 1. S.S. *Sandbeach* Destroyed by an Explosion
Highlands, Heatherton, St. Fintan's,
Colliers, C. Bay -- 1

Chapter 2. *Ida Campbell*: Stranded on Wood's Island
Wood's Island, Bay of Islands -- 9

Chapter 3. Disappearance of *Francis Robie*
Wood's Island, Bay of Islands -- 13

Chapter 4. The Long Walk - *W.E. Morrissey*
Bellburns -- 17

Chapter 5. *Wimoda*: Crushed by Arctic Ice
Belle Isle, Cape Bauld -- 21

Chapter 6. *Armistice* Goes to Davey Jones' Locker
Englee -- 25

Chapter 7. Whatever Happened to *Stanley Parsons*?
Lush's Bight, Long Island -- 31

Chapter 8. *Alma*: Casualty of the Labrador Fleet
Triton, Winterton -- 39

Chapter 9. *Sidney Smith*: A World War One Victim
Twillingate -- 45

Chapter 10. *Dorothy Baird*, Holed by Her Own Spar
Fogo -- 51

Chapter 11. Wreck of *F. ancis P. Duke*
Fogo, Badger's Quay -- 55

Chapter 12. *Percy Wells* and Others "Lost at Sea"
Horwood -- 59

Chapter 13. *Rose M* off Fayal, Azores
Fogo, Norris Arm -- 65

Chapter 14. No Survivors on the *Mollie*
Carmanville, Grate's Cove -- 69

Chapter 15. *Mab*: Seven Days Adrift
Newtown, Portugal Cove South -- 73

Chapter 16. Last of her Kind, *Maxwell R. Corkum*
Badger's Quay, Valleyfield _____________ 77

Chapter 17. Seeking Shelter at Lumsden
Lumsden _______________________ 81

Chapter 18. Wreck of the *Majestic*
Wesleyville, Cabot Island ______________ 85

Chapter 19. Loss of the *Nerette*
Greenspond ______________________ 89

Chapter 20. *Athlete II* and *Tishy*: Wrecked on the Same Night
St. Brendan's, Shambler's Cove,
Bonavista Bay ____________________ 93

Chapter 21. Victim of a Storm: *Blue Blossom*
Dancing Cove, Bonavista, Brigus _________ 97

Chapter 22. Abandoning the *Cento*
Catalina, Bonavista _________________ 101

Chapter 23. Two Fine Vessels: *Revenue, Albert J. Lutz*
Catalina _______________________ 105

Chapter 24. Debris from the *Effie M* at Old Perlican
Trinity, Old Perlican, T. Bay ___________ 111

Chapter 25. Adrift: Fate of Ryan Brothers' Schooner *Sperry*
Trinity, T. Bay ____________________ 115

Chapter 26. Tragedy at Trinity
Trinity, T. Bay ____________________ 121

Chapter 27. Flares from the *Edward VII*
Random ________________________ 127

Chapter 28. "Gone from our Midst" *E.B. Phillips, C.A. Hubley*
Heart's Content, Heart's Delight, New Perlican_ 133

Chapter 29. Captain Ellis Janes' Story of *Catherine B*
Hant's Harbour ___________________ 137

Chapter 30. Tragedy at Burnt Point: *Warren M. Colp*
Silverdale, Burnt Point ______________ 143

Chapter 31. Long Voyage of the *Maggie Bell*
Carbonear, Freshwater, Perry's Cove _______ 149

Chapter 32. One of Newfoundland's Most Beautiful Ships
Carbonear, St. John's ________________ 155

Chapter 33. *Freedom*'s Crew Long Row to Barbados
Brigus ______ 159

Chapter 34. Tragedy in the Narrows
Lethbridge/Brooklyn, St. John's Narrows ______ 165

Chapter 35. *Phoebe*: Wrecked at St. John's Narrows
St. John's Narrows, Random Sound ______ 173

Chapter 36. *Red Gauntlet* Goes Down
St. John's ______ 177

Chapter 37. Abandonment of the *Ruby W*
St. John's ______ 181

Chapter 38. Disastrous Voyage of the *Kinsman*
St. John's ______ 185

Chapter 39. *Evelyn*: Lost with Crew (1924)
St. John's ______ 189

Chapter 40. Capt. Abe Kean's Ships: *Cecil, Jr., Little Stephano*
St. John's, Flower's Island ______ 193

Chapter 41. *Cape Freels* Burns
South east of St. John's ______ 199

Chapter 42. *Evelyn*: Fearless Men of Ferryland (1913)
Ferryland ______ 205

Chapter 43. No Survivors from the *President Coaker*
Cappahayden, Port Union, Catalina ______ 211

Chapter 44. *A.B. Barteau*'s Ordeal by Ice
off Cape Race ______ 219

Chapter 45. Loss of the *Fond Return*
Trepassey, Bay Bulls ______ 225

Chapter 46. S.S. *Tolsby*'s Wreck at Drook
Drook, Portugal Cove South, Trepassey Bay ______ 229

Chapter 47. *Jennie Barno* Disappears
Trepassey ______ 233

Chapter 48. S.S. *Morien* Finally Located
Placentia, St. Bride's ______ 237

Chapter 49. *Clintonia*'s Captain: Ordeal in Water and Fire
Placentia, St. John's ______ 243

Chapter 50. *Beatrice K*, Sunk by a Derelict
Red Island, Burin 247

Chapter 51. Nineteen Hour Struggle: *Joan Ellamae*
Burin

Chapter 52. Steamship Rescues Six
St. Lawrence, Burin 251

Chapter 53. *Ontario*: Death at Lawn
Lawn, St. Lawrence 261

Chapter 54. Two Fishermen of Fortune
Fortune 265

Chapter 55. *Workman*, Cut Down off Spain
Grand Bank, St. John's 269

Chapter 56. When Two Ships Collide: *Flirt*, *Marshall Frank*
Halifax, South Coast 275

Chapter 57. February Storms
off Newfoundland and Nova Scotia 283

Chapter 58. *Vogue*: One Ship and One Life
English Harbour West 289

Chapter 59. *Florence Swyers*, Victim of the Deeps
English Harbour West 295

Chapter 60. Fire on the *Jean and Mona*
Boxey, Connaigre Peninsula 299

Chapter 61. *Inez G* of Burgeo Capsizes
Burgeo 303

Chapter 62. Mission Boat Tragedy off West Point/Lapoile
Lapoile 309

Chapter 63. *Izetta*'s Wreck
McDougall's Gulch, Wreck House 313

Appendices 317

Sources 327

Vessel Index 331

Town Index 333

Foreword

In the course of researching and writing about ships and men of the South Coast I accumulated a file of about thirty or forty accounts of ships lost on other shores of Newfoundland — in Bonavista Bay, Conception Bay, the Avalon Peninsula, the North West Coast and so on. As I looked through these clippings and scraps of information, I realized they, combined with others I may locate, would form the basis for a collection of sea stories and marine mishaps. It would feature lesser known schooners, the small harbours scattered around our coast from which these ships sailed and, most importantly, the hardy crews — our Newfoundland forefathers who manned the schooners.

Many well-known ships have met their end on Newfoundland's coasts: *Truxton, Pollux, William Carson, Newfoundland, Caribou, Southern Cross, Waterwitch, Viking, Anglo Saxon* and *Ethie* to name a few. Much has been written about them and rightly so, for the wreck of these vessels involved heroic deeds performed in trying circumstances or the calamity would have resulted in greater loss of life. But the vessels in *Survive the Savage Sea* are more obscure and have not been documented to any great extent, yet the heroism or tragedy is no less intense.

Moreover, when I looked through the information available for *Survive the Savage Sea,* often it listed the crews of the work-horse schooners that plied our coast. And that was important to me; these hardy mariners — our toilers of the sea — helped form the basis of Newfoundland's seafaring history and their names must be recorded.

Less than two-three generations ago, our little ships passed over the horizon, were wrecked, abandoned, or disappeared from our ken. Sometimes a vessel obituary in the form of a short news article appeared in the *Daily News* or the *Evening Telegram* and with that good-bye, their day was done; their story gone. Occasionally, and especially when loss of life was involved, the tale was preserved by the local poet/singer.

It became my goal to try to flesh out each story beyond a brief newspaper account and to compile them under one cover.

Shipwrecks have been a fact of life and death as long as men have sailed the oceans. The marine disasters that have occurred around our province's shores since John Cabot's time have been many; just how many may never be known. Recently, late historian Keith Matthews and Captain Joe Prim estimated 10,000 to 15,000 vessels have been lost on or near Newfoundland and Labrador. Professor Thomas Nemec has focused on one area, the southern end of the Avalon Peninsula, and documented more than three hundred shipwrecks in that location. White's Newfoundland shipwreck map shows scores of ship losses which happened prior to 1903.

To be added to any compilation of wrecks are the hundreds of Newfoundland vessels abandoned at sea. *Survive the Savage Sea* documents several of these — often crews were rescued, but more tragically, the men and schooners are posted "Lost at Sea". And such stories tend to be briefer for there was no survivor to tell the tale.

Ours is an era when almost every part of our earth is within easy access. Even inhospitable environments like the ocean deeps or the Antarctic are accessible because of advanced technology. Telephone, television, computers, internet and global communications can bring distant countries and foreign cultures past and present into our living rooms.

Yet when the tall ships visit our island ports, Newfoundlanders tune out today's technologies and turn out in thousands to admire and to marvel. White-winged miracles these ships are and they move silently like dignified ghosts from a forgotten era drawing us like magnets to waterfronts and wharves.

No wonder, for the sea is still in our blood. There is scarcely a Newfoundlander today who can not trace his or her roots to a schooner owner, captain, seaman or bank fisherman. Newfoundland schooners and our forefathers who sailed them laid down the designs of settlement and the protocols of island trade that gave our rock-girt Newfoundland its present culture. We wish to see more of those masted mirrors that have helped shape our present and will influence our future.

More so now than a generation ago are we more wondrous of the ingenuity of our forefathers who, with few resources other than manual skills and traditional knowledge, built schooners all around our shores. Today, we want to know more of the builders and the seamen who sailed the treacherous highways with little safeguards beyond efficiency, natural instincts coupled with physical and mental toughness. Such men as these, our forbearers, we may never see again. We can only read about them, and then in tantalizing small amounts, and admire their character and courage.

This book takes us around the island clockwise beginning on the west coast and ending near Cape Ray. It covers a period roughly of one hundred years. Each story (of around one hundred thirty ships) within these covers is true; however, all are subject to the vagaries of human memory and fallibility of newspaper reporters.

As far as recording the sea-faring exploits of our ancestors is concerned, *Survive the Savage Sea* merely scratches the surface and leaves as much unsaid as said.

Acknowledgements

I would like to thank the following for their information, help and encouragement: Oakley Johnson, North Harbour; Jack Keeping, Neil Piercey, George Combden, Fortune; Roland Abbott, Musgrave Harbour; Gerald Hiscock, Rupert Morris, Trinity, Trinity Bay; Ron Maye, Lewisporte; William Acerman, Cupids; Ruth Gosse, Coley's Point South; Captain Michael Croke, Captain Edward "Ned" Kean, Newton Morgan, Peter Cook, Dan Pugh, Eva (Anstey) Martin, Patrick Duke, Frank Bennett, St. John's; Les Butler, Manuels; Leo Slaney, Spanish Room; William Lockyer, Peter P. Rogers, John Kelly, Marystown; Edith Burrage, New Perlican; Gertrude Pelley, Hant's Harbour; Fred Hancock, Manuels; Reg Collett, Baine Harbour; George S. Spencer, Hamilton; Mark Johnson, Arch Stead, Catalina; Les Buffett, Mount Pearl; Jack Hackett, Terrenceville; Winifred Flynn, Lanoraie, Quebec; Rev. Vernon Cluett, Robert Keeping, Dartmouth; Captain Alex Rodway, Ontario; Georgina Froats, Williamsburg, Ontario; Harold Simms, Norwell, Massachusetts; Grand Bank Librarian Mildred Watts, Southern Seamen's Museum Curator Gerald Crews, Stan Savoury, John Ben Anstey, Natasha Melendy, George Buffett, Calvin Coombs, Alex Hardy, Clayton Adams, Don Hollett, Dave Hatcher, John Wells, Gordon Weymouth, Fred Rogers, Grand Bank. Some of these men of the sea and gifted storytellers have since passed away.

I appreciate the help and co-operation of the staff at the Newfoundland Reference Section of the A.C. Hunter Library, and at the Marine Archives, Elizabeth Avenue, St. John's.

To those who loaned or supplied me with photographs of schooners/seamen, I am deeply grateful for the opportunity of re-producing them for this work. I have made every effort to identify rightful owners and to obtain proper permission to reproduce them. If any errors occur in this regard, in the information given, or in the citing of sources, please notify the author and efforts to correct them will be made in any subsequent editions.

William Chapman, Grand Bank, read over my early manuscript and gave perceptive advice. To my manuscript readers and editors, a thank you. Where the text runs smoothly and without obvious grammatical, historical, or geographical errors, it is entirely to their credit. The rougher edges are mine.

Chapter 1

S.S. Sandbeach Destroyed by an Explosion

Highlands, Heatherton, Fischells, Colliers

The wreck of His Majesty's Ship *Raleigh* on August 8, 1922, is an often-told story of shipwreck and drowning on Newfoundland's shores. Not so well-known is the disaster surrounding *Sandbeach*, a tug involved in the salvage of *Raleigh*'s remains in 1932. A Newfoundland seaman from Conception Bay played a final and fatal role.

Raleigh, a twelve-thousand ton cruiser in the British naval squadron, visited Corner Brook in August of 1922 and then proceeded to steam to the Labrador coast. As she travelled north through the Strait of Belle Isle, a combination of the fog, icebergs and faulty navigation put *Raleigh* on the rocks near the Point Amour lighthouse. At the time of her summer cruise, she carried between six and seven hundred men.

To get a lifeline to shore a number of her crew launched the ship's cutter, but it upset in the choppy waters throwing all occupants into the sea. Eleven drowned, but the survivors attached a rope from the stranded ship to the shore. Using a life raft pulled along the line the remaining crew reached shore.

Raleigh's crew salvaged several small and easily transported items from the wreck; then, she was left for residents of the area to take what they could. Local businesses and schooners salvaged larger and more valuable items, like copper, lead, fixtures and lifeboats. Some fishermen discovered several puncheons of rum in the ship's stores making the winter of 1922 a cheerful one.

In 1926 the vessel *Stanhill* carried a demolition team to Point Amour to complete the damage begun by the sea. When *Stanhill*'s work was completed and *Raleigh*'s remains were scattered on the seabed, she carried seven of *Raleigh*'s fifteen-inch guns to Halifax.

T.F.& M. Salvaging and Wrecking Company, whose agents were W.A. Murray of New York City, made one of the final attempts at large-scale salvage of H.M.S. *Raleigh*. It was an ill-prepared undertaking. The ship chartered to do the

Courtesy H. Stone Collection, Marine Archives

With her stern below waterline, H.M.S. *Raleigh*, (above) lies stranded and a rusting hulk at Point Amour in the Strait of Belle Isle. On September 16, 1889, thirty-three years previous to the loss of *Raleigh*, another of His Majestey's warships, *Lily*, was wrecked in Forteau Bay, not far from the site of *Raleigh*.

work was S.S. *Sandbeach*, based in Halifax. *Sandbeach* left Halifax on September 25, 1932, went directly to the wreck site, and prepared to gather salvage from the bottom and shoreline.

Built in Thompkins Cove, New York, S.S. *Sandbeach* was a wooden screw steamer of two hundred forty-eight ton, single decked, and measured one hundred nineteen feet long and 9.3 feet deep. She was owned by Rockaway White Sand Company and registered in New York.

Captain B.M. Moody of New Brunswick was in charge of the ship while Lieutenant J.A. Tardiff, representing the navy, was a British subject. Other crew members were: cook Andrew Berg, Saskatchewan; Rene and Antoine Bouchard, St. Francois, Quebec; chief engineer G.J. (Thomas) Shortt, Oscar Bennett, James McCall, G. Butt all of Halifax; Gus and Wilfred Sampson, Nova Scotia and John Costigan. Costigan, of Colliers, Conception Bay, was the lone Newfoundlander aboard. He had once been employed by the Bell Island Steamship Company and had been a crewman on *Pawnee*, the Conception Bay passenger/supply ferry that operated from Portugal Cove.

Salvage was great. Using divers, floating platforms and explosives, the professional wreckers aboard *Sandbeach* took a full load to Corner Brook, a stopover port for fuel as *Sandbeach* headed for Halifax and New York.

In early December, when *Sandbeach* arrived in Corner Brook, her owners were slapped with a court summons by the Newfoundland railway. Apparently the salvage company owed for coal, crew's wages and demurrage — money owned from failure to load or discharge on time. The case came before the Supreme Court in Admiralty in St. John's and, on an order from the court, *Sandbeach* was released.

Through a twist of fate, the proceedings of the brief court trial cost Captain Moody his life. Both he and R.S. Grant, who represented the Salvage Company, bought tickets at the St. John's railway station and were preparing to leave for Corner Brook. Lawyer R. Gushue, legal counsel for the company, suggested Grant stay over in case he was needed in any further proceedings. Captain Moody used his ticket in a fateful rendezvous with the S.S. *Sandbeach* awaiting at Corner Brook.

Those who recalled the steamship's departure from Corner Brook remembered her as very heavily laden, not only with material from the hulk of *Raleigh*, but from wrecking equipment and a considerable quantity of explosives.

At this point, the final tragic scene of the tale of *Sandbeach* changes to a small uninhabited stretch of shore, Little Friars Cove, about twelve miles west of Highlands and a hundred kilometres southwest of Corner Brook on Newfoundland's west coast. The date: December 5, 1932, and for a few days after that day, clues to a sea mystery had to be pieced together from debris and mutilated bodies.

Two men of the town of Highlands, John Flynn and Richard McEachern, who knew nothing of *Sandbeach* nor her activities, discovered a lifeboat and the body of a dead man on the beach in Little Friars Cove on Monday evening of December fifth. Two life belts were also found, one considerably blood stained. The dead body bore no scars and the men assumed the blood belonged to another seaman. They reported that the name on the lifeboat was "S.S. Sandbeach" and it had drifted in sometime Sunday night or Monday morning.

The seventeen-foot boat was bottom up in the landwash and the body nearby, face down on the sand. The dead man was around one hundred seventy-five pounds in weight, around thirty-five years of age and evidently had been in a hurry to leave the ship. He was dressed in an ordinary lounge suit with a white shirt, low shoes and rubbers. It seemed as if he had died on the shore.

One oar, but no food, was found in the lifeboat and it seemed as if others might have been in the lifeboat as the row-locks had been used. The grisly discovery was found in a gulch surrounded by towering cliffs and scarcely any beach. The nearest law authority, Constable Dawe at St. Fintan's who had been told of the gruesome find, ordered no one to touch the evidence despite the fact that a high tide or waves might wash the body out to sea.

News spread through the West Coast towns of Highlands, St. Fintan's, Maidstones and Heatherton, but no one knew of a missing ship nor of the identity of the seaman.

That same evening at seven o'clock another man's body was picked up at Fischells. He seemed about sixty years of age and the only identification items within his clothes were a knife, a key-wind watch and personal papers, one a letter addressed to Captain B.M. Moody. On December 9, it was determined the remains were those of Captain Moody and his body was sent to New Brunswick for burial.

From that evidence the ship and crew were soon positively identified. In the next days more proof that the S.S. *Sandbeach* and her crew had come to a quick and lethal end appeared at Heatherton, a small town a few miles northeast of Highlands: shattered wreckage found along the shore, broken parts of a wheel, pieces of decking and part of a cabin stranded near the shore. As well two more bodies with the marks of scalding apparently from steam on the arms and faces. Several lifebuoys also drifted in to the beaches.

In the following weeks the Newfoundland Justice Department initiated an enquiry headed by Magistrate O'Rielly of St. George's. By December 23, 1932, the report of the loss of *Sandbeach* concluded:

> "It is the opinion of the Court the *Sandbeach* was destroyed by an explosion. The shattered wreckage...point to the conclusion. In addition there were marks of scalding from steam on the corpses... but death was due from drowning." (Note: the more graphic details of mutilation have been deleted.)

Richard Grase, the supercargo of *S.S. Sandbeach*, who supervised the cargo and loading but had not sailed on the missing vessel, identified the ship, her cargo and the bodies. In his evidence Grase thought that the clothing indicated the

Courtesy of Calvin Cocmbs

.Produced by the Mission to Deep Sea Fishermen in England, copies of this painting (above) of the Gospel Ship hung in many homes, ships and institutions. It connected Bible verses and moral truths to the parts of a ship. Each sail had a word and an appropriate Bible quote; e.g. Destination, Eternity, Crew, Passengers. The quote for Time of Sailing is "Behold, Now is the Accepted Time."
The Mission to Deep Sea Fishermen sponsored Sir Wilfred Grenfell when he came to Northern Newfoundland and Labrador in 1892 as a young pioneer doctor.

men had left the ship in a hurry. Abrasions, cuts, scalds and broken bones signified that some of the crew had been struck with flying objects and steam.

According to Grase's testimony, the steamship had been carrying nine full cases and three broken cases of dynamite. This was stored near the engine room in the lazarette, or the afterpart of a ship's hold used for stores. No concrete proof could be established as to exactly where or when an explosion destroyed the S.S. *Sandbeach* and her crew.

The body found on the shore at Fischells was that of the captain; the two at Heatherton were Shortt and Sampson. The boat which drifted in at Little Friars Cove had contained the body of the cook, Andrew Berg. Presumably the body of Costigan, the Newfoundland sailor aboard *Sandbeach*, was not found.

At the enquiry, McEachern and Flynn, farmers of the Highlands, described the difficulty they had in recovering Berg's body and in getting it to St. George's. They enlisted the help of six other men.

On Wednesday, two days after discovery, using ropes they lifted Berg's remains up over a seven hundred-foot cliff, then tied the body in canvas and brought it on their shoulders to Paul's Gulch, a distance of eight miles. From there the corpse was transported by boat to the Highlands, then carried by horse and cart to St. Fintan's and finally put on a train for transportation to St. George's.

Their work took from Wednesday to Saturday with the most difficult section from Little Friars Cove to Paul's Gulch, a wild and remote section of the coast. They had to blaze and practically make a trail through virgin woods and brush sleeping in improvised shelters as they went.

Thus, after the enquiry report, the snippets of a sea disaster and bits of news surrounding the mysterious end of steamship *Sandbeach* faded from the Newfoundland papers. Today her remains, as well as the valuable fittings, brass, copper and salvage of His Majesty's Ship *Raleigh* lie somewhere on the bottom between Highlands and Fischells.

Chapter 2

Ida Campbell: Stranded on Wood's Island

Wood's Island, Bay of Islands

The year 1932 was almost at a close when the rocks around Wood's Island in the Bay of Islands on the west coast claimed another ship; a wreck that occurred few days after the loss of *Sandbeach*. The five crew of a little schooner, who had escaped to an uninhabited island when their vessel smashed on a rock, kept themselves alive and fashioned their own rescue.

Around four pm Monday, December 19, 1932, Captain James Watts left Corner Brook with supplies for McIvers. His schooner was *Ida Campbell* and his crew was James Brake and Fred Clarke. Also on board was E.A. Elliott, the manager of the local business of Clarke and Company.

On the way Watts stopped at the oil plant to load drums of fuel for the fishermen at Wood's Island. It was a beautiful evening and by seven pm *Ida Campbell* had docked at McIvers and discharged the cargo. Seeing the evening was clear and calm, Watts decided to make Wood's Island in order to discharge the fuel in time for the local fishermen to use in their next day's fishing.

On the way to Wood's Island, a gale sprang up from the southeast and Watts ran *Ida Campbell* down by the island. By this time the weather had deteriorated to a blinding snowstorm with a heavy sea running. On sighting a small island near the larger Wood's Island and realizing the storm had yet to reach its height, Captain Watts decided to anchor under the lee of the island until weather conditions improved.

From eleven pm until five am Tuesday morning, Watts and his crew lay under the lee of the island. When the wind dropped slightly, Watts prepared *Ida Campbell* for a safe harbour. He had all canvas double reefed.

No sooner was the anchor aboard than the fickle wind shifted to northwest and blew with redoubled force. Pinned as *Ida Campbell* was by the full fury of gale pushing her against the island, there was little doubt the schooner would be wrecked.

In less than two minutes she struck the rocks broadside on. Fortunately the dory was on the leeward side of the wrecked vessel. The crew jumped in, reached a rock and from the rock scrambled ashore. In less than ten minutes the wrecked schooner was broken up by the mountainous seas and disappeared completely.

Watts, Elliott, Clarke and Brake succeeded in making a signal fire in the hope of attracting the attention of people on Wood's Island. It was not seen.

The little island had no trees for shelter; the men had no axe and no ship's canvas had washed ashore to make a rough tent. The four men had no alternative but keep walking in order to combat the cold. A half dozen apples, a carrot, a turnip and an onion washed ashore and that represented the only food the four weary men had for their stay on the islet.

All the next day, Wednesday, *Ida Campbell*'s crew was held captive on the island by the raging seas. Eventually their sufferings from cold, hunger and thirst became so acute that it forced them to take a desperate chance to reach Wood's Island in the dory.

The bottom of the dory had been damaged on the rough ride to shore, but after crude repairs effected without the aid of tools, the men launched out. In a struggle in high seas in a leaky boat, *Ida Campbell*'s shipwrecked crew landed in Humber Cove on Wood's Island; then it was only a matter of time before they reached Wood's Island homes.

Chapter 3

Disappearance of Francis Robie

Wood's Island, Bay of Islands

Sixteen years after the wreck of *Ada Campbell*, Wood's Island became the centre of another marine misadventure, this one with more tragic results. On November 4, 1946, the auxiliary/sail vessel *Francis Robie* left Halifax to call at North Sydney to load coal. The thirty ton motor vessel was powered by two sixty horsepower engines and when the wind was right she could be sailed. *Francis Robie* had two masts with a foresail and a jib which could also push the little vessel along in fair weather.

North Sydney was to be the final stop en route to Wood's Island and the Wee Ball Fisheries located in Bay of Islands. *Francis Robie* was partly loaded with fishing equipment; the weather was fair and the vessel was well constructed. What could prevent Captain Charles Benoit from reaching his destination?

Francis Robie failed to report and no plausible explanation for her disappearance was acceptable. Winds were high, but nothing the vessel could not handle. No other ship reported a collision at sea and no wreckage was found along Newfoundland or Nova Scotian shores despite an extensive search. Missing were Captain Benoit, age fifty-one and married; engineer Jerry O'Connell, thirty-eight, married and father of five; seamen Michael O'Connell, twenty-nine, married, father of three and Frank Duffy, twenty-four and single.

In a November fourteenth edition of the *Evening Telegram*, the vessel was officially declared lost; she had been missing for ten days on a voyage normally completed in several hours.

Other Wood's Island Wrecks

On December 22, 1906, word came from the Bay of Islands that schooner *Mindora* was wrecked on Wood's Island. *Mindora* was eighty tons net and had been purchased two years previously by her Captain I.R. Parsons and James Butt. Captain Frank Carter chartered *Mindora* to carry green codfish and barrelled herring to Boston. *Mindora,* under the command of her owner Parsons, was towed out of harbour on Friday, December fifteenth, by *Potomac. Mindora* left with several other vessels, but when a short distance out of the bay, a storm of southeast wind and thick snow forced the schooner to return to port. While entering port in the blinding snowstorm, she struck on a shoal off the northern end of Wood's Island.

In the gale, *Mindora* heeled over. The cabin stove upset and caught the vessel afire. The crew barely had time to get into the boat before the vessel was in flames and saved little belongings. On Saturday *Mindora* drifted over to Lark Harbour and grounded on the north side just outside the harbour limits. A number of Lark Harbour men went out to salvage what they could and succeeded in bringing in her bowsprit, foremast and part of the mainmast.

Carranza, owned in Pushthrough by John Rowsell, was bound from North Sydney to Argentia in September 1930 when she was struck and split by lightning while sailing through an intense electrical storm. With her weight of coal she heeled over and sank, taking ten men with her: Captain Joshua Matthews of Grand Bank, cook John Bobbett of Bay de East, as well as eight fishermen from Garnish returning from Lunenburg, Samuel Moulton, Thomas White, Stephen

Grandy, Frank Legge, Joseph Grandy, Joseph Newport, Arch Adams and John C.M. Cluett.

Six — *Carranza* crewmen Alex "Sandy" Mullins, Nathan and Charles Roberts of Pushthrough, passenger/fishermen George Aaron Cluett, Thomas Cluett and Charles Fleming — survived by clambering into a dory that floated off *Carranza*'s deck and were rescued seventy hours later by the Jersey Harbour schooner *Vignette*, Captain John Buffett.

Eight years later Wood's Island became the final resting place for *Vignette*, Captain John Myles (the adopted son of John Buffett), when she stranded there on October 24, 1938.

10 DROWN IN VESSEL SPLIT BY LIGHTNING

Six Escape in Dory From Foundered Schooner Off Cape Breton—Drift 70 Hours.

64 IN SCOTTISH WRECK

Breeches Buoy Takes 40 From British Ship on Rocks and Surfboats Save Others.

Special to The New York Times.

SYDNEY, N. S., Sept. 23.—The schooner Carranza, bound to Argentina, N. F., with a cargo of coal, was struck by lightning off Scatary Island, on the Cape Breton coast, Thursday night, and foundered with ten of her passengers and crew. Six of those aboard were saved and were brought to North Sydney this morning by the schooner Vignette, which had picked them up off St. Pierre.

The vessel sailed on Thursday night from North Sydney and, according to one of the rescued sailors, had a good run, with all sails set, to within forty miles of Scatary, when a violent storm broke over the craft.

Thomas Cluett, one of the rescued passengers, stated that he saw smoke rising from the binnacle and simultaneously there came a terrific report. The vessel was smothered in a curtain of blinding light, her timbers cracked and sails ripped as she heeled over and sank. She had been struck amidships by a bolt of lightning which tore out her main mast and practically ripped her to bits.

Two Swamped at Last Moment.

Six of the passengers and crew scrambled into a dory, which was floating on the windward side, and were swept to sea. Mr. Cluett said that as the dory slid away he saw two of the passengers attempt to climb through the companionway, but they went down with the schooner. The dory drifted for seventy hours in a heavy sea before the survivors were picked up. They had no food or water during that time.

The passengers lost were Thomas White, Samuel Moulton, Stephen Grandy, Frank Legge, Joseph Grandy, Joseph Newport, Archie Adams and John C. M. Cluett, all Newfoundland fisherman who had been sailing out of Lunenburg during the Summer in the Grand Bank trade. They had been paid off before leaving the Nova Scotia port

Continued on Page Three.

This how the *New York Times* headlined one of the most unusual marine disasters in Newfoundland's seafaring history which eventually had a connection with Wood's Island.

Chapter 4

W.E. Morrissey — The Long Walk

Bellburns

In the first decade of the 1900s the Bay of Islands on Newfoundland's west coast was visited yearly by many foreign schooners. In some years up to seventy United States vessels, usually from Gloucester, Massachusetts, and Canadian vessels mostly from Nova Scotia pursued the lucrative herring stocks of Bay of Islands.

Often American schooners hired Newfoundland crews to help catch the herring or they bought the fish directly from West Coast fishermen. In 1908, for example, fifty-seven U.S. vessels bought over one hundred thousand barrels of cured or salt bulk herring from Newfoundland markets, located chiefly on the west coast. With all the traffic plying the routes in and around Bay of Islands, marine mishaps were bound to occur.

In 1911 the schooner *W.E. Morrissey* came to ruin near Bellburns, a small community located between Daniel's Harbour and Port Saunders on the western side of the Great Northern Peninsula. Her home port was Gloucester, a thriving United States city with modern conveniences including the various forms of land transportation, train, cable cars, horse and buggy. Boston, a bustling city near Gloucester, had the first underground subway system in 1897 and the famous

New York subway opened in 1904. In Bellburns, Newfoundland, as *W.E. Morrissey*'s crewmen discovered, finding conveyance was more difficult.

Trapped on a lee shore in adverse winds, the Gloucesterman *W.E. Morrissey* was bound to Bay of Islands or Bonne Bay for a cargo of herring on January 11, 1911. Drift ice prevented the vessel from swinging out to make headway and at two o'clock in the morning she struck a ledge near Bell Burne (as reported by Captain Daly) pounded in over it and was driven up onto a beach.

Daly and his crew of Henry Bustan, Leslie Nickerson, T. Perry and the cook scrambled ashore by climbing along the bowsprit which projected over the shore and jumping to the beach. Surviving the cold January night was first priority and since the schooner was full of water, it offered no refuge. With no houses in sight, the five Americans went into the woods, protected themselves with boughs as best they could and shivered until daylight. During the night Captain Daly's hands and feet were badly frozen; the cook suffered from a frost-bitten face.

Next morning a resident, who lived three-quarters of a mile away and had come down to view the wreck, escorted *W.E. Morrissey*'s crew back to the nearest house. To Captain Daly it seemed as if he were in the middle of nowhere without roads and a system of communication whereby he could contact help. He was anxious to find the quickest route home.

They were given directions to the nearest transportation centre. The nearest point to reach a railway and thus to get to a passenger steamer was at Birchy Cove, one hundred twelve miles away!

They were in desperate physical condition and were poorly clad to make such a journey. The captain and cook had suffered the most from frostbite and were in agony, but there was no other alternative. *Morrissey*'s crew began their arduous one hundred and twelve mile tramp, without snowshoes, through snow and over rough roads.

Courtesy Natasha Melendy

Rusted hulk of *Bernier* wrecked in 1963. While delivering coal at Red Bay, Labrador, *Bernier* blew a piston. The owner's father stayed aboard to care for the ship as she lay anchored in Red Bay harbour. Another ship manoeuvring around the vessel went aground on Saddle Island. *Bernier*, in the attempt to tow the stranded boat off, weakened or dislodged its moorings. That night a storm blew *Bernier* to her final resting place; a short distance from the Red Bay archaeological dig.

Not long into the journey, their rubber boots chaffed and blistered their feet and they pleaded with a man of the area to go the nearest store to buy moccasins. Daly and his men put the moccasins inside the rubbers and this gave them a modicum of comfort. When they finally reached Birchy Cove, they met Mr. Hall who was an agent for the Gorton-Pew Company, owners of *W.E. Morrissey*.

Hall advanced cash for any further expenses. The five shipwrecked Americans bought tickets for the train trip to Port aux Basques, secured a passage on the S.S. *Glencoe* to Nova Scotia.

It was February eighth when they reached Nova Scotia, almost a month after they lost their schooner. In Louisbourg they went to the American Consular General who arranged transportation to the United States.

Almost a year later Gorton-Pew, an American fish procuring business based in Massachusetts, lost another schooner, *Miranda* of Gloucester. On December 20, 1912, Captain Joe

Kean of the coastal steamer *Portia* reported blizzard conditions in Bonne Bay. Due to the high velocity of wind and driving snow, he was unable to reach port and had to return to Bonne Bay.

On his way down the coast, Kean also saw an American schooner stranded on the shoreline two miles east of Trout River. He thought the crew was safe as no signal or sign of life was seen by him or his crew. This was *Miranda,* which had been at Trout River collecting fish; in the southwest gale she had broken moorings, struck the rocks and was totally wrecked. *Miranda* had collected about two hundred fifty quintals of fish before her chains parted. Her American crew was safe in Trout River.

Chapter 5

Wimoda: Crushed by Arctic Ice

Belle Isle, Cape Bauld

Luck was with marooned sealers when the motor ship *Wimoda* was crushed by heavy pack ice. After the men left the ill-fated wooden ship, they erected improvised tents and spent the night of April 26, 1949, marooned on Arctic drift ice east of Belle Isle at the tip of the Great Northern Peninsula.

Prior to leaving the ship the crew took with them the ship-to-shore radio telephone and generator. Thus, they were able to keep the lines of communication open to three other sealing ships in the area: Motor Ships *Linda Mae, Terra Nova* and *Newfoundlander*. The latter ship was owned and under the command of Captain John H. Blackmore, who had the misfortune to lose a ship, bearing his name at the ice floes the previous year.

Because of ice conditions *Terra Nova,* situated approximately one mile north west of White Point on Belle Isle, wired her owners that she had been unable to respond to the plea for help from *Wimoda*'s captain Ben Andrews. *Terra Nova* reported she would be unable to reach the sinking sealer unless wind conditions changed; then she would try to reach to the east side of the island.

H.W. Dawe of Cupids, owners of *Wimoda,* also received a message late in the night of April 26 from Captain Fred Carter of *Linda Mae* saying that radio reports from *Wimoda*'s crew indicated they were well and fairly comfortable. Indications were that the sealer *Newfoundlander,* lying in open water, would be the first to reach the men.

Disaster fell upon *Wimoda* when rafting ice tore away the rudder and opened seams. As water poured in Captain Andrews gave the order to abandon ship. The final story of *Wimoda*'s wreck is best told from an examination of her logbook: she left Cupids on April thirteenth for her second trip to the ice. *Wimoda* made a good run northwards until she reached Cape Bauld where the craft encountered heavy ice.

Built at Trinity, Bonavista Bay, the motor vessel *Wimoda* was bought by Dawe's business in 1947; prior to that she had been operated by the Monroe Export Company. Her name was formed from the first two letters of the surnames of her original owners — **WI**nsor, **MO**nroe and **DA**vis. In 1943 Captain Arch Thornhill of Anderson's Cove (later Grand Bank) skippered *Wimoda* in relief of her regular captain. On *Wimoda*'s first voyage in 1949 she had a full load of seals. Each crewman cleared $327 and made another one hundred on the sale of seal flippers.

On her final voyage to the ice, log entries up to April 25 were mainly routine describing the search for seals. That day began stormy and with *Wimoda* jammed in ice. Captain Andrews wrote that it was the stormiest weather he had seen for many years. All the seals killed previously were stowed down which gave the sealer a catch of about seven hundred pelts.

A little after midnight the situation was more serious. The engineer reported to Andrews *Wimoda* was taking on water. A large pan of ice under the starboard quarter put the vessel under a list to the port until her rail was level with the water. Another small berg ripped away the rail and a portion of the stern; as well, the rudder and stern post were torn off.

With *Wimoda* filling with water, Captain Andrews gave orders to get the dories and supplies ready; then he told the crew to leave the vessel.

After the crew set up camp on an ice pan not far from their crushed ship, they saw the final death throes of *Wimoda*: slowly she twisted until her bow was below water and her stern thrown high into the air. Held in this grip she stayed suspended for forty-eight hours.

The deck cookhouse and stove which the men had removed from *Wimoda* was set up on a pan of ice and all canvas available was made into tents. The generator, lighting plant and ship-to-shore radio were salvaged and put to good use. Within a few hours Captain Andrews made contact with the other vessels in the area.

At one am on the 27th, the lights of *Newfoundlander* could be seen. Lightkeeper Roberts on Belle Isle had also put on the light and directed it towards the shipwrecked men. Five hours later the rescue ship, plugging through heavy ice, still had not reached the marooned men.

A little before seven am, Andrews gave the orders to leave everything on the ice and walk to *Newfoundlander*, about four

Courtesy Marine Archives, Captain Harry Stone collection.

Wimoda, (above) lost at the ice on April 27, 1949, seen here moored by the Irving Oil premises in Halifax harbour.

miles distant. Rough ice made the trek a difficult one, but within three hours they were at her side. All told *Wimoda*'s men were stranded on Arctic ice thirty-one hours. Fortunately the weather was exceptionally fine.

Captain Blackmore in *Newfoundlander*, which had crew of seventy-one and now with an extra twenty-six men aboard, stayed at the hunt for a week adding over a thousand seals to her catch. On May fourth, Blackmore bore up for home and arrived at Port Union the next day.

Several of *Wimoda*'s crew remained on board *Newfoundlander* as no arrangements to house them could be found. Those belonging to Bonavista and vicinity left on S.S. *Northern Ranger*. *Newfoundlander* also brought the body of Ambrose Butt of Pouch Cove who had been accidentally killed about three weeks previously aboard M.V. *Terra Nova*.

Wimoda was the fourth sealer victimized by rafting ice within two years: *J.H. Blackmore*, *Teazer* and *Monica Walters* — the latter two went down while sealing in the Gulf of St. Lawrence.

Courtesy of Ron Maye

The ninety-foot Willing Lass, owned and operated by Captain Harold Parsons of Springdale, was the last fishing schooner in Newfoundland. Early in the vessel's career Parsons fished with his father at Belle Isle at the tip of the Northern Peninsula. *Willing Lass* burned off Southern Labrador in the early 1990s.

Chapter 6

Armistice Goes to Davey Jones' Locker

Englee

By 1922 owners were lamenting the loss of their foreign-going fleet; especially the tern schooners employed in the European trade. In early January 1923, A.E. Hickman Company of St. John's, received word via a telegram from Lisbon, Portugal, that their tern schooner *Armistice* had gone down in the mid-Atlantic.

Armistice had been built in 1919 at Englee, a town on the eastern side of the Great Northern Peninsula, by J. Norris. According to local tradition, in the early 1850s four families inhabited Englee but most of the original settlers came between 1870 and 1900. French fishermen were active in the area in the 1860s and 1870s.

In the late 1880s the first fishing establishment was built and operated by Baxter Crocker and it was still operating the 1980s as John Reeves Limited. In 1940 Canada Bay Cold-Storage Company began a fresh salmon business in Englee. Today Englee's population stands at a little less than a thousand.

In the era of sail, adequate stands of timber gave rise to a small shipbuilding industry when schooners like *Armistice* were built. Netting one hundred ninety-eight ton and with an overall length of one hundred eight feet, *Armistice* was given a name that indicated the patriotic feelings of victory in World War One. Several schooners built in this era bore names like *WintheWar, Victory Chimes, Over the Top* and *Ricketts, V.C.*, the latter named in honour of Thomas Ricketts who had earned the Victoria Cross.

Armistice, under the command of Captain Jerry Petite of English Harbour West, left St. John's with a full cargo of fish bound for Seville, Spain. On December 6, 1921, Petite loaded salt and sailed for home. Born in Mose Ambrose, Petite was the son of Jeremiah Petite who had moved to English Harbour West from Mose Ambrose just after the turn of the century and established a salt-fish exporting business there. Around 1934 the Petites switched from the coasting and foreign-going voyages to bank fishing and had new vessels like *Ethel M. Petite* built.

Petite and his crew of six encountered the brunt of an early winter storm that lasted several days. On December 23, with his tern schooner sinking beneath him Petite hailed a passing ship and requested to be taken off.

Between 1917 and 1921 several large schooners destined for the foreign trade were constructed in Newfoundland in smaller communities like Englee, Marystown, Grand Bank, Glovertown, St. George's, Port Blandford, Charlottetown, Fortune, Burgeo, Placentia, Port Union and others. Unlike ships built on the American seaboard which used harder wood like oak and had copper fastenings, Newfoundland-built schooners were constructed with the softwoods — spruce and fir. John Parker in his book *Sails of the Maritimes* summarizes the Newfoundland shipbuilding trade:

> The schooners constructed during this period in Newfoundland were not of good quality and with a few exceptions did not last long. To repeat a few of the faults — they were built of unseasoned timber of poor grade, were too light in design and were insecurely fastened. On the other hand, quite a few were lost as a result of stranding, but this was the fault of navigators and not the construction of the vessel.

Terns launched in Newfoundland that lasted a year or less were: *Pauline Martin,* built in 1917 at Norris Arm, lost December 1918; *Nina L.C.*, built in 1918 at Port Union, lost on her maiden voyage; *General Knox*, built in 1919 at Marystown, lost on her maiden voyage; *Violet Buffett*, built in 1919 at Marystown, lost on her maiden voyage; *John E. Lake*, built in 1919 at Fortune, lost on her maiden voyage; *Neerod*, built in 1919, Norris Arm, lost December 1919; *Monchey*, launched in 1920 at Harbour Grace did not make it across the Atlantic on her first voyage.

Armistice lasted four years before Atlantic storms opened her seams; then, as was so often the case, the crew manned the hand pumps, but the pumps sometimes clogged with salt brine and could not handle the inflow of water. Captain Petite and his crew arrived back in Newfoundland sometime in January of 1923.

Courtesy Rev. Vernon Cluett

Misty Star, (above) on the builder's stocks in 1917 at Shelburne, Nova Scotia, was owned by Harvey and Company for their fish exporting interests at Belleoram. Three vessels were built around the same time for Harveys each with colourful, imaginative names —*Sparkling Glance*, *Sunset Glow* and *Misty Star*, at two hundred seventeen net ton, one hundred thirty-one feet long and fully rigged before launching. A stock of extra masts, spars and booms lie in the foreground.

Although constructed with the best of materials, reinforced knees, copper fastened and copper bottomed, *Misty Star* lasted less than three years. In 1920 she was stranded on the coast of Europe without loss of life.

But not all the news from the foreign-going fleet was as encouraging as the safe arrival of *Armistice*'s sailors. On June first, 1923 a schooner owned by James Baird interests of St. John's was presumed lost at sea with crew. *Herbert Warren* left St. John's in November 1922 for Seville with a cargo of fish.

James Baird Ltd. originated in 1873 when Scottish immigrant James Baird established a retail and wholesale business in Newfoundland devoted almost to the fishery and marine trade. Baird relocated to Water Street after two fires damaged his business. After the death of the founding father in 1915, the business continued and expanded into the foreign trade under the guidance of two sons.

It was the second time in less than four years *Herbert Warren* had been overdue for an extended period while on a voyage to Europe. In April/May of 1919, while under the command of Captain T. Janes, she had left Spain laden with salt. While the voyage eastward was made in good time, *Herbert Warren* encountered heavy ice off Newfoundland. With a crewmen posted on the bow keeping a constant lookout for bergs, she eventually made St. Pierre, discharged the salt and continued to St. John's.

On her fateful voyage in 1923, ships' agents knew *Herbert Warren* had reached Spain, discharged her cargo and early in the new year loaded three hundred ton of salt at Cadiz. On January 20, 1923, *Herbert Warren* left for Newfoundland.

No one had any doubt that the schooner was well-founded and capable of making her transatlantic voyage: she was fully provisioned and, in case her canvas was blown away in severe ocean storms, had an extra set of sails. A year previously *Herbert Warren* had undergone extensive repairs at Lunenburg including a re-built bottom. Total repairs exceeded nine thousand dollars and as a result Baird's schooner was upgraded and re-classed as a more capable vessel by Lloyd's insurance company. *Herbert Warren* had been formerly commanded by Captain Gerald Doyle who claimed she was a splendid sea boat and fast under sail.

After one hundred and thirty days with no report or sighting by another vessel, *Herbert Warren* was posted "Missing with Crew":

Capt. Axel Ringman age	35	of Sweden, resident of St. John's
mate Lawrence Hollihan	30	Wickford Street, St. John's, married
cook Edward Wakeham	30	Finn Street, married
seaman Thomas Power	22	Moore Street, single
E. Noseworthy	29	Harbour Grace, resident of St. John's
Timothy Walsh	24	Catalina
bosun Gus Johnson	42	of Norway, single

Lillian M. Richard, a well-known vessel along the eastern side of the Great Northern Peninsula, in White Bay, Green Bay and Notre Dame Bay, had a long career in Newfoundland. In the photo above she is tied on at Beaumont on Long Island. A cord of birch firewood is on the left and lobster pots are on the stagehead to the right.

Built in Nova Scotia in 1911, *Lillian M. Richard* was purchased by Patten and Forsey of Grand Bank in 1915. She fished out of that port for around twenty years under a number of captains — John Thornhill, Joe Grandy, Michael Augot, Hubert Grandy of Garnish and others. Eventually she was sold to the Hounsell family of White Bay and was skippered for a number of years by Steward Hounsell. In 1961 she was destroyed by fire.

Courtesy Ron Maye

Nina W. Corkum moored at Three Arms awaiting a shipment of salt-dry fish. Prip props, logs used for support columns in mines, in are stacked on the schooner's afterquarter. In the foreground several yaffles (armloads) of fish are spread on a wooden flake to dry.

Courtesy Ron Maye

Pleasure yacht Daydream, built by the Rideout shipbuilders in Three Arms, Green Bay, for Captain Wallace Batstone, after Batstone retired from his years at sea and had sold the *Freeman*.

The three arms — the fishing towns of Middle Arm, Three Arms and Western Arm — are a series of long, narrow indrafts in western Notre Dame Bay. In 1993 only Western Arm was populated (the town of Harry's Harbour). The fishing village of Three Arms, which first appeared in Newfoundland *Census* of 1845 with a population of twenty-nine, is today abandoned.

Chapter 7

Whatever Happened to the Stanley Parsons?

Lush's Bight, Long Island

The coastline of Newfoundland, some six thousand miles long, has been the site of hundreds of shipwrecks throughout the last three-four centuries. It can be said with some assurance that a high percentage of wrecks came in the era of the schooner, roughly 1870 to 1970. In this time frame practically every community had a schooner fleet relative to its size and each town felt the pangs of loss of life and suffering on the treacherous sea. One example of the many disappearances which touched the lives of practically every resident in a small Newfoundland outport was the loss of a vessel that operated out of Lush's Bight on Long Island, Notre Dame Bay.

The schooner *Stanley Parsons* left St. John's in the late evening of Monday, December 4, 1932, laden with freight for Notre Dame Bay —barrelled flour and sugar, vegetables, shop goods and general cargo for Twillingate, Springdale and Little Bay Islands. Captain Sidney Parsons, with a crew of five and one passenger, carried some freight for his small home port of Lush's Bight on the western end of Notre Dame Bay.

Generally the voyage from St. John's to Long Island or Little Bay Islands lasted between one to two weeks and was completed in stages or legs. The first stop was Catalina where crews would rest; then the next morning they sailed to Seldom on Fogo Island. The third leg was from Seldom to Herring Neck and Twillingate. On this leg cargo was discharged at various ports until schooners like *Stanley Parsons* reached Little Bay Islands.

By December 12, *Stanley Parsons* was overdue and her owners knew she had not reached Catalina nor Seldom. No debris of a shipwreck had been found nor had news of a shipping mishap been reported. As word of the overdue vessel reached other harbours in Bonavista Bay and Notre

Courtesy Ron Maye

Skippered by Lloyd Wiseman, the one hundred thirty-eight ton schooner *James Strong* (above) leaves Little Bay Islands for the Labrador fishery in July of 1952. Built at Little Bay Islands for Sid and Harold Wiseman, she was later registered to Strong's Limited and was the largest vessel in their fleet.

Samuel Hull began the construction of *James Strong*, but due to illness he was forced to stop and the vessel was finished by Robert Wiseman. In the 1960-70s she sank or was beached in Little Bay Islands harbour and her bones rest in the bottom silt today. One of her last masters was James Locke.

To the right of *James Strong* is a section of the community of Little Bay Islands; behind the schooner looms Black Rock.

Dame Bay, seamen and captains who had often sailed the route taken by *Stanley Parsons* speculated on her fate.

On December 13 and again on December 15, St. John's papers described a storm as one of the worst to hit the northeast coast in many years. Vessels bound north had felt the brunt of the storm: *Nina Beatrice* of Catalina was delayed at Brigus and *Spitfire* arrived at King's Cove reporting high winds with snow. *Maneco,* a government public service vessel operating on the Bell Island Tickle, could not get the mail and passengers through for the first time in her career.

Yet, veteran seamen assumed *Stanley Parsons* was not driven off to sea by the heavy weather of mid-December as no other vessels plying the route in the same time period had gone through that ordeal. Nevertheless, as a precaution, messages were sent to transatlantic steamers to ask them to be on the lookout for the missing schooner.

When other seamen discussed the possible route of *Stanley Parsons,* they surmised she may have struck the Old Harrys, a renowned navigational hazard (another shoal called Old Harry is found off Cape Spear, near St. John's). Located about three quarters of a mile off Cape Bonavista, the Old Harrys are two shoals about three quarters of a mile wide which, although they are not out of water, break in high seas. Ships steer a wide course around them.

Also headed north and sailing in company with *Stanley Parsons* was *Athlete II,* Captain Ernest Burry of Safe Harbour, who parted ways with the schooner during the voyage northward. Burry had only to round the cape to Safe Harbour; Parsons had a longer journey. Captain Burry knew the date and hour of *Stanley Parsons'* departure Burry's account was made public in a news item in the December 22, 1932, *Evening Telegram*:

> At midnight with the Catalina light showing west northwest and ten miles distant, he could see the schooner *Stanley Parsons* about one mile astern but did not see the schooner after that. Elliston lights were seen at 1:30 am.

STILL NO REPORT MISSING VESSEL

Captain Burry Saw Schr. Stanley Parsons on Night She Left—S.S. Hansi Has Not Yet Reported

Yesterday the Minister of Marine and Fisheries received a telegram from Captain Ernest Burry of Safe Harbour, giving some information as to the movements of the schooner Stanley Pasons, which left this port December 5th for Little Bay Islands and has not been reported since that date.

Midnight of Monday Dec. 5th Captain Burry reports, with Catalina light showing west north west, and 10 miles distant, he could see the schooner Stanley Parsons, about one mile astern but did not see the schooner after that. Elliston lights were seen at 1.30 a.m. Tuesday, and he saw nothing until Offer Gooseberry Island was picked up at 8 a.m. Capt. Burry was of the opinion then that Captain Parsons bore up for Catalina, as there was plenty of time to get in before the weather got thick.

Captain Hounsell, of S.S Home, wired the same department yesterday morning, that the steamer left Tilting and went as far eastward as the Funks and vicinity of the Wad-

This is how the *Daily News* of December 22, 1932 reported the disaster.

Burry saw nothing until Offer Gooseberry Island was picked up at 8 am.

Captain Burry was of the opinion Captain Parsons was bearing up to harbour in Catalina, as there was plenty of time to get in before the weather got thick.

Cape Agulhas, a fisheries research/survey trawler which operated out of the Bay Bulls research laboratory, was requested to search northward for debris or wreckage of the mysterious disappearance. Her captain, Gabriel Fudge, zigzagged as far as the Cabot Island on the north side of Bonavista Bay, but saw no sign of *Stanley Parsons*.

Captain Thomas Hounsell of S.S. *Home*, the government coastal vessel, wired the Department of Marine and Fisheries on December twenty-first saying he left Tilting and looked as far westward as the Funks and in the vicinity of the Wadhams.

Visibility was good for ten miles, but there was no sign of the schooner or of wreckage.

When *Stanley Parsons* was purchased and brought to Newfoundland by James Strong Ltd. of Little Bay Islands, she carried the name *Lelia E. Norwood* and had been built in Boothbay, Maine, in 1884. In 1923 she was rebuilt by Skipper Jobie Parsons at Lush's Bight and her new owner re-named his prized acquisition. When brought down from the States, *Norwood* had a durable oak bottom; thus, only the top was replaced with new stanchions, rails, deck and deck beams. In Notre Dame Bay and along the north east coast the ninety-one ton schooner with her newly painted shiny smooth oak hull was considered a fast and able sailing vessel. *Stanley Parsons*, approaching fifty years old and well past the average age of wooden schooners, toiled in the spring/summer Labrador fishery and laboured in the fall coastal trade between Notre Dame Bay and St. John's.

Stanley Parsons never arrived at her home port on Long Island. The vessel and its crew disappeared without a trace. All six crew and the lone passenger belonged to Lush's Bight: Captain Sidney Parsons, married with four children; mate James Maye, age fifty-one, married with four children, three girls and a boy; cook Uriah Miller, married with six children; the deckhands were all single, Cecil Hollett, age twenty; Thomas Caravan, twenty-five and his brother Wesley Caravan, age nineteen.

Alwin Parsons, the passenger, had a business in Lush's bight and came to St. John's to buy winter provisions for his store. He secured a passage back home on *Stanley Parsons.* He was married with two children.

Needless to say, the shock and gloom of the loss of seven men, who left sixteen children as orphans, cast a pall over the town which at that time had a population of about three hundred. For years after, Mrs. Caravan, the mother of Wes and Tom, would get distressed each time she heard the church bell ring.

Each disaster carries its own poignant footnotes and the loss of *Stanley Parsons* was no exception. James Maye's son, Ron, was scheduled to sail on the schooner's final trip for the fall of 1932, but didn't go. Captain Sidney Parsons, who was having stomach problems, had gone to the doctor who said he would probably have an operation in St. John's. Captain Parsons wanted James Maye, an older and more experienced seaman, to make the trip to bring back the schooner in case the captain had to stay in St. John's for surgery.

James Maye, who was also a skipper and a good navigator, had been in foreign-going trade carrying fish to Europe and taking schooners around the coast of Newfoundland. In his early years Maye was a crewman on two other vessels that had been shipwrecked before he lost his life: *Harry and Ralph*, lost off Herring Neck with no casualties.

Another marine mishap he had was in the eighty-ton schooner, *Grace Parsons* and commonly referred to simply as *Grace*, owned by Peter Parsons of Lush's Bight and commanded by Captain Hounsell. In the fall of 1918 she was bound north with general cargo when she was forced to harbour in Deadman's Bay on the Straight Shore. Hounsell ordered out the two anchors, but weather and seas forced him, Maye and the other crew to abandon ship.

According to a report in the 1978 *Newfoundland Quarterly*, it was on a Sunday afternoon when *Grace* began to drag her anchors giving every indication she would come ashore. Anticipating a wreck and potential salvage, the church lay reader cut the evening service short and dispensed with the prayer meeting altogether. *Grace* did drift ashore and was wrecked on the rocks of Muddy Pond Point. Although a watchman was placed on her, the plunder was great and it is said even the watchman joined in.

Wreck Commissioner for the area, Arthur Hounsell, wired the Minister of Marine and Fisheries to say: "The schooner *Grace Parsons* has become a total wreck at Deadman's Bay. Crew all safe."

Courtesy Ron Maye

Joseph and James Strong established a business in Little Bay Islands in the 1870s. After it was incorporated in 1923 as James Strong Limited, it grew to be one of Newfoundland's largest fish-packing and exporting businesses. By the 1940s Strong's Limited had owned around thirty ships; several bore the name of family members including *Norman W. Strong* (above). On October 2, 1923, Strongs lost *Norman W. Strong*, Captain Fred Wiseman, at Castle Hyde, near Little St. Lawrence.

On February 8, 1922, *Norma B. Strong*, built in 1918 at Little Bay Islands and owned by Monroes of St. John's, was abandoned at sea. Her crew of Captain Stephen Penney of Carbonear, cook A. Simms, bosun M. Penney and seamen H. Kingale, J. Sutton and E.A. Penney left Europe for Newfoundland. Thirty miles from Cape Race, the ship met adverse winds which blew her back across the ocean. The crew abandoned the leaking schooner when they neared the Azores and then reached Fayal safely.

Like the other families of Lush's Bight, the Maye family was appalled and distressed by the loss of a husband and father. James' wife, Janet, was in total denial that *Stanley Parsons* was gone, probably because there was no sign of wreckage. She thought for a long time the schooner had drifted off course and would one day come sailing back into Lush's Bight. The youngest child, Lydia then aged six (now a resident in Fortune), kept asking for her father who was going to bring her back a new set of play dishes for Christmas. The eldest child Ron, at nineteen, was now responsible for the whole family and he became a capable breadwinner.

Over sixty years have passed since the disappearance. In shipping rosters, appended next to the name *Stanley Parsons*, are the words "Lost with Crew". Three brief words that

Courtesy Rev. V. Cluett

Another schooner owned in this area of Notre Dame Bay was the schooner *Betty & Molly* (above). In the late 1930s she was registered to T.J. Hewlett of Port Anson, Halls Bay and skippered by Sidney Jones and later by Wilbert Wellman.

Betty & Molly was also owned by W.G. Nott's business of the South Coast and her captain was Zina Keeping of Belleoram. In this photo she is moored at Kearley's wharf in Belleoram. She was wrecked at Eastern Cove near Francois on December 12, 1954; her crew rescued by schooner *Trinity North.*

perhaps indicate how often disasters like this occurred in Newfoundland, but the complete story and details of what actually happened and when and where will never be known. See Appendix C for the Poem "Loss of the Stanley Parsons"

Chapter 8

Alma: Casualty of the Labrador Fleet

Triton, Winterton

For several days, the exact location of the wreck of the schooner *Alma* remained a mystery. In mid-October in 1907, the shipping news in Scilly Cove, Trinity Bay, centred around *Alma*'s disappearance somewhere near Triton Island, an island about 250 kilometres north west, as the crow flies and several days voyage by boat.

There had been no official reports of wreckage, no news indicating *Alma*'s crew had survived the death and destruction that stormy seas and rocks can deal out and, until enquiries reached the captains of the Labrador fleet based in Conception Bay, no one in Scilly Cove knew much about the fate of *Alma*.

Scilly Cove (renamed Winterton in 1921), one of the first sites on Newfoundland's northeast coast to have been settled by English fishermen, first appears on an official census in 1836 with over two hundred residents. The shore fishery, largely conducted to the north and east of the community or at Baccalieu Island, was supplemented by involvement in the Labrador fishery. While the harbour was neither deep nor large enough to accommodate a large schooner fleet, Winterton became known as a boat building centre.

The thirty-five ton banker *Alma*, owned by Henry Piercy of Winterton, was under the command of Captain George Piercy. He employed a Winterton crew: Arthur Piercy, William Andrews, Henry Pitcher, John Coates, and William Banton. All were married except Coates and Banton.

The Piercys of Winterton had been involved in fishing prior to the turn of the century. Captain Sam Piercy moved to Grand Bank from Winterton in the 1890s and took foreign-going schooners overseas to Europe. The *Evening Telegram* of November 25, 1898, shows the season's fishing voyages for all vessels in Grand Bank in 1898 and indicates Sam Piercy landed seven hundred quintals of salt fish. For a year or so prior to 1911, he skippered the banker *Arkansas* and in 1917 owned the tern schooner *Mary D. Young*. He had the tern schooner *Myrtle Piercy* built in 1919.

Alma was one of the large fleet of schooners based in Conception Bay and Trinity Bay that fished the Labrador cod stocks from early summer to October. However Captain George Piercy had not done well with the Labrador fish in the summer of 1907 and finished the fall voyage out of Conche in the area designated as the "French Shore". Located on the eastern shore of the Great Northern Peninsula, Conche was a favoured haven near the once prolific inshore fishing grounds.

In early October a schooner owned and captained by J. Evans arrived in Hant's Harbour and reported seeing *Alma* on the French shore when he left.

As well, Captain Norman of Bay Roberts in the schooner *Dolphin* had been on the Labrador fishing and around the last of September had left for Bay Roberts. On the way home he put into Conche where a number of other vessels harboured from the weather. *Alma* was one of them.

On the third of October the wind was favourable and the eastbound vessels left for home at daylight. According to Captain Norman, *Alma* weighed anchor a short while before *Dolphin*, but the latter vessel overtook *Alma*; yet, both schooners kept together, Captain Norman in the lead within hailing distance almost the whole way.

Both vessels crossed westward — inside the Grey (Grois) Islands —and kept off north of Cape John. Up to this time the other vessels, which had left the eastern side of the Great Northern Peninsula at the same time had kept by the same course. By this time, however, the wind began to freshen, or increase in strength, with every indication that a storm was brewing.

All schooners except *Dolphin* and *Alma* steered for Pacquet and neighbouring harbours. Night was closing fast when both schooners reached Gull Island, Cape John. Moreover the wind was now strong enough that Captain Norman ordered foresail and mainsail reefed and as he could see from *Dolphin*, the crew of *Alma* had also reefed canvas. Both vessels still kept within sight for some hours.

Both ran south of Bishop's Rock; *Dolphin* hauled in for Shoe Cove, a fishing community about ten kilometres southwest of Cape St. John on the Baie Verte Peninsula. Although the waters around Cape St. John are relatively clear of charted rocks and reefs, the currents are very strong and generally set to the south. Combined with fall and winter storms the area around Cape St. John is dangerous for ships.

Captain Norman realized the difficulty in giving his ship adequate and safe sea room and it appeared to him that *Alma* was also making headway to harbour in Shoe Cove. But it was at this point the hand of fate separated both vessels. *Dolphin* had difficulty negotiating the harbour and Shoe Cove Rock, but with quick manoeuvring and sail handling, Norman finally dropped anchor in Shoe Cove. It was now dark, but he could see *Alma*'s light coming astern.

In the common courtesy and regard for mutual assistance on the sea, Norman ordered the lantern to be kept aloft as a guide to the approaching schooner. His guiding light failed to help for *Alma* and her crew disappeared. This account, written some days after the tragedy, speculated on the fate of the schooner:

> The last time the light of the *Alma* was seen it was dangerously near Shoe Cove Rock which is a considerable distance off the cove. For a minute or two in the hurry and hustle of getting the *Dolphin* safely secured for the night, the approaching light was lost sight of. When Captain Norman looked again the light had disappeared and as there was not time for the *Alma* to be out of sight around the land, it was his opinion the ill-fated vessel met her doom on Shoe Cove Rock.

Then word came down from Triton Island of evidence of a sea disaster. On October 14, wreckage which was first seen near the base of Shag Cliff drifted into gulches and coves near Triton. Two days later a bag of clothes with the name "J.W. Andrews" on it washed into Stag Gulch. By this time major portions of the wreck, even the hull and masts, had gone to pieces. Residents of Triton made a fruitless search for bodies, for they knew it was near impossible for anyone to survive Shag Cliff where the derelict *Alma* had struck. Pieces of the wreck were found fifty feet up on the cliff.

Courtesy Ron Maye

Owned by Sam Roberts of Triton, schooner *Julia F* entering Three Arms, in Green Bay, for lumber in 1927. She was then skippered by Joe Mitchell of Twillingate with his crew of James and Ron Maye, Herb and Charles Morey and Walter Heath of Lush's Bight.

Several years later *Julia F* sank in Seal Bay near Triton. She left port at six am; five hours later, she sprang a leak and went to the bottom. Dorman Rideout, who was her captain at this time, and his crew escaped without incident.

Chapter 9

Sidney Smith: A World War One Victim

Twillingate

During World War One a three-masted barquentine involved in the overseas trade disappeared. *Sidney Smith*, at one hundred seventy-seven net ton, was built in Wales in 1895 and was later purchased by Newfoundland interests. The story of her Newfoundland career begins in Twillingate a few years prior to the Great War.

On September 12, 1912, *Sidney Smith* reached Twillingate laden with coal from Scotland consigned to William Ashbourne's business. The coal was taken out and on October 7 Ashbourne's began to load a cargo of Labrador fish that had been collected by the Twillingate business and destined for Europe.

By December 12 *Sidney Smith* was ready to leave: the hatches were battened down, food supply aboard and, since she was sailing to a foreign port, customs and shipping papers were in hand. On that day a northeast wind which blew directly into Twillingate harbour, stalled sailing time. As the day progressed the weather got worse and soon increased to a full gale.

Another attempt was made to moor the schooner. Her anchors dragged and she drifted down on the schooner *Invincible* and this craft lost her bowsprit, jib boom and much of her head gear in the accident.

Sidney Smith suffered most from the collision and the captain and crew abandoned ship early that evening. As the gale increased *Sidney Smith* continued to drag and two hours later struck, stern first, on Harbour Rock in Twillingate harbour.

Ashbourne's bought the wrecked ship and its cargo from the insurance company. All cargo and movable gear was salvaged. The next spring the new owners stripped the gear from *Sidney Smith*'s sails and masts. By now she was just a hull with three masts, but despite several efforts to refloat her, it failed. Finally she was beached on the north side of Twillingate harbour near the premises of Hodge Brothers business. Work and repairs slowed up until the spring of 1914, the outbreak of World War One.

In August, *Sidney Smith* was hove down, or tipped on her side near the shore, pumped out and refloated enough to get her to Gilesport. Gilesport, a small harbour about one mile from Twillingate, provided enough shelter and materials to complete the repair job. Then another problem plagued the owners — the hauling gear for moving the schooner gave out.

Apparently *Sidney Smith* lay idle until the spring of 1917, four and a half years after she was stranded on Harbour Rock, when she was actively refloated and ready for work.

Captain Augustus "Gus" Taylor of Carbonear was hired to re-rig the vessel. This job lasted well into the fall. By this time Ashbourne's supply of Labrador fish was ready for shipping and five thousand seven hundred ten quintals were loaded. Captain Taylor, who had gone to Carbonear for a few days, returned. He and his crew bent on the schooner's new sails.

At four-thirty pm on December 14, 1917, *Sidney Smith* and her five man crew sailed out through Twillingate har-

Courtesy Marine Archives, Harry Roberts' Collection

Sidney Smith, prior to her wreck in Twillingate harbour. This vessel was a barquentine, that is with at least three masts and square rigged on the foremast.

bour, past Harbour Rock, where five years previously almost to the day she had been wrecked, and squared away for Gibraltar.

But the litany of mishaps and accidents which had accompanied the beleaguered vessel for most of her sea life continued. More of the circumstances of her numerous accidents have been recorded than the account of her final hours. No crew survived her last voyage.

Not long after *Sidney Smith* left Twillingate she vanished without a trace and probably went down somewhere in the North Atlantic in December 1917. The cause remains unknown: faulty repairs, a mid-Atlantic storm or an encounter with an unfriendly German submarine. Her crew, with the exception of the captain, hailed from Twillingate and vicinity: Eli Hawkins, son of Mary Hawkins; Henry Porter, son of Nina Porter, both of Change Islands; cook Stewart Hull, son of Andrew Hull, and mate Bert Wells, son of Philip Wells, were from Twillingate. Captain Augustus Taylor was thirty-four years of age.

Two Other Losses with Twillingate Connections

According to local stories originating from Change Islands, the two-masted schooner *Herbert and Ruby*, owned in Burin by E.M. Hollett, sailed for European ports on the same day as *Sidney Smith*. Late fall, 1917, *Herbert and Ruby* loaded salt codfish at Change Islands at the premises of Elliott & Company, a branch business of Harris' interests at Grand Bank. On December seventeenth, when favourable winds came, she set sail for Portugal.

Shortly after she cleared port a vicious gale of south-west wind sprang up unexpectedly and it was assumed *Herbert and Ruby* went down in the gale. Her master was Charles Hollett of Burin, the cook an Eastman and the cook's son Harvey Eastman were crewmembers on the schooner. The remaining two or three men, whose names are not recorded, probably hailed from the Burin area. In March 1920 relatives and friends surrendered all hope of ever hearing news of the schooner.

Saucy Arethusa: A Wreck at Halifax

On November 13, 1929, local papers reported the wreck of a Twillingate schooner; this one with a happier ending and no loss of life. While entering Halifax on November ninth, *Saucy Arethusa*, Captain Bennett Oxford of Twillingate, grounded on "Broad Breakers" north of the Sisters Bell Buoy near Sambro, Halifax. The schooner heeled over on her beam ends and partly submerged forcing Oxford and his crew to abandon ship in boats.

Formerly called *Arethusa*, she had been built at Essex, Massachusetts, in 1907 and grossed 157 ton. She had been owned by Captain Clayton Morrissey as part of the Gloucester fishing fleet.

Ashbournes purchased her in 1928, renamed the vessel with the word "Saucy" and installed an engine in hopes she could engage in the seal hunt. The schooner was then an auxiliary/sail vessel, but in her trials "at the ice" during the spring of 1929 *Saucy Arethusa* obtained only a few seals.

In November 1929 *Saucy Arethusa* left Harbour Grace headed to Halifax to land fish at W. & G. H. Mitchell's firm when, on the approach to Halifax harbour, disaster struck. Oxford related what happened:

> We were approaching Halifax after a good passage of six days in a normal sea, clear and in a light southwest wind. The four lower sails were set and the auxiliary engine was in operation. On account of the hazy appearance of the land we thought that we were further out to sea than was our actual position.
>
> The schooner was turned to enter Halifax harbour and was in "stays" making headway at about three miles an hour when she struck amidships.
>
> Shortly afterwards the vessel commenced to fill and it was not long before the cabin and engine room were flooded and the sea was forcing its way into the hold.

Oxford gave orders to abandon ship. With time to collect all personal effects, the crew boarded the dory and the small boat. Shortly after harbour tug *Ocean Osprey* picked up the crew —Oxford, Cecil Anstey, Stewart Cooper, Frazer Blake, George Lilly, W.J. Young, A. Morey all of Twillingate and area — and carried them into Halifax. *Saucy Arethusa,* valued at $15,000 and her cargo of twenty-seven hundred quintals of dry fish worth $16,000, was a total loss.

The crew stayed in the Navy League Building; then boarded the steamship *Nerissa* bound to St. John's.

Shipwreck was nothing new for many of the crew; Cecil Anstey, for example, was shipwrecked six times over the course of his seagoing career including the wreck of the steamship *Ethie* at Cow Head on December 11, 1919.

Chapter 10

Dorothy Baird, Holed by Her Own Spar

Fogo

A fight — a fifteen day battle against the demanding ocean by the Newfoundland crew of the three-masted schooner *Dorothy Baird*, disabled by a mid-Atlantic storm en route from Brazil to Newfoundland — was not enough to save the ship.

Originally a Portuguese banker which had been purchased in 1923 by James Baird Limited of Water Street, St. John's, the three hundred nine ton *Dorothy Baird* was Baird's main workhorse in the foreign trade — the Caribbean and Brazil. She had previously been skippered by Captain George Brown.

However, on her final voyage she was under the command of Captain John "Jack" Willis. She left Pernambuco, Brazil, on January 4, 1930, with her crew: Captain Willis, his cousin Harvey Elijah Willis, Fred Gill, all of Fogo; Wallace Smith, Trinity Bay; William Pridham, Petty Harbour; a seaman named Dillon and a Portuguese sailor.

Terns like *Dorothy Baird* required seven (sometimes six on smaller terns) men to work the sails and masts. Four men — the captain, mate, and cook exempt — were deck hands or sailmen and each had his mast to look after. Younger sailors were given the foremast, most difficult mast to work due to its exposure to wind and its extra rigging, to look after. Senior men, who had already put in their time and experience, worked the mizzen and main masts. When the men were aloft they held on tight to the ropes and quickly learned the meaning to an old saying: One arm (to work) for yourself; the other for the company. On *Dorothy Baird*'s last voyage, the crew had more than their share of strenuous labour, not only aloft, but also at the pumps.

Not long after leaving port a storm carried away the mizzen mast and the sails; the spar struck the bottom of the vessel causing the tern to leak. Mountainous seas swept the ship before the storm and the crew pumped around the clock. Within a few hours, sand from the ballast clogged the pumping mechanism and water steadily rose higher. Captain Willis recalled what happened:

> Finding ourselves in a desperate situation with our pumps clogged, our vessel leaking and our only lifeboat smashed to pieces in the storm, we kept a constant lookout. We hoped day after day for the sight of a ship. At night we burned our straw beds to attract attention. Five days after the mast was gone, we sighted the dim lights of a vessel and signalled desperately, but our signals must have gone unnoticed.
>
> It was only when the situation looked hopeless and we had just about given up that we sighted the British vessel *Valour*. I have never seen a more welcome sight. The ship (*Dorothy Baird*) would not have kept afloat another two days and our only lifeboat had been smashed in the storm.

When the passing steamer found *Dorothy Baird* on February 10, 1930, the crew was working the pumps, but water had gained on them and was eight feet deep in the holds. Captain Willis and his six men were taken aboard the S.S. *British Valour*, bound for Holland, on February tenth at latitude 39.42 North, longitude 53.07 West about five hundred eighty miles south of Cape Race.

Hunger etched the memory of the ordeal firmly in the minds the crew. *Dorothy Baird* had been supplied with sufficient food for a regular voyage, but this trip extended weeks beyond that. The cook, Harvey Willis, who had to literally scrape the bottom of the barrel to try to serve a square meal to the weary crew, related his version of the loss of the schooner:

> We were sailing in heavy weather and ten to twelve days out we lost the full suit of canvas. All we did was lie around for a few days while we set up a new suit and then carried on. This time the three sticks came out of her with her canvas and we knew then we were in a bit of trouble.
>
> I think it was the Portuguese sailor who broke his leg when the vessel split in two.

Dorothy Baird, as cook Willis termed it, "split in two" and, dismasted with opened seams, she was blown about the Atlantic. Her drift took her out of the usual shipping lanes, but the same storm that punished *Dorothy Baird* also pushed the vessel *British Valour* off course and close to the sinking tern. The officer on watch sighted the Newfoundland schooner and the steamer came within hailing distance. After *Baird*'s crew were safely plucked off their sinking schooner, the *British Valour*'s officers issued dry clothing, fed and offered up a dash of Nelson's Blood to any seaman who wanted it.

Cook Willis summed up his experiences at Rotterdam, Holland: "They looked after us at something like a YMCA for a few days. Then we went on to Belgium and then to the port of Liverpool in England. We took a passage home for St. John's from there. We got back to our Fogo Island homes late in March, 1930 from a voyage that lasted a little longer than anyone expected."

Fogo Island, 260 square kilometres, lies fifteen kilometres off the northeast coast of Newfoundland. It is connected across Hamilton Sound by ferry to the mainland. The name, Fogo, comes from the Portuguese word, *fuego,* meaning "fire". The Portuguese were among many European fishermen who visited the island from the early 1500s. Until the late 1700s the island was a summer retreat of the now-extinct Beothuck Indians. Fogo Island had English settlers as early as 1680; many dependant upon the sea for a living.

The island, with combined population of over 2000, now supports ten settlements including Joe Batt's Arm and Fogo, the oldest and the island's unofficial capital with its population of approximately 1200 people. Each summer Fogo celebrates its Brimstone Head Folk Festival, a major tourist attraction.

Chapter 11

Wreck of the Francis P. Duke

Fogo/Badger's Quay

In the marine history of Newfoundland there are many accounts of storms that have spread devastation and destruction along the island's rugged shore. A little over fifty years ago, a shipwreck near Badger's Quay claimed a small ship and six men.

On Tuesday morning December 16, 1947, the fifty-ton *Francis P. Duke* left Fogo bound for St. John's with a cargo of fish. Owned by Pat Miller of Fogo, she carried a crew from her home port: Captain William Miller, his brother Ignatius "Nish" Miller, Max Payne, Augustine Pickett and Steward Keefe. Passenger Alfred Mullins hailed from Rencontre East on Newfoundland's South Coast. Knowing there was a Christmas social or "time" scheduled for Fogo the following week, *Francis P. Duke* left Fogo early to deliver the cargo in order to get back for the event.

Apparently when heavy weather came on, Captain Miller ran back along the coast trying to reach a sheltered harbour. The snow storm was so severe that people attending a concert in the Orange Lodge in nearby community were forced to spend the night in the hall—the snow was too thick to get home.

Sometime Wednesday night Captain William Miller must have attempted to steam up Shag Rock Tickle between Pool's Island and Badger's Quay and apparently hit a shoal. The tickle, full of jagged rocks that litter the nearby coastline, is a dangerous run even in moderate weather.

On Wednesday morning, December 17, residents of Pool's Island, Greenspond, Wesleyville and Badger's Quay found the spars and masts swinging on the anchor chains. The wooden hull, planking and bulwarks were torn away. A major part of the hull of the schooner with the nameboard *Francis P. Duke* on it drifted ashore in Hermit Cove, a beach not far from the site of the wreck. Broken dories and part of the deck were located near Badger's Quay.

Two men, Captain Ambrose Howell of Badger's Quay and Herbert Dyke of Pool's Island, both sent messages to marine authorities in St. John's advising them that a schooner had been lost with crew at Shag Rock Tickle and the search for bodies was underway. Examination of the position of the schooner's anchors found with the wreckage led to the belief that *Francis P. Duke* had anchored for the night, dragged her anchors in the storm and struck Shag Rock Island or one of the other rocks in the region.

Stormy weather and high seas temporarily postponed the search for bodies on Thursday and Friday, but later the body of the cook and the two Miller men, sons of the owner, were found. Police Constable Bursey, stationed at Greenspond, instructed Captain Wheeler of S.S. *Glencoe* to carry the bodies to Twillingate and thence to Fogo.

Francis P. Duke was built for Wareham's business of Spencer's Cove, Placentia Bay. Originally named *Alice Adams* after relatives of the owner, she freighted for Wareham's as a sailing vessel. It was during the vessel's winter tie-up in St. John's that Isaac M. Duke of Ship Harbour saw the schooner and bought her. The Duke business renamed the schooner for Francis and Patrick Duke, installed a Drott diesel engine and employed her on the Grand Banks as a five dory banker.

Photo courtesy Frank Bennett

Alice Adams on her launching, 1935. Built by Peter Connors under the Commission of Government shipbuilding incentives at Burdeaux Island near Arnold's Cove, *Alice Adams* was to be operated by Nelson T. Adams. In 1936 there was no one to supply or outfit the vessel for fishing and Aaron Reid used her for freighting; then she was purchased by Isaac Duke who renamed her *Francis P. Duke*.

Prior to the acquisition of *Francis P. Duke*, the Duke family owned *Landscape*, a thirty-ton schooner built in 1906 in Lance Cove, Smith Sound, and subsequently sold her to Newell Piercey of Fortune.

As an ironic footnote to this tragic marine mishap, there remains another aspect of the story. About a week before she was lost, *Francis P. Duke* was involved in a life-saving rescue on the ice floes. A pilot of a plane searching for seal herds spotted a lone figure of someone stranded on an ice floe about twenty miles off Fogo Island. Signalling frantically, the castaway seemed to be on the verge of collapse. Details of his position were relayed to Fogo and the Miller seamen immediately steamed to the area. Within hours the person was located, but *Francis P. Duke* jammed in heavy ice before he could be reached. Eventually freed, *Francis P. Duke* picked up the young man, Christopher Cobb of Barr'd Islands, who had been adrift for two days.

Author's collection

Walter G. Sweeney, as seen here on her launching day in 1946, became another vessel owned by Captain Pat Miller of Fogo. The two hundred sixteen ton *Walter G. Sweeney* sank on October 31, 1961, when water leaked in and flooded the engines. Navy tug *St. John* out of Sydney came by, pumped out her engine room and took her in tow, but she sank fifty miles off Cape Breton, Nova Scotia.

Walter Sweeney's crew was Pat Miller of Fogo; Everett French, Coley's Point; Willis Bath and Gerry Andrews of Horse Islands; Lance Short, British Harbour; Lloyd Landry, Sydney, Nova Scotia; Samuel Power, English Harbour West and a cook from Valleyfield whose name was not available.

Courtesy William Lockyer

On April 1, 1960, the Miller business lost the sealing vessel Camperdown when she sprang a leak in the ice floes off northeastern Newfoundland. Captain Pat Miller and his crew were rescued by the Canadian icebreaker *Wolfe* and taken to Lewisporte. As seen here in a photo taken from the deck of *Wolfe* by William Lockyer of Marystown, *Camperdown* is down by the stern. Her lifeboats and other moveable gear are on the ice.

After the heavy fittings like the anchor and chains were removed, *Wolfe* rammed eighty-six ton *Camperdown* to ensure the derelict would sink; however, the tough old sealer wouldn't go easily. *Wolfe* steamed up to ram the vessel and although *Camperdown* rolled down past her mastheads, she bobbed back up. Finally on the third or fourth attempt, *Camperdown* went to the bottom.

Chapter 12

"Lost at Sea" Percy Wells and Others

Horwood

In 1921 the number of local vessels wrecked or abandoned at sea was the highest for many years. Over fifty of the foreign-going fleet went to the bottom; many taking their cargoes with them and, even more tragically, several disappeared with full crews. Two whose crew and fate is still shrouded in mystery are the schooners *Douglas H. Adams* and *Helen C. Morse*.

Douglas H. Adams, with six crew, left Lisbon early in the spring of 1921 headed for Twillingate, but had never reported. She was in trouble several times before her final departure for Twillingate. On two occasions after attempting her westbound voyage she was forced to return to Lisbon for repairs to damage caused by rough weather.

On October 29, Newfoundland papers reported a violent storm that lashed the island's north coast. On the day previous to the storm the one-hundred ton *Helen C. Morse* departed Little Bay Islands for St. Anthony. Nothing further was known of her except some wreckage — a lifebuoy, fog alarm, part of her nameboard — picked up at Exploits Island a few days after she was due in port. It was presumed she foundered in the gale. Her six crew disappeared with the ship: Captain Ray Wiseman, age twenty-four, G.D. Wiseman,

Courtesy Marine Archives, Harry Roberts' Collection.

Ariceen (above), owned in Twillingate by Ashbourne's firm, was stranded to total loss in the same gale that probably claimed *Helen C. Morse*. On November 2, 1921, laden with several hundred ton of coal, *Ariceen* hit a rock in Twillingate harbour and eventually broke up. Words on the bottom of the painting read: *Ariceen* John Churchill, Master.

twenty-two, Arthur Hustins, twenty-six, all of Little Bay Islands; Alfonso White, twenty-nine, Tilt Cove; Adolph Morey, twenty-five, Boat Harbour, Notre Dame Bay and Jacob Moores, Flower's Cove.

In early December the tern schooner *Jean and Mary* was wrecked on the Penguin Islands on the northeast coast. None of her crew of six, all from Grand Bank, survived. The same December storm that claimed *Jean and Mary* also took the lives of six crew and a lady passenger of the Greenspond schooner *Passport*, wrecked at Caplin Cove near Carbonear. (See chapter 19 "Loss of Nerette")

By December 30, 1921 the tern schooner *Percy Wells* was entered on Lloyd's of London Shipping Registry as "Lost at Sea". She left New York on September 25 for Newfoundland with a cargo of coal in the holds and on deck. Built in Hare Bay in 1919 by Thomas Wells for the Horwood Lumber Company, in the fall of 1921 the one hundred nineteen ton *Percy Wells* was commissioned in March for several oceanic trading voyages.

With Captain F. Hanham in command she loaded molasses at Barbados for Campbellton, Notre Dame Bay, discharged and left Campbellton with a load of lumber for New York. At New York she loaded coal for Dog Bay in Hamilton Sound on Newfoundland's north east coast.

According to tradition one of the first permanent settlers in Dog Bay was George Hodder of Fogo who followed the lucrative salmon fishery. Other early family names were Godwin, Simmon, Cull, Croucher, Stone, Baker, Freake, and Russell. Around the turn of the century logging became a major industry in the heavily-timbered bay and the Horwood Lumber Company built a steam-driven lumber mill nearby. In 1911 Dog Bay was renamed Horwood in honour of William Frederick Horwood, the founder of the mill and the lumber business.

Horwood was the last Newfoundland port *Percy Wells* sailed from as she returned to New York with another load of

Horwood lumber. Again on her final voyage for the year, hard coal was her cargo destined for the mill in Dog Bay.

Captain Hanham was born on Newfoundland's west coast, but resided in St. John's with his family; mate Solomon French, married with a family, belonged to Bay Roberts and the four other crew were cook Luke Feltham, sailors Charles Brown, Peter Noftall, and A. Snow of Spaniard's Bay.

No plausible explanation for *Percy Wells'* disappearance was acceptable to grieving relatives: a vessel only two years old, well-constructed and fully equipped. The schooner *Aviator*, owned by the Gorton-Pew Company, was towed into Boston and reported that on October second she encountered a sudden and tremendous storm. During the gale she was dismasted, nearly sank and was eventually brought to safety. Possibly *Percy Wells*, heavily burdened with coal, disappeared in the same storm.

In addition to the wrecks and abandonments which seemed to mark 1921 as "the year of shipwrecks", three other Newfoundland vessels were lost with crew between February and December. *General Horne*, owned in Grand Bank was reported missing on a run between Seldom Come By and Change Islands in February 1921. This tern schooner was later located, floating bottom up, in the Atlantic with no sign of her five crew: Captain Berkely Rogers of Grand Bank; William Brooks and Randell Mayo, Fortune; Otto Ledrew, Change Islands and two other unidentified seamen. Moulton's tern schooner *County of Richmond* out of Burgeo with five crew — Captain Leonard Hare and his young son, Wilson and Charles Spencer, James Hare, all of Burgeo and Joe Benson — capsized off Ramea on February 21, 1921, with no survivors.

Because of the exceptional number of losses among the local schooner fleet, marine insurance rates had been increased substantially by December 1921. Only the best foreign-going schooners were insured and only then at new and higher rates. This severely affected Newfoundland shipowners who were unable to compete with Canadian and American businesses. The latter captured the lion's share of marine trade.

In turn, master mariners and seamen were unemployed; shipowners were willing to sell their large tern schooners if a buyer could be found. Owners belated the fact that the large profits of the war years (1914-1918) had disappeared. Competition kept shipping values down and the demand for the large tonnage of tern schooners was nil. As a result, by the new year 1922, the effect of insurance rates, competition, cost of vessel upkeep and low profits meant shipowners were fast losing money.

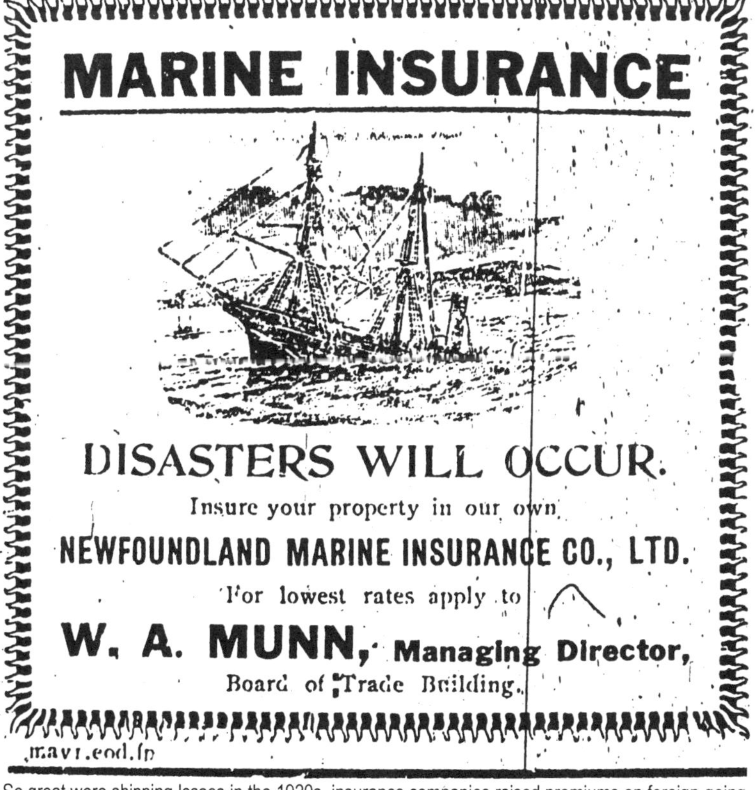

So great were shipping losses in the 1920s, insurance companies raised premiums on foreign-going bottoms. Orders for freights were scarce, costs of maintaining idle ships soared; thus, rumours were rampant vessels were intentionally scuttled to collect insurance, but there is no direct proof of illegal practices.

This is a 1920 advertisement of a Newfoundland insurance company.

Chapter 13

Rose M off Fayal, Azores

Fogo, Norris Arm

Built in Norris Arm by the Norris Arm Shipbuilding Co. Ltd. in 1918, the schooner *Rose M,* like many other Newfoundland foreign-going vessels, had a short life in the foreign trade and went to the bottom in 1922. When she left Fogo in December of 1921, *Rose M,* a one hundred and forty-seven ton schooner, was fully equipped with good sails and tackle and was well-manned for her intended voyage to Portugal carrying seven crew under the command of Captain John Kendrick. The mate on the voyage was Captain S.M. Kendrick.

Laden with dried fish owned by the Newfoundland and Labrador Export Company, *Rose M* sailed with all canvas out and full sails until two or three days out when heavy winds and seas strained the ship's planking. *Rose M* leaked enough that some cargo had to be thrown overboard.

Leaks, together with the loss of the schooner's fresh water and damage to the sails, compelled Captain Kendrick to bear up for the nearest port to repair and refit. The official log of *Rose M* at this point read:

> January 1st, 1922; Lat. 43.14 north, Long. 27.41 West. Ship leaking badly and sails damaged; short of water and drinking water damaged by sea water; put ship South for the

Courtesy Y. Andrieux

On a St. Pierre quay, French gendarms (police) question seamen about the discovery of the grisly remains of a victim of the sea. Often the unrelenting ocean gave up her toll. A makeshift coffin (centre) has been prepared for the body.

Azores the nearest port, for benefit of all concerned for ship and crew.

Rose M arrived off the island of Fayal in the Azores on January 13 and the captain passed the Semaphore Station at Capellinhas on the western end of Fayal. He made no attempt to communicate with those manning the station or to hoist the ensign to indicate trouble.

From the time *Rose M* passed the Fayal semaphore station until she sank, the captain kept the schooner tacking back and forth between the station and the Horta breakwater at Fayal. But Kendrick had no choice: winds were unfavourable, the schooner was waterlogged, and no harbour tug was available to tow the disabled schooner into port. All day Friday 13th, Saturday, and Sunday the 15th of January no great effort was made to reduce the water in *Rose M*'s holds below four feet nor were distress signals displayed from the schooner's mast head.

On Sunday, according to the captain's log, water rose to five feet in the hold. On her last tack on Sunday afternoon, as the master attempted to enter Horta and was standing near shore, the captain gave the order to the helmsman to keep off. With battling winds and in her waterlogged condition, *Rose M* did not respond to the wheel.

Seeing his schooner was too close to the shore — about four or five hundred from the breakers — Kendrick ordered anchors dropped. But it was too late! *Rose M* grounded. Within a few hours she broke apart and her name was added to the growing list of ships lost in 1922. Most of her fish cargo was lost; five hundred quintals were saved and well as the schooner's masts and spars which were sold to insurance underwriters.

From Fayal, Kendrick and his crew found transportation to Providence, Rhode Island and eventually arrived in St. John's on February 28 on the steamship *Kyle*.

Chapter 14

No Survivors on the Mollie

Carmanville, Grate's Cove

After a severe winter storm that raged over the northeast coast on the night of December 19-20, 1944, the people of Grate's Cove awoke in the morning to find their small Trinity Bay town inundated with snow. A blizzard, a hurricane of northeast wind, put two or three feet of snow on the ground all over the Avalon Peninsula. It was no night for any human being to be out exposed to the elements, much less a small ship on the high seas.

But several vessels had been caught in the storm as they plied the trade route bringing supplies from St. John's to Trinity Bay, the Straight Shore and Bonavista Bay: *Neva Belle* of Carmanville reported on the twentieth covered in ice and snow; *Mazeltov* reported sometime later — stormbound in another small harbour, but there was no news of Captain Ross Chaulk's *Mollie*.

On December 19, Chaulk had left St. John's in *Mollie* filled almost to capacity with shop goods and general cargo destined mainly for Carmanville and Horwood. The first leg of his journey would take him along the St. John's/Torbay shore, across Conception Bay, through Baccalieu Tickle, past Grate's Cove (at the tip of the peninsula), across Trinity Bay and to Catalina by nightfall. There he would anchor for the night and finish the journey the next day.

Courtesy Roland Abbott.

A cutwater schooner, *Mollie* (seen here entering Carmanville), was over forty years old at the time of her loss in a storm which blew up on the night of December 19-20, 1944. Apparently, for there were no survivors to tell the tale, the schooner, in high winds and heavy snow which blocked all visibility, was pushed onto the rocks of Grate's Cove.

In the morning of December 20, as the storm was abating, residents of Grate's Cove discovered wreckage of a vessel and debris floating in the cove which forms part of the town. Closer investigation revealed part of a spar, bales of hay, general cargo of every description and the unmistakable debris of a schooner. A piece of the nameboard on which part of the name *Mollie* was located as well as personal belongings. Searches of a nearby gulch and beaches revealed no bodies or survivors.

The first message of major loss of life and wreckage was sent that evening from Grate's Cove to Sir John Puddester, Commissioner of Public Health and Safety at St. John's. It read: "Wreckage Schooner *Mollie* of St. John's drove ashore Grate's Cove today. No sign of crew."

By the next day, December 22, the people of the ill-fated schooner's home port of Carmanville still had not heard of the whereabouts of the vessel. Concern, although still unspoken, crossed many anxious minds. The storm had abated, other vessels had reported in, but there was still no word of Captain Chaulk and his Carmanville crew.

Carmanville, situated along both sides of North West

THE EVENING TELEGRAM, ST. JOHN'S, NEWFOUNDLAND,

FRIDAY, DECEMBER 22, 1944

Seeking for Wreckage Of Vessel Mollie

Reported Illfated Schooner Had Young Woman Passenger

Up to this forenoon the local authorities have had no further information regarding the schr. Mollie, believed to have been lost on Tuesday night in Baccalieu Tickle whilst en route northward from St. John's. Boats from Grate's Cove and vicinity are searching for wreckage and sign of the crew. It is reported that in addition to the crew of five an eighteen year old girl took passage by the boat.

MAGISTRATE'S COURT

(Before His Honor Judge Browne)

While patrolling George street

This is how the *Evening Telegram* of December 22, 1944, reported the loss of *Mollie*.

Arm in Rocky Bay on Newfoundland's northeastern coast, first appears in the census reports as Rocky Bay in 1825 with eleven people living there. By 1884 the population had risen to one hundred and seventy-one with fishing, raising animals and gardening as the chief occupations. On June 18, 1906, the name of the community was changed to Carmanville after the Rev. Albert Carman, the General Superintendent of Canada's Methodist Church.

Although some offshore fishing (to the Labrador, Funk Islands, Wadham Islands and Penguin Islands) logging remained a major industry in Carmanville during the first half of the Twentieth Century, but a major forest fire in 1961 dealt a severe blow to that industry. In the era before the TransCanada highway Carmanville, like many Newfoundland towns, sent its small schooners — like *Mollie* — to St. John's for supplies.

Carmanville received the news of the disaster through the Gerald S. Doyle News Bulletin, which was aired every evening to bring information and announcements from all over Newfoundland into people's homes via the radio. As many heard on the radio, which was later confirmed by local clergy who brought the unpleasant news to several Carmanville homes, *Mollie* was lost with crew.

Built in Lunenburg, Nova Scotia, around the turn of the century, *Mollie* was acquired by Jasper Chaulk of Carmanville in the early 1930s. By the 1940s she was passed on to Ross Chaulk, his son. As was the custom, when the Labrador fishery finished in the fall, many schooners of the northeast coast were put into the trading run.

Sailing on *Mollie* with Chaulk, age twenty-six and unmarried, were mate James Ellsworth, twenty-five, unmarried; John Goodyear, sixty-one and his two sons Reginald, thirty-two, Charles, twenty-six, both unmarried and Otto Hicks, a widower with one child. All belonged to Carmanville except Hicks who was a resident of Musgrave Harbour. In a search that lasted four days, residents of Grate's Cove recovered all bodies.

Courtesy Seamen's Museum

Neva Belle (above) which survived the storm that claimed *Mollie*, is tied on in front of A.H. Murray's premises in St. John's. In 1932 this schooner was brought down from Mahone Bay, Nova Scotia, by Arthur Samson of Flat Islands. His son, William, later took command. *Neva Belle* claims the record for the most dried fish brought to the north east coast from Labrador, thirty two hundred quintals. She was sold around 1940 to Frank Collins, Carmanville. During the war *Neva Belle*'s work was servicing the many lighthouses on Newfoundland's west coast until 1942 when she was wrecked in Bonne Bay.

Tied on outside *Neva Belle* is the sixty ton schooner *Maggie G*, built by the Glovers of Bragg's Island and skippered by Lewis Glover.

Chapter 15

Mab: Seven Days Adrift

Newtown, Portugal Cove South

For seven days and nights, Captain John Parsons and his crew, who hailed from Newtown, Bonavista Bay, battled the worst elements the North Atlantic could throw at them. According to Parsons' story, it was the most severe storm he had ever experienced in his sea-going career. He was surprised his little forty-seven ton *Mab* had kept afloat for as long as it did.

Mab sailed from St. John's on December 5, 1926, with a full load of general cargo for Newtown, Bonavista Bay. Under normal circumstances she should have been home sometime during the following day. Located near Cape Freels on the western headland of Bonavista Bay, Newtown consists of several little islands joined by bridges. It was not until 1891 that Newtown appeared in *Census* with a population of five hundred eighty-three; by 1921 it was six hundred and twenty-eight. Like most towns along the northwest coast, it depended on local schooners trading to St. John's for winter supplies and food.

When Parsons and his crew — Hedley, Kenneth, Victor and Albert Parsons, James Way, Samuel Clark and Arthur West — did not show up, relatives in Newtown grew increasingly anxious. They sent word to St. John's inquiring for the schooner *Mab*. Authorities sent the S.S. *Watchful* out on two occasions to search for the missing schooner. *Watchful* scoured the seas off northeastern Newfoundland but reported no sign of the little vessel. No other ship had seen them and fears surfaced in St. John's and Newtown that *Mab* was lost with all her crew.

After *Mab* left St. John's she made good time northward in a strong southwest wind. That night the wind veered westward. Although Captain Parsons and his crew could clearly see the light on Cape Bonavista, it was considered too dangerous to run into Bonavista Bay.

Early the next morning, as the wind rose to gale force, *Mab* was buffeted by heavy seas. Low in the water and well-laden with cargo, her decks were by now frequently running with white water. That night Parsons had the schooner run under bare poles, that is without canvas. By then she was about sixty miles from Cape Bonavista.

On the morning of December seventh winds turned more to the captain's liking and he decided to make another run for Newtown. Before the crew could hoist canvas, kerosene oil had to be poured on and worked into the ropes and sails to make them more flexible. Course was set to the west northwest and with full canvas, *Mab* made good headway.

As daylight broke there was no land in sight. Wind had changed to the westward again and the sea was rough. Again Parsons was obliged to run back under bare poles. Conditions did not improve the next day and to make matter worse, several seams in the little schooner opened. Now the crew was forced to pump to keep water from rising in the holds. By then, as Parsons reckoned, they were about sixty miles off Baccalieu.

On December tenth, weather conditions deteriorated. *Mab*, a fishing/coasting craft designed to pursue a career close to land, was driven seventy miles out into the open Atlantic. Mountainous seas pounded the vessel. And now the seven men wondered, not if they would reach Newtown, but at which moment the mad Atlantic would swallow them and their small schooner. The crew worked the pumps day and night.

"To pile on the agony" as the old saying goes, whitecaps breaking over the schooner smashed the cabin house, damaged the steering gear and high winds blew away the mainsail. Around mid-day, as the wind shifted west northwest, Captain Parsons made another attempt to reach land — any Newfoundland shore.

However, a thick snowstorm dashed any hopes. *Mab*'s crew were exhausted contending with storm conditions and pumping, but they had no recourse — only pump and man their stations.

About six pm, the weather settled; Parsons had *Mab* "hove to". A steamer passed about a half mile away. Other ships had been sighted throughout the day, but were too far to signal. Although Parsons was not ready to abandon his vessel just yet, he thought that if he could contact a steamer, officers would give them their position and send a message to Newfoundland that the schooner *Mab* had been sighted.

Flares, which were run up to the masthead, must have gone un-noticed for there was no response to the signals from the beleaguered *Mab*. A second ship was sighted, this one about a mile away, but again gave no reply to signal fires.

As the morning of December 12 dawned and the wind veered, Parsons and his weary crew shaped their course for northwest-by-north. After a few hours sailing, a faint smudge of land was sighted and soon the crew recognized Cape Race in the distance.

One of the men reported to Captain Parsons water had filled the cabin and the holds. *Mab* was slowly sinking. Up to this time Parsons fully believed the schooner could be sailed into a port. Now he decided to run her on a beach in an attempt to save their lives. Late in the evening of December 12, 1926, *Mab* ground to a halt several feet off shore in Portugal Cove South, a small town four or five miles east of Trepassey on the Southern Avalon.

Meanwhile the crew had collected their belongings, put them in the schooner's small boat and launched the boat over the side. All hands rowed safely to land and were taken to the home of Joseph Coombs. Exposed to the heavy breakers and high winds *Mab* split in two parts. The cargo — salt pork, salt beef, apples, sugar, flour — contained in barrels washed ashore or drifted away. The schooner, which had been built in Bonavista Bay, was insured, but not the cargo.

Eventually the eight Newtown men made their way to St. John's arriving there on December fourteenth. The shipwrecked crew were met by Captain W.C. Winsor, Minister of Marine and Fisheries who took them to a place of lodging until transportation could be arranged to Newtown.

Chapter 16

Last of her Kind, Maxwell R. Corkum

Badger's Quay, Valleyfield

Built of wood in Nova Scotia and destroyed by fire on the Labrador Coast forty-six years later, *Maxwell R. Corkum* was one of the final survivors of the sailing schooner era. In 1925 she slipped down the ways at the Smith and Rhuland yards, the same Nova Scotian enterprise that launched *Bluenose*. *Maxwell Corkum*, a one hundred fifty ton two-masted vessel, first came to Newfoundland when she was purchased by Foote's of Grand Bank exclusively for the bank fishery but, like most vessels in lean times, she was converted to a coasting schooner hauling coal and dry goods from mainland ports to Newfoundland.

In time *Maxwell* was purchased by Reeves Limited of Englee who sold her in 1967 to Captain Edward S. "Ned" Kean, a vessel owner and businessman born in Badger's Quay. Badger's Quay, found on the western side of Bonavista Bay, first appeared in the Newfoundland *Census* in 1891 with a population of eighty-seven. In the early 1900s other families — Winter, Starkes, Sturge, Kean, Blackmore, Hunt and Roberts — came from Pool's Island, Flowers Island, Cape Island and Wesleyville to settle in the town.

Although its proximity to the seal herds was the primary reason for early settlement in Badger's Quay, after 1920 most

Courtesy Alex Hardy

An indistinct photo of *Maxwell R. Corkum* taken at sea and bank fishing with her riding sail up — a small sail used to keep a vessel's head to the wind while at anchor.

Captain tom Harris was the master and part owner during her stay in Grand Bank. After she was sold to Reeves in the 1940s, she was skippered in various years by several well-known northeast coast captains: Ralph Roberts, Ernest Penney, Willis Hopkins, William Russell, Alfred Pollard and William Sturge.

people turned to the inshore cod fishery or logging. In the 1960s the fish plant opened; twenty years later it employed two hundred people at its peak.

In the late nineteen sixties, fish procurers brought the fish from the inshore fishermen and from the Labrador to be processed in Newfoundland. Kean also owned the coaster *Saval,* which like *Maxwell Corkum* was once registered to a business in Grand Bank. *Maxwell Corkum* had been rebuilt in 1960 at Englee: she was made a little longer and higher, and two Caterpillar engines were installed. But the ex-Nova Scotian banker still maintained her beautiful lines while becoming a great carrier of freight.

In June 1971 Captain Kean was getting ready for the provincial election contesting the Labrador South riding as a Progressive Conservative. That spring, as he had done the four previous springs, Kean had *Maxwell Corkum* engaged in the salmon business travelling the Labrador coast buying salmon from the fishermen. Captain William Sturge of Valleyfield had a crew all from Valleyfield: engineer Pierce Penton (formerly of Norris Arm), cook Wilshire, mate Ed Burry and seaman Ed Burry, Jr.

On June 15, she was anchored just offshore at Southeast Bight, Long Island, off Cartwright, Labrador. John Russell, the salmon buyer from Bonavista, was aboard. A few minutes after the anchor was weighed, a fire broke out aboard *Maxwell Corkum*, apparently started by an oil stove.

Although the crew tried to fight the blaze, soon the fire was out of control and they were forced to abandon ship in a small motorboat. The crew and Russell could do nothing but watch as the old workhorse went up in flames. *Maxwell Corkum*'s remains and anchors are still on the bottom near Southeast Bight.

Chapter 17

Seeking Shelter at Lumsden

Lumsden

In the era of sail, when schooners shaped a course northward along the Strait Shore after rounding Cape Freels, the first good harbour they reached was Lumsden — once called Cat Harbour and renamed Lumsden at the beginning of the century. The Newfoundland and Labrador Pilot describes the harbour as..."small and dangerous; it is only available for small vessels with local knowledge in fine weather. It is entered between Inner and Outer Cat Island, which are situated close to the coast. Outer Cat Island is seventy feet high."

It was not a harbour easily or readily ventured into by masters of sailing ships but, according to R.W. Guy writing in *The Newfoundland Quarterly* (1978), many a crew has run in there to save their lives during adverse weather. "In most cases they were successful, but the ships were doomed. Very few ships going ashore at Cat Harbour were ever refloated."

An example of the validity of this claim happened on December 2, 1929, when two schooners — *Erema H* and *Toukalou* — were caught in a winter storm at Lumsden. *Erema H* was wrecked; the latter survived.

Erema H parted her chains and drifted on South Cat Harbour Island. Owner and captain Theophilus William

Courtesy Rolland Abbott, Musgrave Harbour

A crewman reaches to the bowsprit of the seventy-one ton *Erema H*, a schooner once owned by Samuel Harris of Grand Bank. Her mainsail and foresail are lashed as the schooner is tied to a St. John's wharf. She was later lost in Lumsden harbour, 1929.

Blackwood and his two brothers, mate Stephen Blackwood, Charles E. Blackwood; cook Pierce Blackwood and Edward Ellsworth, all of Carmanville and Roland W. Abbott of Musgrave Harbour, passenger — escaped without injury.

Captain John J. Chaulk of Carmanville, master of *Toukalou*, was more fortunate. In company with other schooners, he had left Loo Cove on December first bound for Carmanville, but by the next evening was forced to seek shelter in Lumsden. Chaulk described the weather and the situation:

> The wind was blowing a hurricane from the northwest. Owing to the heavy sea running it took all our time to keep spring tackling on our chains. Just at daylight we had to leave the schooner.

On the night of December second Captain Chaulk witnessed the wreck of *Erema H* and narrow escape of her crew. For two weeks Chaulk and his men were forced to stay at Lumsden all the while watching anxiously as *Toukalou* strained at her chains in the storm. *Toukalou* came through and Chaulk, grateful to the people of Lumsden, wrote a letter which appeared in December 27 edition of *The Fisherman's Advocate*:

> **Thanks People of Lumsden**
> I wish to thank the good friends and my relatives of Lumsden for their kind hospitality shown to me and the crew of the schooner "Toukalou" while anchored there. For two weeks recently we had to stay on shore or run the risk of our lives by staying on board.
>
> ...Just at daylight we had to leave the schooner. When we reached the shore, the sandy beach was crowded with men. We were all glad to find a comfortable home in Lumsden. We were met with welcoming faces and found comfortable beds and good food which we appreciated very much. We wish the kind people a Merry Christmas and a Happy New Year.
>
> J.J. Chaulk, December 18, 1929

Chapter 18

Wreck of the Majestic

Wesleyville, Cabot Island

One of the greatest hazards to ships that ply the northeast coast in winter are strong currents and winds that veer or change quickly. Within a few minutes wind and weather can roil relatively shallow coastal water and that, combined with jagged rocks, underwater ledges and numerous small islands, sank scores of sailing vessels. Any error in seamanship or judgement could prove disastrous to men and the hard-working vessels that carried them.

One example of what unpredictable wind patterns and rocks can do to ships happened to the schooner *Majestic* on Sunday night December 9-10, 1906. Owned in Twillingate by G.J. Carter, the ninety-nine ton vessel was eleven years old and under the command of Archibald Roberts with mate William Hanrahan. Captain and crew hailed from Twillingate and vicinity.

While en route northward from St. John's laden with food, shop goods and supplies *Majestic* was within sight of Cape Fogo when the jumbo stay broke. Roberts and his crew "bore up", ran past the Wadham Islands and "hove to" until four pm Sunday evening. By this time they had drifted back until they were about four miles north of Gull Island, Cape Freels. Roberts intended to make a safe harbour in Bonavista

Bay, wait until the strong westerly wind moderated and then make any necessary repairs to *Majestic*. The temperature had dropped to below freezing.

But the erratic currents around Cabot Island carried *Majestic* off her course. When Captain Roberts discovered the dangerous position, he tried to retreat but the schooner mis-stayed or drifted back while changing tack. Despite all efforts the ship was drifting onto Gull Rock near Cabot Island.

Roberts and his crew abandoned ship about six thirty; within a half hour *Majestic*, her bottom torn out by one of the many jagged ledges, sank. When the crew jumped into the small boat, mate Hanrahan leaped from the schooner's deck to the boat, but fell across the gunwale with his legs in the water.

When the mate got into the boat he seemed all right; although wet and cold, he was apparently uninjured and took an oar to help row to land. After an hour and a half he asked to be relieved. Now it appeared to the rest of the crew Hanrahan had internal injuries and was suffering from exposure. They picked up the pace in their rowing. The mate refused to give in taking his turn on the tiller.

It was a cold winter's night and *Majestic*'s crew rowed for six hours in an open boat. When their schooner went down they were only a short distance from Cabot Island. Although Cabot Island (actually two small islands) was never a settled community, it is listed in the census of 1911 as having a population of eleven people, most likely the lighthouse keepers and their families. Located about five and a half miles southeast from the South Bill of Cape Freels, Cabot is remote and relatively inaccessible and because of its rugged shore, *Majestic*'s crew couldn't land there and made for Flower's Island, the nearest settled community.

Around twelve-thirty Monday morning the weary crew arrived on Flower's Island; all the while the rapidly failing mate had only complained of feeling tired. He died while they were removing him from the boat to the land.

Two of the other men had frostbitten hands. No one saved anything from the wreck except the wet and cold clothes they stood in. The survivors left Flower's Island for Wesleyville on Tuesday morning carrying the body of their shipmate with them.

Residents of Flower's Island and Wesleyville took them in and gave them whatever assistance they could. At Wesleyville authorities sent a message to Sir Robert Bond, the Prime Minister of Newfoundland at that time, who made arrangements for the S.S. *Falcon* to transport the crew to Twillingate. To make sure the shipwrecked sailors were made as comfortable as possible Bond sent the following message to George Roberts, M.H.A. for the district:

> Have heard with profound regret of the loss on Sunday night, at Cabot Island of the schooner *Majestic* of Twillingate. Crew landed at Wesleyville, badly frozen, and one poor fellow died just after landing. Have instructed Magistrate Mifflin to do all possible for their comfort. Convey an expression of my sincere sympathy to their friends.

Captain Roberts and his remaining crew arrived at Twillingate by skiff from Herring Neck on Thursday, four days after the schooner *Majestic,* laden with winter supplies for the people of Twillingate, Herring Neck and other towns on New World Island, went to the bottom off Cabot Island.

On December 13, food — ten packs of sweets, a box of biscuits, two carpet brooms, box of cocoa, twenty tubs of butter, hams, rolls of paper and a number of other articles — drifted into Keels, Bonavista Bay.

Chapter 19

Loss of the Nerette

Greenspond

As published in a brief newspaper article datelined Sydney, Nova Scotia, for November 4, 1919, the story of eleven people who nearly went down on their sinking schooner became known. According to the report, seven crewmen and four passengers, including one woman, of the schooner *Nerette*, owned in Greenspond, were saved from a watery grave by the steamer *Germanicus*.

Situated on the northwest side of Bonavista Bay, Greenspond is an island town about a kilometre offshore on Greenspond Island. First settled as a fishing-station in the 1690s, Greenspond is one of the oldest continuously inhabited outports in Newfoundland. Due to its strategic location, it became a major settlement and a commercial centre earning the nickname "The Capital of the North".

Greenspond has always had a substantial population — in 1874 over fifteen hundred people lived there and thirty years later numbers had risen to over seventeen hundred. Thereafter the town experienced a steady decline caused mainly by out-migration and a drop in fish stocks. Today between four and five hundred make Greenspond their home.

Early settlers were predominantly from England's West Country and, as in many Newfoundland communities, certain family names are well-represented: Bishop, Brown, Burry, Chaytor, Easton, Green, Harding, Hunt, Kean, Oakley, Oldford, Osmond, Parsons, Rogers, and Wornell. Indeed, *Nerette*'s crew, who all belonged to Greenspond, have surnames closely associated with the town: Captain W. Carter, first mate W. Carter, seamen E. Carter, L. Carter, A. Pond, R. Keats and L. Acreman; passengers Mrs. Carter, the captain's wife; Q. Carter, the captain's son; A. Carter, the captain's nephew and E. Crocker.

While bound from St. John's to Greenspond the fifty-seven ton *Nerette* was overwhelmed by a gale on Thursday, October 30th. When the wind chopped northerly, the crew had no choice but reduce sail and run before the wind. The force of wind on the sails and rigging caused the masts to work loose until they broke or fell out.

For sailing vessels headed northward in the fall months which harsher weather prevailed, to be driven out to sea was not an unusual occurrence. Often the wind abated within a couple of days and the schooner, which may have drifted between one to two hundred miles, could beat back to coastal ports. Many schooners engaged in the Labrador fishery or coastal trade were old, poorly rigged and a few were not able to withstand raging Atlantic gales. *Nerette* was no exception and the heavy pounding and buffetting opened seams and the schooner slowly settled lower and lower until her deck was awash.

For four days Carter's crew fought to keep the vessel afloat. By that time *Nerette* was driven out into transatlantic shipping lanes. Monday morning at daylight, the steamer *Germanicus* came in sight. Carter, knowing his schooner was doomed, had already decided to abandon ship. Heavy seas gave the steamer's crew manning the lifeboat a difficult time, but eventually they plucked the eleven from the sinking schooner.

In the four days of trying to keep *Nerette* afloat and in their haste to leave the sinking vessel, all the people aboard lost personal belongings including their money and any extra clothes. When they landed in Sydney, Nova Scotia, on Tuesday, November 4, they were practically destitute.

Loss of the Passport

One of the most poignant tragedies affecting Greenspond occurred during the storm of December 5-7, 1921, when several vessels were wrecked on the northeast coast; two with full crew.

In the evening of December 5, *Passport*, in company with several other schooners including a Carbonear schooner *Pet*, Captain Art Osmond, left St. John's laden with winter freight and Christmas supplies. Winds were light and southerly off St. John's, but by the time the little flotilla reached Cape St. Francis, the wind had veered to a strong southeasterly with snow.

By the next day, Captain Art Osmond's *Pet* had harboured safely in Bristol's Hope; *Passport* went on apparently to make Carbonear, but was wrecked at Caplin Cove with a loss of several lives: Captain Lewis Bragg, married with two children; Pierce Burry, married; William Peckford, married, one child; Christopher Rogers, married, three children; Thomas Button, married, one child, and Joseph Stratton, single. In addition to the six crew, *Passport* carried an unidentified lady passenger. Captain Bragg, Peckford, Burry and Stratton were of Greenspond; the others resided in towns near Greenspond.

A sixty-nine ton, six-dory banker, *Passport* was built in Grand Bank at the turn of the century and was registered to Thomas Foote of Grand Bank before she had been purchased by Greenspond interests.

Through the December blizzard and spray watchers on the cliffs near Caplin Cove saw a schooner unsuccessfully attempting to beat her way off the rocks, but were powerless to help. On the morning of December 7, Magistrate Vatcher

In a photo credited to Holloway, banking schooners leave for sea sometime prior the advent of engines. When there was not enough wind to fill the sails, the crew, manning the vessel's dories, were obliged to tow the schooners outside the headlands.

at Old Perlican wired this message to the Deputy Minister of Justice in St. John's:

> Nothing further ascertained regarding fate of crew of vessel lost at Caplin Cove in Monday's storm. Vessel completely broken up. Two hours after being discovered, small fragments of wreckage were picked up, on which were vessel's name "Passport."
>
> Everything points to previous theory, that crew were drowned in attempting to land in vessel's boat. Every effort being made to recover bodies, but up to present unsuccessful. Search will be continued as long as any hope of recovery exists.

Chapter 20

Athlete II and Tishy: Wrecked on the Same Night

St. Brendan's, Shambler's Cove, Bonavista Bay

Two well-known motor vessels, virtual workhorses of Bonavista Bay, — *Athlete II* and *Tishy* — were both wrecked within a few miles of each other and on the same night: December 6, 1950. *Athlete II*, the last vessel to be near the ill-fated *Stanley Parsons* eighteen years before, was bound to ports on the north side of Bonavista Bay from St. John's. *Stanley Parsons*, a freighting schooner from Lush's Bight near Bay of Islands, disappeared while en route from St. John's to Lush's bight in November 1932. (See Chapter 7 "Whatever Happened to Stanley Parsons")

On *Athlete II*'s final voyage, all had gone well until darkness fell and fog capped all lights in the area. This weather condition was in direct contrast to *Athlete II*'s journey with *Stanley Parsons* in December 1932, eighteen years previously. That night was clear and *Athlete*'s captain saw the Catalina lights, the Elliston light and the Offer Gooseberry Island. He also kept in contact with *Stanley Parsons* and the last to see the missing schooner.

Now as Captain John Burry steered in the dense fog for Greenspond, Bonavista Bay, he had no beacons or lights to guide him. The one hundred thirty-two ton *Athlete II* piled into rocks near the Offer Gooseberry Island and sank almost immediately.

The crew barely had time to throw the dory over the side and abandon ship before *Athlete II* sank. Seaman Walter Pope of Pool's Island was struck by an oil cask sustaining severe bruises in the abdomen. None of the crew saved any clothes or personal effects. Pope, in addition to his injury, lost eighty dollars in cash which was in his wallet in the forecastle. The schooner broke up so quickly he was unable to get below to retrieve his wallet.

Athlete grounded about 8:30 pm and after rowing four and a half hours in a dory, the crew reached Dock Cove at St. Brendan's on Cottel Island about midnight. In the few hours they were there, the crew was well cared for. That day they joined S.S. *Glencoe* for their homes at Safe Harbour and Pool's Island.

Although Burry did not know it at the time, *Tishy*, owned and commanded by Captain William Blackmore of St. John's, came to grief on Smart Island at the entrance to Shambler's Cove near Greenspond. *Tishy* lies on the bottom on the east side not far from the remains of seventy-seven ton *Lloyd Jack*, burned July 14, 1952. Built in Nova Scotia in 1899, *Lloyd Jack* had various Newfoundland owners, but at the time of her loss was under the registry of merchant Wesley Pittman, Pilley's Island.

Built in 1920, *Tishy* was constructed by the Palfrey shipbuilders of Placentia. In the previous year, Palfreys had constructed two large tern schooners for G.C. Fearn and Son: *Elizabeth Fearn*, two hundred forty-six ton and *Herbert Fearn* three hundred twenty-five ton. Out of the pieces and material left over, they built a smaller tern schooner *Mollie Fearn*, at one hundred eighteen ton and one hundred two feet long. James Baird Limited bought and renamed the schooner *Tishy*. One of her subsequent Newfoundland owners installed auxiliary engines which increased her tonnage to one

Photo courtesy Marine Archives, Harry Stone Collection and *The Newfoundland Ancestor*.

Tishy, from a photo probably taken in the late 1930s when she was owned by Baird's Limited, waiting in Baird's Cove to take on a shipment of lumber. The St. John's Courthouse dominates the background view.

Commanded for many years by Captain William Dillon, *Tishy* was a three-masted vessel built in Placentia and later converted to a motorized two master designed for the coastal trade.

hundred thirty net. Eventually *Tishy* came under the registry of W.B. Blackmore.

One seaman, Vince Mallay of Marystown, recalled his voyage to Oporto in September 1933 on *Tishy*. Baird's branch business in Marystown consigned her to load salt fish at various Placentia Bay ports: Harbour Buffett, Marystown and Burin. Needing one more deckhand, Captain William Dillon hired Mallay at $22.50 a month. The trip over lasted twenty-two days and the westward voyage laden with salt, twenty-eight. Others in the crew were all from St. John's; seamen Michael Maddigan and Walter Hodder, a cook and a mate whose names are not recorded.

Both *Tishy* and *Athlete II* were in the coastal freight business supplying firms and stores along the North East coast with winter supplies. For example, Bown and Company of Badger's Quay had goods on board both vessels valued at $5,000 which included one hundred cases of oil and a motor car. Some goods were insured, but Bown and Company stood to lose considerably.

By this time in the development of Newfoundland towns, much of the stands of trees and firewood close to communities had been depleted. Coal had replaced wood as fuel. The small coasting schooners of Newfoundland regularly visited North Sydney to load coal for local depots and businesses. In rural Newfoundland using coal depended on availability of work. Many men were employed seasonally or year-round the lumber woods; thus, most people had the ready cash to buy coal. Since employment in the logging industry required men to work away from home in the winter months, which was the season to cut firewood, they depended on coal to supplement winter's fuel.

The loss of the two coasting vessels had a direct effect on coal supplies on certain towns on the northeast coast. By December of 1950, for example, National Stores of Wesleyville and Bown & Company, Badger's Quay expected a cargo of two hundred ton. In contrast Fishermen's Protective Union Limited store at Valleyfield had had a large stock in October, but fall sales dwindled the supply leaving some Bonavista Bay families with a fuel shortage.

In addition to the loss of her coal cargo, many of the crew of *Athlete II* had winter food and clothing aboard for their families. Each family would have extra burdens that winter.

Chapter 21

Victim of a Storm: Blue Blossom

Dancing Cove near Bonavista, Brigus

Two men of Brigus lost their life at Dancing Cove, Bonavista Bay, when the schooner *Blue Blossom* was pounded by a mid-November storm in 1920. From all over Newfoundland came reports of damage, but shipwrecks were more extensive along the northeast segment of Newfoundland's coast. The official report of the tragedy at Dancing Cove came to Inspector General Hutchings of St. John's from acting-ser geant Gardner of Bonavista:

> "**November 15, 1920** Unknown schooner anchored in Dancing Cove late this evening, two men tried to land in a dory and were drowned. Four other men still on schooner. If wind does not abate, little hope of saving schooner or men."

Hutchings immediately got in touch with the Ministry of Shipping in St. John's who wired the captain of the steamship *Watchful* to proceed to the site. Once there *Watchful*'s crew were to attempt to rescue the stranded men or to take the schooner in tow. Subsequent reports to St. John's by the next day at one thirty pm stated that *Watchful* had arrived at Port Union with schooner *Blue Blossom* in tow. The two lost men were identified as Captain Thomas Hayes and seaman Harold Linthorn of Brigus.

According to the story related later, when the schooner stranded a short distance offshore, Hayes and Linthorn made an attempt to reach land with a line in a small boat. In the high winds and raging seas the boat swamped throwing the two occupants into the sea. It was impossible for the remaining four men on *Blue Blossom* or for those standing on the shore to attempt a rescue.

Reports of strandings, wrecks and narrow escapes came nearly every area of Newfoundland: from Old Perlican came notification of a Twillingate schooner *Marion,* Alex Hodder master, a total wreck at Daniel's Cove, a resettled town once located at the tip of the Bay de Verde Peninsula. The owner of this particular vessel had insured his schooner in Twillingate Mutual Company for four thousand dollars as well as with another company, Home Mutual of St. John's, for three thousand dollars. *Marion*'s crew had escaped the wreck without incident.

At Englee three schooners laden with fish cargoes were lost. The Justice of Peace at Conche, J. D. Fitzgerald, sent brief particulars in this message:

> "Schooner *Ada Mildred,* Captain Robert Bragg (owned by David Barry), lost at Englee, crew all safe. Schooner *Chips,* Captain M.H. Roberts (R.G. Rendell, owner) lost at Englee, crew all safe. Schooner *J.A. Mclean,* Captain Cross (George Bragg, owner) lost at Englee, crew all safe. All three were total wrecks in a terrific gale of westerly wind."

These were vessels bound home from the Labrador fishery and, at the outset of the gale, had taken shelter at Englee. They had broken moorings and were driven ashore.

The extent of damage reached as far as the South Coast where schooner *Edith Pardy,* owned in Grand Bank by Patten and Forsey, was wrecked at Lamaline. In addition to shipwrecks reported around the coast, out of Harbour Breton came a report of an extensive fire burning out of control on

Courtesy Y. Andrieux

Evidence of a shipwreck. With only the planking and ribs peeking above the sand and gravel, a horse stands on all that remains of a Newfoundland schooner.

the north side of Broad Cove, a community two miles east of Harbour Breton. Unable to extinguish the blaze due to high winds, the people had to let it burn itself out. The report also said that the fire was likely to destroy ten homes which represented about half the small settlement of Broad Cove.

Chapter 22

Abandoning the Cento

Bonavista, Catalina

In 1920 P. Templeton's Ltd. of Bonavista sent their schooner *Cento,* under the command of Captain W.J. (James) Edgecombe of Catalina, to Malaga, Spain, with a cargo of dry cod. *Cento,* a ninety-ton vessel, left Catalina where Templeton had a branch business, on October sixth and made the run eastward from port to port in twenty-six days. However, the return voyage was arduous and when the battle against the elements ended, *Cento,* one of Templeton's foreign-going fleet, was abandoned in mid-ocean. In addition to Captain Edgecombe, only one other of his six-man crew is known: Caleb Edgecombe of Catalina.

The Templeton business on Newfoundland's northeast coast had a long and unique history. At the age of thirteen Philip Templeton worked in his father's store which had just begun to branch out into fish buying. In 1887 he purchased the premises of the Saint business, a central location in Bonavista, and later bought property in nearby Bayley's Cove. By 1890 Templeton opened his first branch outside of Bonavista, at Catalina and, with the acquisition of banking schooners, soon began to ship salt fish to Europe through vessels like *Cento.*

P. Templeton's Ltd., a major supplier to the Labrador and French Shore fisheries, also had branch businesses in Labrador. By 1913 Templeton's establishments was one of the leading fishery and supply businesses in the country. In the Depression years, the firm faltered and in 1936-37 eventually phased out. Templeton's Bonavista premises were subsequently bought by J.T. Swyers.

Cento left Malaga on January third, putting into Gibraltar five days later and finally set sail for Bonavista and Catalina on January tenth. Six days out, the schooner sprang a leak and every crewman was kept at the pumps constantly for eighty-seven hours. Water rose so quickly pumps could not keep up with the inrush and Captain Edgecombe decided to abandon ship.

Before this decision was made, Edgecombe ran distress flags up to the top mast hoping a passing ship would see them. Within a few hours the steamer *Massillon Bridge* spotted the signals. She came by, took the crew off, and the wallowing *Cento* was abandoned. Her position when she dipped her bow below the Atlantic was latitude 39.04 North, longitude 19.02 West.

Now the crew had to make a circuitous route to get back home: *Massillon Bridge* was eastbound and took them back to Gibraltar, the place they had left more than a week previously. From Gibraltar they found a passage to St. John, New Brunswick, on the S.S. *Otira*, travelled to Louisbourg, Nova Scotia, by train and joined the Newfoundland steamship *Kyle* for Newfoundland. *Cento*'s crew finally set foot on Newfoundland soil at Port aux Basques on February 11, 1921 — one hundred and twenty-eight days after putting out of Catalina.

Cento's crew experienced the misfortunes which was often the lot of foreign-going sailors. As Edgecombe related later:

> [We] were very fortunate in having gotten clear of the *Cento* so quickly as in another couple of hours we would have been compelled to take to the boats. Being about 400

> miles from land when we abandoned ship, there would have been poor hope of making shore with both wind and sea against us. Luckily the timely arrival of the *Massillon Bridge* saved the hazard of the open boat.

Cento's crew had a short, comfortable voyage on *Massillon Bridge,* but when they reached Gibraltar, each man was, in essence, stranded and destitute. Edgecombe had high praise for the officers and crew of S.S. *Otira* who supplied the shipwrecked mariners with food, money and clothing.

Chapter 23

Two Fine Vessels: Revenue and Albert J. Lutz

Catalina

On November 11, 1918, World War One officially ended. Germany had surrendered. The enemy submarine and warship threat on the high seas between Newfoundland and Europe was no longer a menace. Undaunted by the presence of hostile submarines and warships, the little ships of Newfoundland transported fish and salt between North America and Europe during the war years.

The Bay of Biscay, off the west coast of France, had been a theatre of ocean warfare and the sea in that area was littered with mines. It was one of these unexploded, stray mines that proved disastrous for a Catalina crew. The schooner *Revenue* sailed from Bay Bulls in the fall of 1918, had gone through the Bay of Biscay to La Rochelle, France and had delivered her cargo safely. On the westward bound voyage from Cadiz, Spain, she was laden with salt. Her crew:

James McLaughlin,	son of Catherine McLaughlin, Catalina
Harry Mullins,	son of Bessie Manuel? of Catalina
Simeon Penney,	son of Catherine Penney, Catalina

Michael Walsh,	son of Bridget Walsh, Catalina
Harold Cook,	grandson of Mrs. Honora Cook of Port Rexton, T.B.
John Sutton,	married, St. John's

Unexplained events abound in the tales of the sea and the disappearance of *Revenue* at the end of the war may have been one of those unsolved mysteries, but for a chance encounter of another Newfoundland schooner. *Revenue* and one of A.E. Hickman's fleet of foreign-going schooners, *Henry L. Montague*, left Cadiz on the same day in November, 1918, bound for Newfoundland.

Off the Bay of Biscay a storm overtook both vessels; Captain George Anstey, a native of Grand Bank, reduced canvas on *Montague*. *Revenue* sailed past in the twilight. The next morning Captain Anstey passed through wreckage of a wooden vessel, slowed to investigate and realized his Newfoundland compatriots would never be seen again. He later confirmed the wreckage was that of *Revenue*.

Situated on the eastern coast of the Bonavista Peninsula in Trinity Bay, Catalina's name probably comes from the French Havre Sainte-Katerine which was later superseded by the Spanish Cataluna. Sixteenth century fishermen from England, France and Spain frequented the sheltered harbour and by 1580 it had a permanent population of one hundred. Fishing remained the main occupation until the 1990s. In 1981 the commercial centre was the site of the largest salt fish businesses in eastern Canada, Mifflin Fisheries Ltd. Today Catalina has a population of around twelve hundred and adjoins the town of Port Union, home of the Fisherman's Union Trading Company established by Sir William Coaker. (See chapter 43 "No Survivors from President Coaker.")

Like most Newfoundland towns emerging as growth centres in early twentieth century, Catalina had schooners regularly plying the coastal run obtaining food, supplies and coal from mainland ports. During a calm spring day in early June, 1919, the schooner *Albert J. Lutz* suddenly capsized off

Cape Broyle and one member of her crew died in the mishap. Registered to Captain Joseph Johnson of Catalina and laden with coal for Philip Templeton's business, the ninety-five ton vessel carried a crew of six: mate Thomas Chaulk, Charles King, Azariah Tippett, Fred King. Cook, William L. Johnson, the captain's cousin, was married and lived in Catalina.

Built in Shelburne, Nova Scotia, in 1908 J.T. Moulton's business of Burgeo acquired *Albert J. Lutz* in 1918. In her brief time on the South Coast — for Moulton sold her to Catalina interests one year later — she was captained by two Burgeo men: George Street and Matthew Pink.

From the time she left Sydney, Nova Scotia, on a Tuesday morning *Albert J. Lutz* made good time in fine weather, a good sea and a moderate breeze. At one o'clock Saturday morning, without the slightest warning, a heavy squall of wind struck the ship and threw her on her beam ends. Four crew were on deck at the time: the captain, mate and two seamen. Captain Johnson was aft at the wheel and was able to hold on as his schooner was thrown down, sails and masts parallel to the choppy sea.

The other three men tumbled into the water trying to hold on to anything within reach. With great presence of mind, mate Chaulk grabbed the dory which floated up from the deck, took out his knife and cut it loose. Otherwise all the crew would have been lost.

The man forward shouted to the two crew still in the forecastle, but it was impossible to give them any assistance, as the forecastle entrance was almost entirely underwater. After several attempts Charles King forced his way up through the companionway through the inrushing seawater, but cook William Johnson, a man of fifty-two years, married with no children, was not able to make it. He went down with *Albert J. Lutz* which sank a minute or two after the others had boarded the dory.

When they took stock of their situation, the five marooned men found the dory had no oars. They figured they were south east of Cape Broyle; but were uncertain of the

Albert J. Lutz on the occasion of her launching at Shelburne in 1908.
Below, *Albert J. Lutz* with all sails full in calm, peaceful days. She capsized off Cape Broyle in June 1919 carrying a resident of Catalina down with her.

Courtesy Canadian Coast Guard and Marine Archives

The historic ports of Catalina/Port Union have harboured hundreds of ships and have experienced several shipwrecks over the years. On January 23, 1922, schooner Smuggler, Captain George Parsons was wrecked at Catalina. Formerly a Gloucester banker and once owned in Burin, *Smuggler* had been bought by Roberts and Parsons firm for $1600. She had loaded 3000 quintals of fish at Little Grey Island, but during a gale she dragged her anchors and went on the rocks near Catalina.

In this photo (above) a vessel of more recent vintage, the eight hundred forty-six ton Fisheries Products trawler *Zaratoga* grounded near Port Union on October 18, 1983, after fire broke out on board. Smoke from her bridge and black and light patches of oil drift away from the burning hulk.

distance. Making the best use of what material was in the small, open boat, they took the thwarts, or dory seats, and made makeshift paddles. With the help of a favourable wind they succeeded in making Renews about five o'clock in the morning.

At Renews, as they related the story of their mishap and of their friend who had disappeared with the ship, the shipwrecked crew were cared for and eventually transported to St. John's. They arrived there Saturday afternoon, less than twenty-four hours after their horrifying ordeal aboard *Albert J. Lutz*.

Chapter 24

Debris from the Effie M at Old Perlican

Trinity, Old Perlican, Trinity Bay

Every few years or so in the era of sail, September (or August) gales pounced suddenly and severely on unsuspecting Newfoundland schooners. The gales were tail-ends of tropical hurricanes that spent their power somewhere in the Atlantic or on the eastern seaboard, but not before they had become a killer storm. On September 17-19, 1907, a great storm battered the east coast of Newfoundland with such ruthlessness, that scores of schooners went to the bottom. Many ships were returning from the Labrador fishery; thus, families not only lost a vessel, but also its valuable cargo and then had to face the winter in economic ruin.

For Trinity (Trinity Bay) and for the several smaller towns nearby, the storm of 1907 left a wake of death: *Effie M*, wrecked at Great Brook near Old Perlican, had sixteen persons on board and not one escaped to tell the tale.

Owned by Joseph Morris of Trinity and commanded by Fred Morris, *Effie M* left Trinity early in the summer to fish off the Labrador with a crew of eleven men and two boys. In relation to other schooners in the same trade, *Effie M* was a larger craft at seventy ton and had been well-maintained. Her canvas was all practically new; thus able to withstand a strong wind.

Captain Morris did not meet with the success he had hoped for and decided to return to Trinity in mid-September with his three hundred quintals — below *Effie M*'s capacity. On the way home he stopped on the French shore, probably at Conche or Croque, to take three passengers, or freighters as they were termed, to Trinity Bay.

En route to Trinity the captain anchored at Seldom Come By for a short while. Since the weather was already threatening, other schooners gathered there to wait out a possible storm, but Morris apparently decided to sail on.

What happened next is pure speculation, but it was possible *Effie M* made Trinity Bight during the storm. In the gale most likely her sails were carried away or she lost her spars. Others believed the schooner would have been stood a greater chance of survival beyond Baccalieu Island and into open water. Perhaps that had been Morris' destination.

All who knew Captain Morris — a man who put the well-being of his crew above personal safety — recognized his superb seamanship. Most schooners travelling the north-east coast while going to and from the Labrador coast tried to hold close to the land as much as possible. Experienced captains believed *Effie M* was close to the safety of Trinity Bight when the fury of the September gale struck.

The following morning wreckage was found floating at Broad Cove, near Old Perlican, on the eastern side of Trinity Bay. People living on that shore neither saw nor heard anything during the night of September eighteenth to signify a disaster. Among the debris searchers located seaman's box marked Woolridge; letters from a schooner's nameboard marked "EF" and marked fishing gear. Within twenty-four hours three bodies were located and identified which proved the ill-fated craft was Joseph Morris' *Effie M*.

Most men aboard were from communities in Trinity Bay: Captain Fred Morris and his son; George Hiscock, single, son of Robert; James Woolridge, married four years previously;

William Miller and his two sons, both single; Walter Brown, son of John; all of Trinity; James Fleet, Cuckold's Cove; Robert Morris, Trouty and Daniel Locke of North West Arm, a widower. James Janes, single, resided in Spaniard's Bay. Perhaps because they were passengers, the home town of four other victims — John Pinhorn, John Ash, Arthur Sexton and his son — were not identified.

Within two days eight bodies were jigged up from the bottom, taken to Old Perlican, coffined and sent to Trinity. Later others were recovered. Describing the sorrow at Trinity, one report said, "The scenes in some houses at Trinity and some small nearby settlements were heart-rending. The wives of the ill-fated crew were distraught — some silent in an agony of grief; others wailing and finding vent for their awful misery in shrieks and sobs."

Other crews exposed to the gale were more fortunate. Although the exact numbers are not clear, estimates say close to one hundred schooners were wrecked: five at Bonavista, twenty-eight at Twillingate, seven at Musgrave Harbour, four at Newtown, four at Eastern Tickle, four at Fogo, five at Keels, three at La Scie and one or two in each of several other towns along the northeast coast.

The toll in lives and ships was staggering. Fall gales and hurricanes, unpredictable in the days of limited weather forecasting, made easy victims of vessels.

Chapter 25

Adrift: Fate of Ryan Brothers' Schooner Sperry

Trinity

Ryan Brothers' business, which originated in Bonavista in 1857, became one of the largest supply and fish exporting firms in Newfoundland. In 1906 the firm expanded to Trinity and soon grew to be the largest enterprise in that community as it supplied the inshore and the Labrador fishery operating in the area. After nearly half a century of successful business the Ryan brothers, who lived in the historic Lester/Garland house in Trinity, closed out Trinity branch on March 31, 1952.

Throughout the years, the Ryans had owned many vessels (according to local knowledge ninety-nine) ranging in size from two-dory schooners to larger coasters. Ryans' ships were engaged in the coastal or foreign trade and in the Labrador fishery. Their largest schooner *Marguerite Ryan*, a tern or three master used in the foreign-going trade to transport dry cod to the European market, was abandoned at sea in February, 1923.

When Ryans set up business in Trinity, the first vessel they owned and operated out of the town was *Flora W. Sperry*, generally called the *Sperry*. *Sperry*, at one hundred six tons and built in LaHave, Nova Scotia, was registered to

Daniel Ryan. In the fall of 1906 *Sperry* took a load of salt fish to Portugal and returned in good time. Six months later, when she sank off Scaterie Island, Nova Scotia, Ryan's schooner became a victim of the hazardous coastal trade.

In the spring, before work with salt fish began for the year, owners often sent their coastal schooners to mainland ports for supplies. *Sperry* left Trinity on April 17, 1907, headed for North Sydney for a cargo of coal. Her crew: Captain Oldford, probably of Elliston, near Bonavista, who had been *Sperry*'s captain when she was transferred from the Bonavista/King's Cove area to Trinity in 1906; mate James Carroll; M. Hanlyn, Trinity East; Ephriam Hiscock of Trinity; John Dewling, Trinity East or Trouty, and John Peddle, Lockston. Today Lockston, or the North West Arm of Trinity harbour, has only summer residents. Some years ago, when North West Arm was to be renamed, there was debate whether the arm would be called Lockston or Peddleton for both family names were equally represented; eventually the town became Lockston.

On Wednesday, May 22, as *Sperry* neared the Nova Scotian shore, she struck a pan of ice about fifty miles east southeast of Scaterie Island. With planking broken or "stove in" the schooner soon filled with water; in fact, pumps were useless against the inflow. Oldford and his crew barely had time to launch the small boat into the ice-filled sea. Oldford, the last to leave, snatched the compass and some hard bread (tack) before he abandoned ship. By then the life boat had drifted a few feet from the sinking schooner. As the captain stood on the rail preparing to jump, the boat drifted too far off and he had to clamber onto a pan of ice and thence to the boat. While in *Sperry*'s small boat, the crew watched their ship go down.

Surrounded on all sides by a seemingly limitless field of ice and with no other boat or land in sight, the shipwrecked men appeared to be in a hopeless situation. They attempted to row toward land, but ice and heavy weather prevented them from making headway. In addition, the little craft was poorly provisioned. With little drinking water and only the hard tack the captain had grabbed, their prospects of survival seemed remote. But Newfoundland sailors are not easily discouraged. They continued to row for twenty-one hours, but by the captain's reckoning were still forty miles south southeast of Scaterie.

Fortunately, they had sailed near the much frequented route of Newfoundland vessels travelling between the island and Nova Scotian ports and, about the time when some of the men were about to give up hope of rescue, they spotted a sail in the distance. *Sperry*'s beleaguered crew hoisted an old shirt as a makeshift distress flag on an oar in the hope of attracting attention.

It proved to be a Newfoundland schooner *Cora* — registered to J.B. Foote's business of Grand Bank and commanded by Captain Harry Lee — returning from a fishing trip from the Grand Banks. In the evening of Thursday, May 23, Lee saw *Sperry*'s lifeboat in the distance and, although *Cora* was a small vessel and was herself bucking seas and adverse winds, he swung around to aid the shipwrecked men. The stranded Trinity men, cold and physically drained, arrived in North Sydney and were immediately rushed to hospital. It was Monday, May 27, five days after *Flora W. Sperry* had gone to the bottom.

The little boat had drifted twenty-five miles from where *Sperry* went down. No crewman had saved any clothing or personal belongings except what they wore when they abandoned ship. Joseph Salter and Sons of North Sydney made the arrangements to have the men returned to Newfoundland via the steamship *Virginia Lake*.

This tale of shipwreck is but one of many events in the long, exciting history of Trinity, one of Newfoundland's oldest settlements. Some of the first English settlers arrived there in 1558 and by the 1800s the town had a population of around four thousand. In the mid-eighteen hundreds, three prosperous businesses were established in Trinity — Slades,

Garlands and Brookings —all based on island trade, fishing, and shipbuilding.

Trinity's harbour, deep and well-sheltered, has approximately twenty miles of coastline and was once well-fortified against the enemies — the French or pirates. Today, remains of extensive fortifications can be seen at Fort Point. Other evidence of Trinity's rich past can be seen in town museums, restored premises and through live theatre. Each summer, troupes dramatize the town's history and heritage for the benefit of visitors.

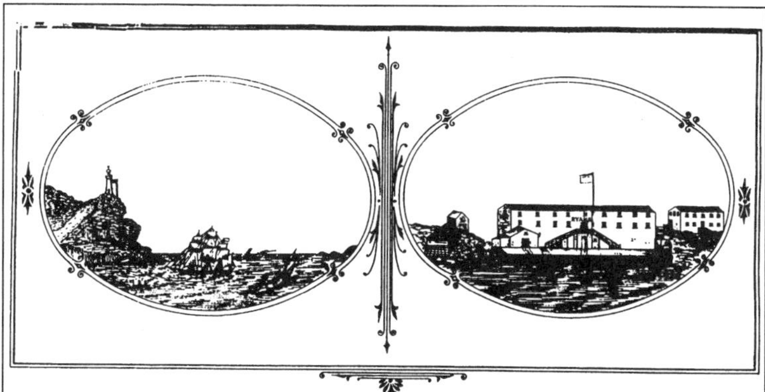

RYANS ✻ EMPORIUM.

RYANS ROYAL PORT EMPORIUM,

(Established over a Quarter of a Century).

BEG to call attention to the large and **varied stock** carried by them of **General Goods** suitable for all sorts and conditions of Men, Women, and Children in this Newfoundland of Ours. They claim a unique position in

BONAVISTA BAY.

1st.—They buy all Goods for **Spot Cash** and get all possible discounts, which they give their Customers the advantage of.

2nd.—They sell all Goods at **lowest margin of profit** consistent with quality of same; and, like the British and Colonial Troops, cannot and will not be beaten.

3rd.—They **guarantee prompt attention**, fair and square dealings, and aim to give general satisfaction to all, high and low, rich and poor.

At this, the first year of the New Century, they cordially invite and ask for your support, and this will be found to benefit both you and them. Their business is increasing every year by leaps and bounds, and the Stock of Goods carried by them runs into Hundreds of Thousands of Dollars for Spring, Summer and Winter Trade, they wish you to remember that they are not flitting, that is here to-day and gone to-morrow, as their Twenty-Seven Years record shows; in good times and bad times, when their Summer Competitors are not to be found, they are at their Old Stand always ready for business. They purchase all the Country's Produce at Market Prices, and Exporting as they do large quantities of Codfish every year they are able to give best prices for a well-cured article.

Remember their places of Business on the Labrador where they keep everything for Sale and buy everything that comes to their Stores, more especially **Codfish, Cod Oil, Herrings, and Fur.**

An advertising flyer produced by Ryan's Royal Port Emporium at the turn of the century to commemorate more than a quarter century of supplying the needs of the residents of Bonavista Bay through this particular outlet..

Chapter 26

Tragedy at Trinity

Trinity

Newfoundland's written history and oral traditions are filled with stories of ships and men who made their living from the ever-demanding ocean. But the remorseless, cold Atlantic often exacted its repayment; this is the story of one ship and seven men who paid the price. It began one November nearly sixty years ago when someone found the unmistakable debris of a wrecked ship and its cargo scattered along the rugged shoreline in Trinity Bight.

On the morning of November 28, 1938, residents of Trinity, Trinity Bay, discovered evidence of a shipwreck near Trinity harbour. The schooner *Marion Rogers,* expected to arrive in Trinity on the late evening of November 27, had not shown up. The following morning there was still no sign of the overdue ship. A typical winter storm with high winds and snow squalls had blown up overnight, but nothing that a vessel like *Marion Rogers* could not handle.

Relatives of Edward McGrath waiting in Trinity were expecting him to arrive for they knew he had obtained a passage to his Trinity home on *Marion Rogers*. To while away some time as they pondered on possible reasons for the schooner's delay, McGrath's kin walked along the beach near Trinity, looking out to sea and watching for her sails to appear around a familiar headland. One of the group spotted a suitcase that had drifted in with other debris in the high tide mark. When opened, the clothes and personal belongings identified the suitcase as that belonging to Edward McGrath — the very person they were waiting for.

It was possible the suitcase had washed off deck while the schooner attempted to make some harbour of refuge. The group, saddened and fearful of the end result, summoned help for a more careful search of the waters along the shore. McGrath's suitcase was the first indication the schooner had likely come to grief.

Within an hour much of the ship's timbers and debris was located floating near the Fort Point fog horn; soon, other portions of the schooner were found for several miles along the shoreline. Some cargo and wreckage drifted in Trinity harbour, but there was no sign of the crew; no word or evidence they had survived, had rowed in or had reached shore anywhere along the coast.

From the position of wreckage and from wind direction that night, it was determined the accident had occurred a few feet from the Trinity fog horn on Fort Point. In those years the lighthouse and horn on Fort Point was manned; that is, tended by a lighthouse keeper. There are many who wonder if there was a problem with the light or the sounding of the horn on that fateful Sunday night. Many residents believe that if Captain Hogarth had any signal from the shore — the horn, a light — he would have realized his dangerous position.

To this day no one is exactly sure how or why *Marion Rogers* was wrecked, but according to local tradition she may have grounded on Fort Point or struck a treacherous rock called Skirwink off Fort Point during the brief winter storm. The wind and snow probably obliterated any lights along the coast or the crew may not have heard the Trinity fog alarm although some wreckage drifted ashore practically in under the structure. Other residents of the area discredit this theory of bad weather. *Marion Rogers'* captain, William Hogarth, was very familiar with the coastline. During any inclement weather, he would have kept well off Skirwink.

Marion Rogers, a forty-one ton vessel, had been built by Stephen and Robert Miller of New Bonaventure, a community on the north side of Trinity Bay about seventeen kilometres southwest of Trinity and was owned by William J. Butler of New Bonaventure. Her crew hailed from the general vicinity: Captain Hogarth and his son, Lester, of Trinity East; owner William J. Butler; three men of New Bonaventure, Alfred Pitcher, his son Simon, and passenger McGrath, a resident of Trinity.

Also aboard was Ellis Butler of Port Rexton, brother of William. Some years previously to 1938 — the year of the loss of *Marion Rogers* — Ellis had left Newfoundland, found work in Boston where he stayed nine years and had married a Newfoundland girl. He and his wife returned home and he began to built a new house in Port Rexton. Ellis Butler had been in St. John's buying lumber and building material and planned to return home by train. However, he changed his mind and joined his brother's schooner *Marion Rogers* for the fateful trip to Trinity.

By the next evening the first official notification was sent to the Minister of Marine Affairs in St. John's by the police constable stationed in Trinity. He reported the schooner *Marion Rogers* had struck the rocks near Trinity lighthouse on the night of November 27-28 and that all aboard had perished.

In a poem "Loss of the Marion Rogers", written by William Dawe of Flatrock and publicized by Levi Butler of Port Rexton who lost two brothers in the tragedy, the cause of the wreck — the eternal nemesis of adverse weather — is exemplified. These are the third to eighth stanzas which tell of wind, heavy seas, and a blinding snowstorm:

The schooner Marion Rogers
She sailed from St. John's town
Deep laden with provisions
To the Nor'ad she was bound.

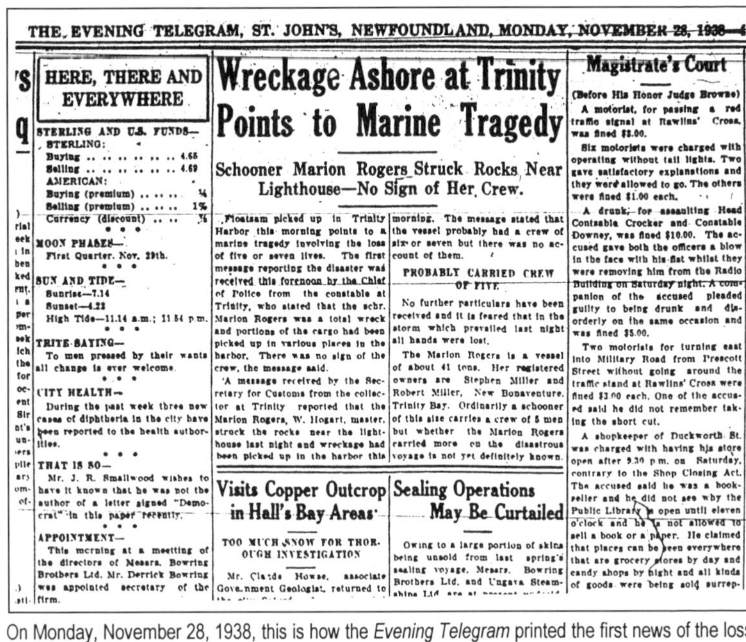

THE EVENING TELEGRAM, ST. JOHN'S, NEWFOUNDLAND, MONDAY, NOVEMBER 28, 1938—4

HERE, THERE AND EVERYWHERE

STERLING AND U.S. FUNDS—
STERLING:
Buying 4.65
Selling 4.69
AMERICAN:
Buying (premium) .. .. .. ¼
Selling (premium) 1%
Currency (discount) .. .. ⅞

• • •

MOON PHASES—
First Quarter. Nov. 29th.

• • •

SUN AND TIDE—
Sunrise—7.14
Sunset—4.22
High Tide—11.14 a.m.; 11.54 p.m.

• • •

TRITE SAYING—
To men pressed by their wants all change is ever welcome.

• • •

CITY HEALTH—
During the past week three new cases of diphtheria in the city have been reported to the health authorities.

• • •

THAT IS SO—
Mr. J. R. Smallwood wishes to have it known that he was not the author of a letter signed "Democrat" in this paper recently.

• • •

APPOINTMENT—
This morning at a meetting of the directors of Messrs. Bowring Brothers Ltd. Mr. Derrick Bowring was appointed secretary of the firm.

Wreckage Ashore at Trinity Points to Marine Tragedy

Schooner Marion Rogers Struck Rocks Near Lighthouse—No Sign of Her Crew.

Flotsam picked up in Trinity Harbor this morning points to a marine tragedy involving the loss of five or seven lives. The first message reporting the disaster was received this forenoon by the Chief of Police from the constable at Trinity, who stated that the schr. Marion Rogers was a total wreck and portions of the cargo had been picked up in various places in the harbor. There was no sign of the crew, the message said.

A message received by the Secretary for Customs from the collector at Trinity reported that the Marion Rogers, W. Hogart, master, struck the rocks near the lighthouse last night and wreckage had been picked up in the harbor this morning. The message stated that the vessel probably had a crew of six or seven but there was no account of them.

PROBABLY CARRIED CREW OF FIVE

No further particulars have been received and it is feared that in the storm which prevailed last night all hands were lost.

The Marion Rogers is a vessel of about 41 tons. Her registered owners are Stephen Miller and Robert Miller, New Bonaventure, Trinity Bay. Ordinarily a schooner of this size carries a crew of 5 men but whether the Marion Rogers carried more on the disastrous voyage is not yet definitely known.

Visits Copper Outcrop in Hall's Bay Areas

TOO MUCH SNOW FOR THOROUGH INVESTIGATION

Mr. Claude Howse, associate Government Geologist, returned to

Sealing Operations May Be Curtailed

Owing to a large portion of skins being unsold from last spring's sealing voyage, Messrs. Bowring Brothers Ltd. and Ungava Steamships Ltd. are at present

Magistrate's Court

(Before His Honor Judge Browne)

A motorist, for passing a red traffic signal at Rawlins' Cross, was fined $3.00.

Six motorists were charged with operating without tail lights. Two gave satisfactory explanations and they were allowed to go. The others were fined $1.00 each.

A drunk, for assaulting Head Contsable Crocker and Constable Downey, was fined $10.00. The accused gave both the officers a blow in the face with his fist whilst they were removing him from the Radio Building on Saturday night. A companion of the accused pleaded guilty to being drunk and disorderly on the same occasion and was fined $5.00.

Two motorists for turning east into Military Road from Prescott Street without going around the traffic stand at Rawlins' Cross were fined $3.00 each. One of the accused said he did not remember taking the short cut.

A shopkeeper of Duckworth St. was charged with having his store open after 9.30 p.m. on Saturday, contrary to the Shop Closing Act. The accused said he was a bookseller and he did not see why the Public Library is open until eleven o'clock and he is not allowed to sell a book or a paper. He claimed that places can be seen everywhere that are grocery stores by day and candy shops by night and all kinds of goods were being sold surrep-

On Monday, November 28, 1938, this is how the *Evening Telegram* printed the first news of the loss of schooner *Marion Rogers*. The article went on to say "...portions of the cargo had been picked up in various places in the harbour. There was no sign of the crew."

Seven good seamen formed her crew
All noble and so brave
And little did they ever think
They'd meet a watery grave.

Aye, little did they ever think,
Goin' down the shore that night,
The hour of death and tragedy
Was the end of a silent flight.

The rolling seas were mountains high
The ocean foaming white,
When those brave seamen met their doom
Upon that fateful night.

The wind it blew most violently,
As on the ship did go,
The land was not visible
Through heavy squalls of snow.

No one was left to tell the tale,
So mournful and so drear,
Of that most awful shipwreck,
The worst one of the year

Many stories of tragedy and shipwreck along our island shores contain elements of omens and tokens; usually, these tales show the compassion and sharing of a race of people who knew well the dangers of "those who go down to the sea in ships". The events surrounding the loss of *Marion Rogers* are no exception. Edward McGrath and George Hiscock of Trinity were good friends. McGrath, who often wore a bow tie, had said that when he died he wanted Hiscock to put a certain black bow tie around his neck.

On the night of November 27-28, Hiscock could not rest well. He fancied he could hear Edward McGrath calling him. He tried to put his friend out of mind and Hiscock eventually fell into a troubled sleep. At daybreak, George Hiscock was called to help search for the men lost in a shipwreck on Fort Point and soon learned his companion was one of those who had perished.

All bodies were found and laid out in the old Trinity Court House. The constable assigned men, including Hiscock, to dress and to prepare the dead for burial or for transport to their home towns. Hiscock noticed the other men were having difficulty securing a tie to the body of Edward McGrath and said to the constable, "I'll do that. I'll put this tie on Edward." And he placed a black bow tie on his friend. Such was the respect and love one man had for another, even in death.

To this day, mysterious lights are seen off Trinity and those who have witnessed the eerie sight claim it is the riding lights of *Marion Rogers* as she veers to make her way into Trinity. The apparition will flicker and slowly fade away; then, those who know the tale of the tragic wreck think back to that stormy night of November 1938 when the schooner and her seven men failed to reach port.

Courtesy of Boyd Coleridge

Taken around 1933-34, some years previous to *Marion Rogers*' loss, this photo shows Trinity from the vantage point of the hill near Olive Hiscock's house. Skirwink is near the headland (left background); while the schooner's wreckage was located behind Fort Point (centre back). The United Church, since taken down, (centre right) overlooks the historic town.

As well on the same night of *Marion Rogers*' wreck, another schooner grounded to total loss at Black Island on the Labrador coast. All four crew of *Monica Walters*, owned by James T. Walters of Petley, Trinity Bay, escaped safely.

Chapter 27

Flares from the *Edward VII*

Random, Trinity Bay

By 1933, Newfoundland was in the midst of a world-wide depression. International markets for her main product, salt dry fish, had practically disappeared. In this era, termed locally "The Dirty Thirties" which lasted roughly from 1929 until the onset of World War Two, there was little money and less work.

In those years, merchants and vessel owners continued to sell or trade fish and fish products for low prices; trading schooners maintained their voyages supplying food and necessities for families all over coastal Newfoundland. Along the south coast and west coast the nearest supplies were mainland Canada. For the communities located along the northeast coast and in the four large bays — Conception, Trinity, Bonavista and Notre Dame — St. John's was the commercial centre.

Most schooners owned along the northeast coast fished the inshore or Labrador fishery in the summer and early fall. In November and up to Christmas when poorer weather generally prevailed, the little schooners brought winter supplies from St. John's to the outports.

On Saturday, November 25, 1933, the schooner *Edward VII* left St. John's laden with supplies and drums of kerosene on deck intended for winter fuel for homes on Random Island, Trinity Bay. The island, about two hundred forty-nine square kilometres, is situated on the west side of Trinity Bay in eastern Newfoundland. Deposits of red shale and limestone once supported large brick factories. Nine fishing communities ring the island which is connected to the mainland by the Hefferton Causeway.

Edward VII's crew all belonged to Random: Captain Wilson Vey, age thirty five; mate Daniel Vey, sixty-six; James Gosse, sixty six; John Barfitt, forty-seven; Llewellyn Barfitt, fifty; George Smith, thirty-nine; Edwin Lambeth, twenty-seven; John Brown, twenty-one and Joseph Drover, who was the youngest on board at nineteen years of age.

For the first leg of the voyage home, up to Baccalieu Tickle, all went well. At eight o'clock that evening *Edward VII* sailed into Trinity Bay and parted company with several other schooners headed for ports further northwest.

A gentle southwest wind blew, but before Captain Vey and *Edward VII* reached any sheltered waters, the wind veered around to westerly and increased in strength. Within an hour or so, the crew was fighting a winter gale.

The mainsail was reefed, the foresail was taken down, and everything moveable on deck was lashed down. Later the crew was forced to haul down the mainsail. The storm quickly turned from bad to worse such that Captain Vey and his crew stayed on deck.

Edward VII shipped a huge sea that washed across the deck taking several drums of kerosene with it. Mate Daniel Vey was struck by a careening drum and knocked down. Drums, like loose cannons rolling across the deck, made it difficult for the crew to work. The helmsman especially was in the most danger.

Vey ordered the heads of the drums beaten in and the contents spilled on the deck. As time wore on throughout the night, the wind veered to northwest. By daylight the schooner was iced up, ropes and canvas frozen solid.

All Sunday the vessel drifted under bare poles for, if the ropes could be worked, no sail would stay aloft in the wind. Sometime later the crew wished to get a sail up to give *Edward VII* some direction and perhaps make land. Mainsail and topsail went up, but the main boom broke in two places. The weary men had no choice; the mainsail had to come down to make the repairs to the main boom and rigging.

A steamer was sighted astern bringing all hands on deck. Signal flares made of rag and kerosene oil, of which they plenty, were raised to the masthead. At first, it seemed the steamer was working its way toward them, but it soon passed over the horizon in the opposite direction.

Despite the fact that the crew was now becoming hardened to working the schooner on the cold open Atlantic, they suffered from lack of water. Water meant to last a day or two in the journey from St. John's to Random was stretched to last several days. In order to survive the cold, the crew was forced to chop down and burn parts of the schooner.

On the night of December third, about ten thirty, their improvised flare went up again for they saw another ship.

Third officer Alex Meyer of the steamer *Maine* observed something burning some distance away and reported to Captain Hausen. Hausen immediately ordered the steamer to alter its course and to race toward the labouring vessel. Within a short while Captain Vey and his eight crew were aboard the Danish freighter *Maine*, manned by Danish officers and crew. She was en route from Hamburg, Germany, to Wilmington, North Carolina, with a cargo of potash.

Vey admitted all hope for saving the schooner was gone; in fact, he believed it would not have stayed afloat another twenty-four hours in the high seas. In the damage done to the schooner's upper structure, seams opened and *Edward VII* was rapidly filling with water.

Out of mutual consideration inherent in all shipwrecked men, Captain Hausen immediately wired Cape Race to inform the families of the men of their rescue. However he could not put into a Newfoundland port and steamed on toward Wilmington. The freighter arrived there on Wednesday, December thirteenth. The Random sailors stayed aboard *Maine* until the British Consul who was stationed at Savannah, Georgia, arrived.

The British Consul, responsible for British subjects as Newfoundland at that time was a British colony, arranged transportation to New York to connect with the S.S. *Rosalind,* bound for Newfoundland. He also obtained extra clothes for the nine destitute sailors who had lost all personal belongings when *Edward VII* went down.

When *Rosalind* arrived in St. John's, relatives of the hapless mariners were there to greet them. Some of Vey's crew stayed in Stanford's Boarding House in St. John's until a passage was arranged to Random.

All in all it was December 22 before the men again touched foot in St. John's — twenty-seven days after they first left there in their schooner. Now Captain Vey and his crew were going home in a time of little money and food, limited resources, and scant winter supplies. They had survived an ordeal on the ocean and were left with only the clothes on their backs. Vey's schooner and its cargo representing potential income and winter supplies lay on the bottom of the Atlantic about three hundred sixty miles east southeast of Cape Race.

TELEGRAM, ST. JOHN'S, NEWFO

lved

ourn-
ecide
otted
mon-
Have
liers

ten-cent
captain

ENTER
IZE
ht)
n. 11
h, Aus-
omplete
m Lon-
r for a
n-with

ATHER
ht)
n. 11

List of Schooners Lost

DURING THE YEAR 1933

Jan. 7th—M. S. Farrell, 31 tons.
May 6th—Democracy (B) 100 tons.
May 28th—H. H. McIntosh, 128 tons.
May 28th.—Dorothy Melita Thornhill (B), 95 tons.
~~June 11th.—Iron Head, 123 tons.~~
June 15th.— Maxwell Roy, 91 tons.
June 29th.—Douglas J. Mosher, 150 tons.
July 3rd.—Lady A. P., 46 tons.
Aug. 10th—Eda, 33 tons.
Aug. 18th—Guide, 39 tons.
Aug. 18th,—Mary H. Gray, 100 tons.
Aug. 25th—T. W. Langley, 71 tons.
Sept. 18th.—Armenia, 48 tons.
Sept. 23rd.—Charlie & Eric, 81 tons.
Sept. 28th.—Ettie Bess, 43 tons.
Sept. 27th.—Rose L., 54 tons.
Oct. 2nd.—St. Helena 36 tons.
Dec. 26th.—Monica Hartery, 66 tons.
Dec. —Marjorie Wareham—tons.
Dec. 21st.—Humourist, (Aux.) 172 tons.
Dec. 4th.—Edward VII (High Seas), 45 tons.
Dec. 16th.—Tritoma, 51 tons.
Nov. 13th.—Topaz, 50 tons.
Nov. 13th.—Excellence (High Seas), 100 tons.
Nov. 22nd.—Freda Hummelman (Aux.), 174 tons.
Nov. 25th.—Eva Mary, 12 tons (?).
Oct. 21st.—Alice M. Brydle, 36 tons.
Nov. 26th.—Exotic, 52 tons.
Nov. 17th.—Ianthe (Aux)., 123 tons.
Nov. 16th.—Vera May, 24 tons.
Nov. 13th.—Mankato, 76 tons.
Nov. 9th.—Alla Ackbar, 30 tons.
N.B.—There are 28 schooners now being built in the various districts, of about 12 to 90-tons.

In January 1934 this *Evening Telegram* tabulation showed the extent of Newfoundland's shipping losses in 1933; *Edward VII* is one of them. Two of those listed disappeared with crew: *Monica Hartery* and *Mark H. Gray*.

Although not recorded, the tern schooner *John Millett*, owned in Fortune and once named *General Jacobs*, was abandoned on July 17, 1933. *John Millett*'s crew was rescued.

Chapter 28

"Gone from our Midst"
E.B. Phillips and C.A. Hubley

Heart's Content, Heart's Delight, New Perlican

In 1994, a poem was featured on an event's pamphlet for the communities of Winterton, New Perlican and Hant's Harbour, three towns in close proximity on the eastern side of Trinity Bay. One side of the pamphlet listed local church events; the reverse side was headed "Our Heritage" and featured a poem submitted by Edith Burrage of New Perlican. The poem told the story of the schooner *E.B. Phillips* which sank on the Grand Banks in 1892.

The poem had been written by Mrs. William Hadden of Heart's Content in the late 1890s shortly after *E.B. Phillips* was lost. The first four stanzas are:

Brothers and Friends
ye have gone from our midst
gone by the boisterous wave.
Taken away in your youth and bloom
to share a watery grave.

How sad to think when leaving home,
wishing their friends farewell

that they would never return again.
Not one to tell the tale.

Six brothers from their happy homes
were taken by the gale,
And next the father, and the son.
None left to tell the tale.

And now they're gone forever.
Drowned in the mighty deep
Leaving their parents, wives, and friends
at home to mourn and weep...

A poem written over one hundred years ago implying the disappearance of several men — brothers, fathers, sons. With the help of Edith Burrage, related by marriage to one of the ill-fated crew, the identity of those lost were recorded as:

Edgar and Archibald Hopkins, brothers	Heart's Content
John Hopkins, their cousin	Heart's Content
Francis and William Badcock, nephews	Heart's Content
Silas and James Ryall, brothers	Heart's Content
Thomas Legge	Heart's Content
Joseph and Reuben Piercy, brothers	Heart's Content
Ambrose and Simon Fost, brothers	Heart's Delight
John Burrage and his son, John	New Perlican

According to local knowledge, it seems as if the banking schooner *E.B. Phillips* was old and not entirely seaworthy, but that was not the cause of her misfortune. She was riding out a gale on the Grand Banks when another unidentified ship, laden with lumber, rammed her. Both vessels went down; only three men from the lumber-carrying vessel saved themselves by jumping overboard and clinging to a pile of drifting lumber.

The September 22, 1892, Thursday edition of *The Evening Telegram* basically confirms local folk knowledge. The newspaper states:

> One of Goodfellow's bankers which arrived here (St. John's) on Monday night brings sad intelligence related to a banker and crew which sailed from Heart's Content being fitted out by Mr. George Moore this summer. The schooner is *E.B. Phillips*, owned by Mr. J. Baird.
>
> Morrissey of Trinity, sailing in another banker that arrived here Monday night says that *E.B. Phillips* had been run down by a lumber vessel and that the crew had met a sad fate. The captain and nine of the crew of *E.B. Phillips* belong to Heart's Content, two belong to New Perlican and two to Heart's Delight. It would not be well to publish anything further regarding this sad intelligence until particulars are known.

A few days prior to this newspaper account, there were reports of a wreck located forty miles southeast of Cape Broyle. Brigantine *Atlanta* from Harbour Grace, Captain Antle, arrived in St. John's after a tedious run from Sydney which took him six days.

On the way to Sydney, Antle passed a wreck, bottom up, with the bottom freshly painted with copper paint. Top sides were white and the bow was partly submerged owing to the dangling chains and anchor which pulled the bow down. Antle claimed it was a schooner, about ninety ton. The wind was high and he could not go close enough to investigate thoroughly. The derelict presented a real threat for sea traffic especially for vessels going to the banks as it lay directly in a much-travelled route.

The same wind storm reported by Antle had played havoc with another Newfoundland schooner, *Henrietta*. Three of her crew, all from Bear's Cove, Witless Bay, had been washed overboard and disappeared: John T. Carey, Cornelius White, and Luke Tobin.

Of *E.B. Phillips*, as the poem says, there was "Not one to tell the tale" of how and on what day she was wrecked. Could the stormy weather reported around the time she was lost have foundered the vessel? Could she have struck the sunken ship described by Antle? Or was *E.B. Phillips* the derelict? If the newspaper and the local tales are correct, and most likely this is the case, why was more information not forthcoming from the three survivors of the lumber-laden vessel which rammed the schooner?

The questions were never satisfactorily answered, but a little over one hundred years ago fourteen men from Trinity Bay disappeared. Their legacy lives on in folk poems and local tales.

It would be forty years after *Phillip*'s loss before the pangs of sorrow over a ship's disappearance would again touch New Perlican. *C.A. Hubley* was last reported off Cape Bonavista on November 18, 1937, by another vessel. Most of *C.A. Hubley*'s crew were New Perlican men — Captain Neddie Seward, his son Walter and the captain's brother Mark. Pierre Ross of St. John's was the fourth person aboard and he may have joined the schooner when she was at Bermuda some time previously.

The New Perlican schooner, light in ballast, left St. John's on November eighth and harboured in Catalina until November 18. She set sail for Groais Islands (Grey Islands), a little south of the tip of the Great Northern Peninsula. At two pm Captain Bragg of the motor vessel *Marie Yvonne*, in bound from St. Anthony, passed *Hubley* off Cape Bonavista.

From that point on *C.A. Hubley* disappeared. Captain Knee of the government steamer *Sagona* searched the seas outside the Funk Islands for it was thought the schooner may have travelled that course to avoid coastal fog. Other ships searched closer to land, but no trace was found of *C.A. Hubley* and her four man crew. According to residents of the area, it is possible she struck the Horse Islands, two rugged isolated islands about thirteen miles northwest of Cape John.

Chapter 29

Captain Ellis Janes' Story of Catherine B

Hant's Harbour

Over thirty years after it happened, Captain Ellis Janes of Hant's Harbour, vividly recalled the loss of *Catherine B* and later retold the story for the magazine *Newfoundland Quarterly*.

In 1923 Samuel Harris of Grand Bank, owner of *Catherine B*, sold this vessel to S. Short and Sons of Hant's Harbour, Trinity Bay. The forty-five ton banker was built in 1919 in Marystown and put into the Labrador fishery out of Change Islands where Samuel Harris had a branch business. With the onset of the "Great Depression", reduced world markets for salt fish, and the decline in family business, Harris sold many of his schooners and closed the branch business at Change Islands.

In the fall of the year many Labrador schooners plied the coasting trade bringing food and supplies from St. John's to Trinity Bay, Bonavista Bay and other northeastern ports of call.

Catherine B left St. John's at four pm on Friday, November 29, 1929 laden with a full general cargo. The wind was blowing a light breeze from the west southwest. Captain

Courtesy Freeman Francis, Hant's Harbour

Catherine B, seen here sailing into Hant's Harbour sometime before 1929, was lost December 1, 1929. As the rescue ship carried the crew across the Atlantic, a young Freeman Francis of Hant's Harbour celebrated his nineteenth birthday on December eighth.

Janes and his crew were all from Hant's Harbour: Charles Green, Wilbert Short and James Loder. As well four passengers — Freeman Francis, Frank Strickland, Wesley and Frederick Short — had booked a passage to their homes in Hant's Harbour.

Outside St. John's harbour, weather soon deteriorated as Captain Janes remembered:

> When our schooner arrived off Sugarloaf the wind veered to the southeast blowing a gale and about two am the main sheet broke. The main boom broke in three pieces so we had to run under a reefed foresail until we sighted Baccalieu light. The wind chopped westerly and we broke our fore gaff leaving the vessel practically helpless.
>
> We shipped a sea which flattened out our dory like a sheet of paper and carried away our bowsprit right in to the bollards.

The wind "veered to a gale" as Janes mildly termed it but, according to newspapers of the day, it was a virtual winter's hurricane. Several other schooners which had left St. John's destined for Bonavista Bay sometime during the day of November 29th were driven off course and out to sea by the vicious storm: *Northern Light, Watersprite, Merry Widow, George K., Neptune II, Gander Deal, Janie Blackwood* and one or two others. High seas and a blinding snowstorm put the small schooners in serious jeopardy.

As for *Catherine B,* after her main boom broke at eleven am on Friday, all hands, passengers as well, worked to heave to under a double reefed foresail. Janes said:

> We drifted all day Saturday and on Sunday we made a mutton cut sail out of the foresail. We poured kerosene oil on the water to make it smooth and then we put up the jumbo, a reefed foresail and riding sail. Under these we made a S.S.E. course and sailed thirty-two miles.
>
> On Sunday the wind rose stronger and we had to haul down the jumbo and foresail using only the riding sail to keep the vessel up to the wind.

The wind changed again to a more wild northwest accompanied by severe frost. The notion of making the run down in Trinity Bay was hopeless; the unmanageable schooner was being driven farther and farther out to sea. At six-thirty Sunday evening, someone in the crew saw the lights of a steamer well off in the distance. Captain Janes recalled how they signalled the ship:

> ...We saw a steamer and we used Brin bags soaked in kerosene oil as a signal of distress. The ship saw our signal and steamed down toward us. They came up on our windward side and we asked them to stand by and take us off in the morning.
>
> The captain asked us if we had a boat, but our boat had been smashed by the sea.

This ship was the S.S. *Holfplein,* an iron ore carrier that had left Bell Island laden with ore sometime on Sunday. She was bound for Rotterdam with Captain Schaap in command.

Steamers carried a limited amount of coal for fuel which was usually obtained on the Canadian or American mainland, thus there was no way she could return to Newfoundland or stand by for eight or ten hours, but had to steam on toward Europe once *Catherine B*'s crew had been rescued.

Captain Janes, in his account to *The Newfoundland Quarterly*, recalled how the transfer from a sinking ship to a rescue vessel was made that stormy evening. Janes thought a salvation in such weather was impossible, but *Holfplein*'s crew pulled it through:

> Captain Schaap asked for volunteers to go to the rescue. The second mate of the *Holfplein* and four members of the crew volunteered for the extremely hazardous task to go in a small lifeboat to the rescue.
>
> It was about 9:30 that night when the lifeboat got alongside the *Catherine B* and one by one the members of the crew jumped safely into the lifeboat.
>
> When the captain told us he was sending a rescue party I thought it would be impossible as the sea was so rough. I took a lantern and held it over the side of the vessel so they would see us.

One of *Catherine B*'s passengers, Frederick Short, was seventy-four years old at the time of this terrific ordeal at sea. He was not able to climb the ladder hanging down from the side of the rescue boat, but was pulled up over with a rope around his waist.

St. John's was eighty miles back; thus Captain Schaap could not land the stranded men there, but had to continue to Rotterdam. Aboard the steamer, the eight Hant's Harbour men were immediately given hot coffee, offered a spare room in the ship's saloon and fed well. What of the little Trinity Bay schooner? Janes recalled:

> Just before leaving the helpless *Catherine B*, wallowing there in the storm, the Captain of the *Holfplein* gave her a bunt in the main chains and thus probably sent her to the bottom.

> After picking us up Captain Schaap notified Cape Race of our rescue and word was sent to our relatives in Hant's Harbour. Had the *Holfplein* not been there to rescue us it is almost a certainty that our little vessel would have foundered.

Three hours after the rescue, the steamer ran into a tremendous winter storm that lashed the ship for thirteen days. Everything moveable on the deck was destroyed or swept overboard. Schaap told Captain Janes it was the worst storm in all his years of sea experiences.

So the crew ended up in Rotterdam, Netherlands, one of the world's largest, most modern ports and with a population in 1929 of a quarter million people. Getting transportation home was no easy matter. If such a rescue mission had happened in today's world, the crew would have several resources open to them: appeal to government agencies to arrange transportation or call home for money to fly home. In the 1920s, most Newfoundland families saw little cash and these options were not there. No government, foreign or local, would issue transportation tickets; there was no money to transfer and the means to send money to Europe was next to impossible.

Most large seaports (including St. John's) had Consuls or embassies and more importantly for sailors, free lodging in buildings generally termed "The Seamen's Institute". The Hant's Harbour men, like so many other Newfoundland sailors stranded on foreign shores, had roundabout trips and delays before they eventually reached their Trinity Bay home. Captain Janes remembered:

> In Rotterdam we were taken to the Seamen's Institute and the next morning the British consul came to see us and took pictures of us. He arranged our transportation to Antwerp and the pictures he had taken were used as our passport into Belgium. Arrangements were made for a man to meet us who took us to the Seamen's Institute where we stayed eight days.
>
> While there we saw the British Consul who arranged

> transportation to Cherbourg and from there to Southampton and Halifax on the S.S. *Pentland* where we boarded the *Silvia* bound for St. John's.

The shipwrecked crew of *Catherine B* finally arrived in St. John's on January 4, 1930. They were thirty-six days on a trip from St. John's to Hant's Harbour which could normally have been completed in eight hours.

Although no lives were lost, the food and supplies badly needed in the small town was gone. S. Short and Sons business was without a valuable schooner for the Labrador fishery. The other schooners caught in the same gale fared just as badly. Five were abandoned at sea; their crews rescued by other vessels: *Merry Widow, George K, Gander Deal, Janie Blackwood,* and *Northern Light,* the latter with the loss of one crewman, Rex Parsons of Goose Bay, Bonavista Bay. The other schooners, *Watersprite, Lloyd Jack, Effie May Petite* and *Neptune II,* after days of drifting reached another port safely or were towed in.

At eight am on the same morning as *Catherine B*'s crew were plucked from a watery grave, *Holfplein* had rescued the crew of the Greenspond schooner *George K* (above). She had left St. John's the same evening as the other schooners, was caught in the gale and driven out of control southwestward.

Because *George K* was abandoned only a few miles off St. John's harbour, her crew — Captain Frank Green, Edward Carter, Mark Parsons, Stanley Mullett and Saul Burry, all of Greenspond and area — did not end up in Rotterdam. *Holfplein*'s captain telegraphed news of rescue to St. John's and arranged for the harbour tug to bring the crew of *George K* back to St. John's while *Holfplein* was outside the Narrows.

Chapter 30

Tragedy at Burnt Point: Warren M. Colp

Silverdale, Burnt Point

Winter of 1930 brought a typical mid-December storm — strong winds laced with sleet and heavy snow — over a wide area of northeastern Newfoundland. Most small craft and schooners had already found a sheltered harbour, but a two-masted schooner, *Warren M. Colp*, was out in the heavy weather trying to complete a voyage from Herring Neck to St. John's.

Warren M. Colp, a craft of one hundred and fifteen ton and built in 1913 at Lunenburg, left Herring Neck on Twillingate Island on December 14. She had five hundred quintals of codfish in bulk collected from fishermen in Silverdale and Herring Neck destined for J.R. Chalker's business in the city; drums and barrelled fish for George J. Carter and a quantity of oil and herring in barrels on deck.

Jointly owned by the Newfoundland Lime Company of St. John's and her captain, she carried a crew that hailed mostly from Green Bay: Captain Randolph Batstone, Joseph Moores, mate Jordan Moores, cook Pierce Moores, all of Silverdale; Fred Fudge, Round Harbour and William Atkinson resided in Herring Neck on Twillingate Island.

Today Silverdale is part of a joint township combined with Jackson's Cove and Langdon's Cove located near the promontory separating Green Bay from Western Arm. A fishing, farming and lumbering community, Silverdale (called Bear Cove until 1921) first appears in the Newfoundland *Census* of 1891 with a population of twenty-nine. Today the three towns have around two hundred seventy residents with Batstone, Kelly, King, Knight, Pynn, Upward and Webber as principal family names.

Warren M. Colp had left Green Bay some days previously making her way toward St. John's. After her stop on Twillingate Island to load, she had put into Catalina on the night of December 14 and left early the next morning. Seeking shelter from the thickening snowstorm, watchers on shore had noticed the schooner passing through Baccalieu Tickle headed for Western Bay Point bound for Carbonear or some other place along the shore. At that point, the fortunes of the schooner changed.

Colp mis-stayed or drifted back while changing tack, and then was seen to veer around, drop her mainsail, but it became impossible for her crew to haul her off the lee shore before she was on the rocks. *Warren M. Colp* was equipped with a deck engine for operating her sails, and her crew tried to use the engine hoist the mainsail. The engine stalled and all attempts to re-start it failed.

The schooner drifted into Job's Cove, hit the rocks of Murphy's Island in Job's Cove Bight, about a mile east of the town of Burnt Point, and eventually grounded under the cliffs near Burnt Point, a fishing community located about thirty-two kilometres north of Carbonear.

The first settlers in Burnt Point were Andrew Layman and John Tucker who came around 1810. Other surnames common by 1835 were Milley, Oliver and Wicks. The population of Burnt Point, ninety-six in 1836, was approximately three hundred a hundred years later, but declined somewhat during the 1930-40s. The economy of Burnt Point was based on the inshore cod-fishery and the seal hunt until the 1930-

40s when the fisheries declined. In 1905 a lighthouse was built on the point and, in 1921, two cod liver oil factories opened there. Today the population remains around two hundred.

Such was the impact of shipwreck and loss of lives in the small town, the story of rescue was told and re-told. Through the passage of time, in the local folk history of Burnt Point and area, the vessel has been mis-identified or wrongly pronounced as *Colf* or *Dekult*, but in fact it was the Green Bay schooner *Warren M. Colp* with her six crew.

When *Warren M. Colp* struck, about two pm, Captain Batstone, Fred Fudge and Pearce Moores crawled out on the bowsprit and jumped for the rocks. The seas washed the captain and Fudge off but Moores maintained his hold and reached the foot of the cliff. There he clung on, not knowing what minute a sea would tear away his grip and drag him into the boiling surf.

Two members of the crew — Joseph Moores and William Atkinson —got into the schooner's dory. In their attempt to reach shore, the towering whitecaps upset the dory and both men went into the frigid sea. Jordan Moores, the last man to leave the stranded schooner, remained on board as long as possible; then, got onto a plank, fastened a determined grip and washed away from the wreck.

The tragic scene of the wreck — a large schooner on the rocks and six lives hanging in the balance — was witnessed by the people of Burnt Point including the local police constable, J. Thistle. Within a few minutes many had gathered on the cliff and, as soon as they saw the threat to human life, tried to rescue the crew. Their efforts were hampered not only by limited visibility and the raging windstorm, but the stranded schooner was under an overhanging cliff making it difficult to reach the wreck.

Rescuers saw the overturned dory slowly drifting away with one man clinging to the bottom. The man on the plank was washing in under the cliff but lay within distance of a heaving line. He was pulled to safety.

Constable Thistle directed rescue operations. Warren J. Bursey and E.B.(Bert) Tucker were lowered down over the cliff to find one man alive, Pearce Moores; he was pulled up by those who manned the ropes on the top of the cliff. The two rescued men were housed in Adolphus Tucker's house at Burnt Point.

Such was the position of *Warren M. Colp* wedged under an overhanging cliff that up to the time of rescue no one was sure of the schooner's name. Within hours the residents of Burnt Point, as well as relatives in the sailors' home port and the vessel's owners in St. John's knew another epitaph of the sea had been written: Schooner *Warren M. Colp* wrecked, four lost, two saved. Residents believe that had all six remained aboard the schooner each life would have been saved as *Colp* did not break up until several days after.

Some weeks after the rescue when he arrived home in Silverdale, Jordan Moores publicly expressed his appreciation to the people of Burnt Point in a letter:

> I am one of the two survivors of the ill-fated schooner, *Warren M. Colp*, which ran ashore on Burnt Point...To those who never had such a hard and trying experience, the thought of being shipwrecked does not always appeal with any special significance.
>
> But I have sailed quite a bit. I have seen the pyramids of Egypt. I have crossed the Atlantic and sailed the Mediterranean. It would take too much space to tell of the countries and great cities I have seen, and of the blizzards and storms I have experienced at sea. But, never did I fully recognize the divine nature of humanity until December 15th when men were revealing man in his noblest character.
>
> I must first thank Constable J. Thistle who was the first to the scene of the tragedy and spared no pains to rescue us from a watery grave. And then to all the other men who came to our assistance with ropes by which they pulled us to the top of the cliff.
>
> And then for their untiring efforts in searching for the bodies of those who lost their lives, and then for the

Courtesy Seamen's Museum, Grand Bank

Josie and Phoebe (above), built 1908 and lost at sea on August 9, 1944. While coming from Nova Scotia with salt, *Josie and Phoebe* sank suddenly twenty-one miles off St. Pierre. She went down so quickly the pressurized air trapped in her holds hit the mainmast out. Her crew — Captain Freeman Pottle of Eastport, engineer Harold Wells, cook Cecil Morgan, Cuyler Acreman and Raymond Dawe, all of Cupids — threw off the dory and were rowing toward St. Pierre when the French cutter picked them up.

Pottle was involved in another wreck less than a year later when the coaster *Gladys Mosher* was wrecked on the West Coast on June 28, 1945.

superhuman respect they showed us by following us in procession to the railway station...

Five years later, in November 1935, the schooner *Theresa M. Gray*, owned by Captain Edward Burton, ran ashore on a ledge in Spaniard's Bay and became a total wreck. *Theresa M. Gray* had loaded lumber at Colinet in St. Mary's Bay and put into St. John's on November 16-17. She left St. John's on the morning of the eighteenth and was entering Spaniard's Bay, having shaped a course for Green Island when a snowstorm came on.

In the reduced visibility *Theresa M. Gray* hit a ledge and ground to a halt. Captain Burton and his crew — Michael

Singleton and John Ryan — escaped the wreck and reached shore.

Sergeant Seward at Bay Roberts arranged for the stranded crew, who had saved nothing but the wet clothes they wore, to be temporarily lodged at the Court House. In the morning Seward and the schooner's crew went down to the wreck to salvage what they could.

Chapter 31

Long Voyage of the Maggie Bell

Carbonear, Freshwater, Perry's Cove

On November 5, 1913, a small schooner, *Maggie Bell*, left Crouse on the French shore bound for Carbonear on the next to last leg of her journey from Labrador to Conception Bay. Owned by Arthur Parsons of Carbonear and commanded by John Parsons of Freshwater, near Carbonear, *Maggie Bell* had completed a productive fall fishery on the Labrador coast.

Aboard was a crew of sixteen floater fishermen and two women employed as cooks for the fishing crew; most on board hailed from Carbonear or neighbouring towns of Perry's Cove and Freshwater. After shipping two barrels of fresh water, Parsons left Crouse in the morning. With the exception of several gallons of partridge berries which crew-members had picked on the Labrador, the boat had very little food aboard, and Parsons intended to call at Twillingate to obtain enough to finish the trip.

Sailing weather was co-operative and *Maggie Bell* passed Twillingate Island at three am the following morning. Captain Parsons walked the deck taking stock of the winds and distance. He decided, since there was a fair wind blowing, to bypass Twillingate and to sail as far as Seldom-Come-By. Although food and water were in short supply, Captain Parsons pushed on past Can Island, near Seldom-Come-By taking advantage of good winds and expecting "a fine time along" — a quick and uneventful run to Carbonear.

However, before the schooner reached Cabot Island in Bonavista Bay, good weather and fortune changed. One of the crew aboard *Maggie Bell*, was William J. Kelloway of Perry's Cove, Carbonear, who later recorded his experiences. He recalled:

> We put in single reefs and raced on, but before daylight, the vessel was a hard looking sight. Our mainsail was going in strips, and our foresail and outside jib started to rip. We were left with only the jumbo. The vessel was making poor way and starting to leak so that it kept one pump going to keep her free.
>
> By now all our drinking water was gone and our two boats washed away. The only food we had left were some partridge berries.

It was now three days since *Maggie Bell* left Crouse. After the schooner left Notre Dame Bay, difficult conditions prevailed —high winds, heavy weather and an unmanageable ship. By this time the schooner was well past her destination of Carbonear and out into the Atlantic beyond Newfoundland.

When the wind dropped, the crew made repairs: mended sails, roped up and double reefed the patched canvas, and swung *Maggie Bell* around to the northwest. Kelloway recalled:

> We were going this way for two days when we sighted land. It was Signal Hill (St. John's).
>
> Suddenly a squall struck *Maggie Bell*, took away all our canvas and left us with nothing to keep her steady. So we were forced to go where the wind carried us, that was an easterly direction.
>
> Shortly after that a large steamer passed us, so close that waves from her washed our deck which by now was getting low in the water. She was leaking so badly that the two pumps could not keep the water out as fast it was coming in.

In effect, *Maggie Bell* was going under. Her crew was slowly starving. Food meant to last two or three days was practically gone and already the eighteen people on board had been to sea five days. But the treacherous sea was not finished yet.

Captain Parsons ordered up distress signals in the rigging, but the passing vessel mentioned by Kelloway failed to see them. It steamed by without taking any note of a small schooner in a sinking condition. *Maggie Bell* continued powerless for three more days. By the fourth day water was over the cabin floor and was gaining on the pumps. The two lifeboats had long since been smashed and swept away taking thwarting even that avenue of escape. The sixteen men and two women realized that unless help came within hours they would be victims of the hungry Atlantic. As Kelloway recalled:

> We all knew that before another day would dawn we would be with the sharks. Late in the evening we sighted a schooner. She was heading straight for us and it wasn't long before she came within hailing distance. Her skipper asked what the trouble was.
>
> It was then we discovered that our mouths and tongues were so dry and stiff that we could hardly speak. The only drink we had after we lost our water was what we caught in a pan running off the cabin house one night when it rained hard. The only food was berries.

The schooner proved to be *W.C. McKay*, Captain William Dean, on her first voyage across the Atlantic with a load of fish. She had left St. John's two days previously with a cargo of fish shipped by G.M. Barr's business. According to Kelloway, Dean was a young man who could handle a schooner with great skill.

Dean took*W.C. McKay* windward of the wrecked *Maggie Bell* and kept her there making the water as smooth as possible. A lifeboat made four trips back and forth until the last of *Maggie Bell*'s compliment was rescued.

W.C. McKay's captain, Dean, then asked if the last off had set fire to the wreck to prevent it from becoming a navigational hazard. While someone explained how they had tried, *Maggie Bell* sank in full view carrying her cargo of Labrador fish to the bottom. It was November fourteenth — nine days after leaving Crouse — *Maggie Bell's* compliment had endured not only the worst nature could throw at them, but near death from thirst and hunger.

The Lunenburg schooner had five men in her crew; now, eighteen more people were aboard and they had not eaten a solid meal nor had little water for over two weeks. The captain had no choice but to postpone his foreign-going voyage, put into St. John's to land the shipwrecked crew and to obtain more food. Kelloway continued:

> We arrived in good time and as we ate up quite a bit of ship's food, we hunted up the member (House of Assembly) for our district to see if he could replace the food we ate on the ship that picked us up.
>
> We were told he could do nothing about it, so the captain had to buy more before he could continue his voyage. We knew then why the steamer passed us by; they would only get into trouble.

The M.H.A for the district did however manage to get train tickets to Carbonear. From the Carbonear station, some of the tired and hungry crew had to walk as far as seven miles to reach their homes in Freshwater and Perry's Cove.

Despite their ordeal, all arrived safely only to find out that neither they nor *Maggie Bell* had been reported missing! No one knew what day the schooner had left Crouse for Carbonear. There was nowhere at Crouse or vicinity where a message of inquiry could be sent and *Maggie Bell* had had no radio or visual contact with any other vessel. The crew had been concerned relatives would be worried about their safely; ironically, no one at home had felt any distress.

The crew, with the loss of their schooner and the summer's catch of cod, had no choice but seek employment elsewhere to help provide a living for their families from the coming winter of 1913-14.

As a tragic maritime footnote to this story of happy ending, the loss five years later of the schooner *W.C. McKay* was more unfortunate. She sailed out of Twillingate during the war years and around January 10, 1918, she went down taking her men with her, probably the victim of a German submarine. Dean was not her captain at this time. *W.C. McKay* had a mixed crew, including at least three Newfoundlanders:

Michael Dooley, son of Patrick Dooley	57 New Gower St., St. John's
Clem McManus, son of Joseph McManus	12 Sebastian St. St. John's
William O'Neill, married	of Battery Road, St. John's
John Stewart, married	of North Strand, Drogheda, Ireland
Arthur Licence	of Ipswich, England
Hubert Evans	residence unknown
Jose Torres	of Chancho, Chili

Chapter 32

One of Newfoundland's Most Beautiful Ships

Carbonear, St. John's

Czarina's first owner was the Imperialist Ruler of Russia. An attractive vessel constructed of oak and teak, *Czarina* was originally owned by the Czar Alexander III of Russia and named for the title of Russia's female ruler. Built in 1877 in England by Camper and Nicholsen for Czar Alexander, the three hundred twenty-two gross ton barquentine/yacht measured one hundred fifty-two foot long, a little over twenty-nine foot beam (wide) and fifteen foot deep.

Czarina was subsequently sold to Arthur Brassey of England, brother to Lord Brassey, and converted to steam power while retaining her beautiful spread of sail. In England, with her main duties as a hospital ship, she was re-named *Sunbeam.*

In May 1916 Monroe and Company, a business founded around the end of the 1800s and based in St. John's, acquired the barquentine and re-modelled her for the foreign trade. One of the most expensively furnished vessels ever owned in Newfoundland, she was given her former name *Czarina.* In St. John's her elaborate fittings were removed and later sold at an auction in the British Hall, fetching very high prices.

Czarina's engine was installed in the schooner *Gordon C*, a vessel which later burned and went to the bottom in 1918. *Czarina*'s crew for a foreign voyage in 1921 is recorded as:

Capt. Colin Taylor	59	Carbonear
Fred Butt	37	Carbonear
William Snow	31	St. John's
Thomas Harvey	45	Witless Bay
Greg Thomey	21	Harbour Grace
Greg Humphries	26	Carbonear
Robert Shannahan	21	Cape Broyle
Hayward Marshall	31	Carbonear

Forty years — the combined length of service under the ruler of Russia and later as an English hospital ship — but she plied only seven years in the hazardous Newfoundland shipping trade. On December 31, 1923, reports reached Monroe and Company in St. John's *Czarina* had gone to the bottom at latitude 39 North, longitude 51.40 West.

On her final voyage *Czarina* left Newfoundland on St. Steven's Day, 1923, bound to Brazil with a cargo of five thousand drums of codfish. Actually she had been ready to sail several days previously, but unfavourable weather and the fact that one of her crew left ship unexpectedly delayed her departure. Her crew: Captain Colin Taylor, mate James J. Connors, bosun William Snow, seamen Aubrey Lang, John Keats, Edward Snow, Reuben Tizzard and John O'Neill.

A storm raging over the Atlantic in December proved too much for the staunch vessel. Captain Taylor reported heavy seas which pounded *Czarina* into submission. On the third day out, she lost her foremast, the mainmast sprung, or worked loose, and this caused excessive leaking. With her stanchions and bulwarks smashed and spars broken or washed overboard, the yacht was doomed. Working in heavy December frost, the crew tried to keep her afloat in hope that some ship would pass close by.

At nine-thirty in the evening the lights of a passing ship could be seen and immediately signal flares were hoisted to

Courtesy Marine Archives, Harry Roberts' Collection

Antoinette of Harbour Grace, sank March 30, 1915 en route from Patras, Greece to Newfoundland. Her crew: Captain George C. Webber, married and William Hoddinott, married, both of Harbour Grace; Edmund Hiscock, husband of Margaret Hiscock of Carbonear; Ralph Neil, son of Richard Neil, Spaniard's Bay; Stephen Shute, married, Freshwater, Bay de Verde; and A. Alflsen, residence unknown (probably Scandinavian).

the topmast. The passing ship proved to be *Cairnmona* bound from England to Portland, United States. By the time the steamer arrived and preparations were made to take off the crew, *Czarina*, nearly a half century old, was going under. Monroe and Company had both vessel and cargo insured.

Chapter 33

Freedom's Crew Long Row to Barbados

Brigus

"We were given up for lost," Andy Short recalled. "We got into the horse latitudes where there was little wind and we drifted with the current. Sunday morning there was a big ship about three miles from us. I had an old jacket and we tore the lining out and put it on an oar for a flag. But she couldn't have seen us."

Andy Short and his crew mates, drifting in an open boat on the broad expanses of the North Atlantic, had left port a month and a half before and relatives back in Brigus were fraught with anxiety. Nothing had been heard from them despite inquires to their intended port of call, Sydney. Short remembered the abandonment of the tern schooner *Freedom* although it had happened fifty-eight years before and told his story in the November 1982 issue of the magazine *Decks Awash*.

Brigus, located in Conception Bay, today has a population of around nine hundred. Its roots are steeped in the sealing and fishing industry and in 1921, three years prior to

Freedom's sailing, Brigus had seven large vessels and seventeen small boats involved in the inshore fishery.

Freedom sailed from Brigus on October 17, 1924, bound for Sydney for coal. The crew landed in Barbados on December first, nearly a month and a half later with *Freedom* on the bottom of the Atlantic six hundred miles east north east of Barbados.

Built in 1908 in the Robie McLeod shipyards at Liverpool, Nova Scotia, the tern netted one hundred ninety-seven ton and measured one hundred twelve foot long. A.S. Rendell, a business based in St. John's, managed the vessel and she was crewed by Captain Sam Noseworthy, mate Thomas Power, cook Fred Rossiter, bosun Thomas Fillier, seamen Andrew Short, John Hearn, and Richard Kenny.

Two days out of port *Freedom* was buffeted by a typical mid-Atlantic storm forcing Captain Noseworthy to heave-to and try to ride out the gale. But the wind intensified and raged for over three weeks driving the tern eastward, further and further off course.

Five hundred and fifty miles out to sea, *Freedom* foundered. Andy Short remembered the damage inflicted. "The sea beat the stern off her," he said. All hands were at the pumps constantly, but soon the pumps malfunctioned. Water began to rise and it was then Captain Noseworthy decided to make a run to Barbados. By November 8 the tern had been battered beyond recovery; she was going down and Noseworthy gave the word to abandon ship.

Two boats were put over the side: Captain Noseworthy, the cook, the bosun and seaman Kenny went in the larger boat with both charts and sextant. The second boat, a fourteen foot boat without food or water and with only a compass as a navigational aid, was put in charge of the mate with Short and John Hearn.

Since only one boat had adequate navigational aids, it was planned that both craft would stay together during the hundreds of miles the captain had charted to Barbados, but as Short recalled:

Photo courtesy Jack Keeping

Mary Ruth (above), moored at Brigus in the early 1970s. *Mary Ruth*, built in Shelburne, Nova Scotia, in 1918, was first operated in Newfoundland by Belleoram's Ben Keeping while owned by Harvey and Company.

Rebuilt in Fortune by W. T. Lake in 1945, she was eventually sold to the Hiscock business at Clarenville, operated for several years in the coasting/fishing trade out of Brigus (and crewed by William Flynn of Brigus in the 1940s), and ended her days a beached hulk at Southport, Trinity Bay.

> On the second night the boats parted company. (We) had been connected by a tow line because the bigger boat sailed faster, but in the dark it had towed the rudder clear off the captain's boat. We had to cut and let him go on to save ourselves. Later we sent up a flare but could see nothing and when day broke we were alone.

A small sail was set; weather was favourable and at least one passing ship was sighted, but it failed to see either small boat. On December first, mate Power's boat altered course slightly and the next day they saw land in the distance.

As they neared the land, Short, Power and Hearn saw an island with a lighthouse but the shoreline was rugged and looked threatening. Yet, Short liked what he saw:

> It was beautiful. Finally with night coming on we made a desperate attempt to beach the boat. We cleared the reef successfully and knew that we were all right. We were on a tiny beach surrounded by vertical cliffs. The first person we met was a small black child and soon a crowd of black people arrived.

It was the first time *Freedom*'s crew had touched land in a month and a half. At that time Short and his two mates had no idea what had happened to the second (and larger) boat containing the captain and three other men. They were escorted to the local railway station where they learned the captain's boat had landed in Barbados. As Short told it:

> By and by here comes two horse police, two doctors and two detectives. The detectives were very suspicious and asked a lot of questions until the doctor realized that (we) had been shipwrecked and he drove the detectives away. He said we were very weak and we didn't think we were as weak as we were.

In fact Short and his shipmates had not eaten for five days. The doctor gave each man half a glass of milk and a piece of biscuit which promptly made them feel worse. Such was their focus on reaching land safely, they had been starving without realizing it. Unknown to Short, the captain had landed on the same island about four pm, but on the opposite side.

Captain Noseworthy had been to Barbados before and knew the man who ran an island drugstore and it was there he went seeking news of his other shipmates. He was told a shipwrecked crew had landed some time before in St. John district of Barbados. Noseworthy could hardly believe his good fortune; all his ship's crew were alive and well. He sent a taxi for them so all would be re-united again.

Short remembered how well the islanders treated them:

> Flags adorned our taxi and the crowds wanted to shake hands with us. We were there a week. Barbados was a place where they'd never see you stuck. They'd ask you if you wanted a cigarette and they knew we had no money, so they gave us a pack of cigarettes. They were really very good to us.

Freedom's shipwrecked crew left Barbados on the steamship *Canadian Otter* en route for Halifax. There the crew spent four days before taking the Red Cross steamer *Rosalind* to St. John's and arrived home safely during Christmas season.

Anxious relatives in Brigus and the other home ports of the missing sailors knew they were coming. On December 4, 1924, within a day or so after the shipwrecked crew reached land, A.S. Rendell & Company received a message from Barbados which read:

"Noseworthy, Fillier, Kenny, Rossiter, reached here today in a boat of the *Freedom*, abandoned 600 miles E.N.E. of Barbados. Power, Hearn, and Short in another boat landed East Coast."

This was the second vessel Rendell lost in 1924, the latter with more tragic results: tern schooner *Hester Hankinson* was abandoned in early December 1924 while on a transAtlantic voyage. Captain Collett of Harbour Buffett and six of his crew were landed at Montevideo, the capital city of Uruguay, after they were rescued from the sinking *Hester Hankinson*. In the battle with winter storms the bosun, Peter Slaney of King-well, Placentia Bay, fell into the sea and disappeared while trying to rig a jury rudder on the disabled craft. He was nineteen.

Hester Hankinson, a two hundred ninety-two net ton schooner built in 1917, left Cadiz on October eighth bound for Little Bay Islands with salt. She had been unreported for several weeks by Rendell's business when news came of the safety of the six survivors on December 11, 1924.

Chapter 34

Tragedy in the Narrows

Lethbridge/Brooklyn, St. John's Narrows

St. John's harbour, with its deep and well-protected basin, is considered one of the world's best seaports. Nearly half a mile long, the "Narrows" or entrance to the harbour, is a channel bounded on the north side by Signal Hill and on the south by South Side Hills. Near Chain Rock, the Narrows is sixty-one feet wide, but deep enough to admit the world's largest vessels.

Around 1770 a chain, which could be raised or lowered and designed to keep out enemy ships, was stretched across the Narrows from Pancake Rock to what became known as Chain Rock. To assist friendly vessels through the entrance, the government built a lighthouse on the south cliff in 1811. The structure was replaced in 1954.

Year by year, decade by decade, hour by hour seacraft of all sizes and types have passed the confined opening; but occasionally, despite guiding lights, helpful harbour tugs, and modern technology, the narrows exact their tribute.

One of the most terrible calamities to happen near St. John's Narrows occurred on November 6, 1896, when the fifty-seven ton schooner *Maggie* collided with the steamship *Tiber*. Owned and commanded by Captain William Blundon, *Maggie* left Brooklyn in Goose Bay, an arm of Bonavista Bay,

Courtesy Marine Archives, Captain Harry Stone collection

On January 17, 1904, the bark *Stella* went ashore at Cuckold's Cove, near the St. John's Harbour entrance. Salvage has already begun as a little boat moves off towing *Stella*'s booms. A gangplank (left) extends from the cliff to the ship.

for St. John's laden with a thousand quintals of fish, eight hundred quintals belonging to Blundon. More tragically, as it turned out, she also had aboard twenty-three people — nine crew and fourteen passengers.

Owing to wind direction, *Maggie* had sailed past the Narrows and was sailing back toward St. John's from the eastward with full sails. S.S. *Tiber*, Captain J. DeLisle, was outward bound en route to North Sydney. James Power was at *Maggie*'s wheel and some crew had gathered aft paying out the main sheet or sail.

When *Tiber* reached Chain Rock in the Narrows, her lights could be seen from the schooner and word passed around a steamer was coming out. *Maggie* kept up to the wind and her crew could see danger ahead as the steamer shaped her course for Cape Spear, but heading directly for the little schooner. It is the law of the sea, powered vessels like

Tiber must give way to sail and, in any case, *Maggie* was pushed along by the caprice of the varying winds.

Usually large ships leaving St. John's steamed straight off a good distance before changing course to the north or south. The St. John's harbour pilot boat with Pilot Richard Vinnicombe had left the steamer somewhere near Hay Cove several minutes previously, but had no knowledge *Tiber* would change course quickly.

As the distance lessened between the two vessels, those on *Maggie* shouted with all their might for the men on the steamer to keep clear and to change course. Despite the efforts of those on *Maggie*, the steamer did not alter course and struck the schooner on the starboard side just aft of the mainmast. *Tiber* cut completely through the schooner severing the stern section.

Twenty-three people — eighteen men and five women — were now struggling for their lives. Although the accident happened near shore, it was too far for anyone to swim the distance. Most of the women and some of the men were in the cabin at the time of contact and were crushed to death or killed. The schooner's spars fell out and she filled with water and sank within a few minutes. Fish, cash and personal effects went with her. Although Mutual Marine Insurance Company had insured the schooner for $1260, the loss of property was insignificant compared to loss of Lethbridge lives.

Lethbridge, a community located about twenty-five kilometres north of Clarenville in Bonavista Bay, today has a population of around six hundred fifty. It was settled around 1870, largely by people of Bonavista and Catalina and first appears in the 1874 *Census* as Hopeville with ninety-five people.

Originally Lethbridge was regarded as part of nearby Brooklyn and was often designated as Brooklyn West. In 1912 the Nomenclature Board of Newfoundland (which often chose or changed names of Newfoundland towns) affixed the name Lethbridge to that portion of Brooklyn containing the railway station and its residences. It was named in honour of James Lethbridge, the oldest resident. Other family names included: Blundon, Diamond, Harris, Oldford, Osmond, Pardy, Russell and Smart.

Early in its settlement the town had relied on the Labrador fishery for its existence. Construction, sawmills and the railway later provided employment. The Goose Bay area has had a long tradition of agriculture and fishing — Brooklyn's excellent harbour made it a fine port in the days of sail. Later, with the development of the A.N.D. Company and the railway, logging employed many residents. Farmers in the area continued to produce hay, potatoes, cabbage, livestock and, in the era of the schooner trade, fishermen caught and shipped salmon, codfish and lobster to St. John's.

Laden with such trade goods — salt fish, hay and lumber — as produced by hard-working Lethbridge/Brooklyn pioneers, *Maggie* made her way to St. John's. Fourteen people, all of Lethbridge and area, went down with *Maggie*:

Crew or Passenger	**Age**	**Married or Single**
William Ash	50	Married, 9 children
William Diamond	73	Married, 5 children
James Power	28	Married, no children
Rhoda Power wife of James Power	20	Married, no children
Thomas Abbott	20	Married, no children
Christopher Lethbridge	24	Married, 2 children
George Blundon	23	Single
Herbert Holloway	18	Single
Moses Lethbridge	33	Married, 5 children
Joseph Diamond	35	Married, 5 children
Annie Blundon	60	Wife of Captain,
Annie Blundon's young son		Single
Sarah Gullage	50	Married, 3 children
Isabella Holloway	20	Single

Two of those rescued boarded *Tiber* without getting wet — David Diamond and Stephen Blundon. Diamond jumped aboard from his schooner's foresail rigging; Blundon ran up the rigging, caught a rope handing over the steamer's side and tried to pull himself up. But another of *Maggie*'s compliment, Thomas Abbott, clung to Blundon's clothes or legs. Diamond, who had an instant before made the deck of the steamer, grabbed Blundon and helped him aboard while Abbott lost his hold and fell into the sea.

Working feverishly, several of *Maggie*'s crew had the punt, which was lashed on the afterdeck, almost ready to launch when *Tiber* plowed into the schooner. The fore boom fell on the punt and smashed it. Two men who were preparing the small boat — James Power and James Lethbridge — jumped into the sea and grasped each other's arms over a bale of hay. As they struggled to say afloat, the hay rolled. The men let go, Lethbridge survived; Power did not.As some of those who could swim or had managed to stay afloat were struggling, the great mainsail and foresail of *Maggie* fell, spread out over them and forced them under. This was how Captain Blundon described the death of his wife. Apparently he held his wife, but the foresail engulfed her and he could not keep her above water.

After some delay in preparation *Tiber*'s men launched a lifeboat commanded by the mate. It ran among the wreckage and several people left alive and holding debris were pulled aboard. Three or four were rescued by a small boat from a Brigus schooner which had sailed near the scene.

Those rescued were: Captain Blundon, Isaac Blundon, Levi Blundon, Stephen Blundon, David Diamond, James Lethbridge, Thomas Holloway, Julius Lane and his wife Clara who were both Labrador natives. The nearest place of authority was the East End police station and when the survivors arrived there, they were cared for: wet clothing was removed and dry clothes provided. The weakest sufferers were laid in the policemen's beds; liquor, supplied to whoever wanted it, was provided by Mr. T.J. Green of Shea and Company.

When a doctor arrived, he ordered Captain Blundon, who was in the worse shape, physically and mentally, to be taken to hospital by the police ambulance. Attorney General William Whiteway and other persons in power immediately set up an inquiry to examine the command and management of S.S. *Tiber*. Captain DeLisle, well known in St. John's, was regarded as an efficient and cautious man.

On the morning of November 7, S.S. *Favourite* with Superintendent Sullivan and harbour pilot Vinnicombe aboard, searched the area where *Maggie* went down. *Favourite*'s crew placed a buoy there to mark the location but, although some soundings were made, no bodies were found. *Favourite* returned to port at nine-thirty to get members of a police investigation team who were going to the site. Several small boats had already searched the area only to find a few articles — one box, a bed, a four-inch rope and several lumber deals floating around.

That evening, at the official inquiry of the fatal collision given before Judge Conroy, Captain Blundon gave this statement (sections have been deleted for brevity):

> On the evening of November 5, 1896, I left Goose Bay...I saw the Cape Spear light last night; the weather was clear and it was a beautiful night with the wind about south southeast.
>
> ...I saw a steamer coming out and she came out fast. I was then more than halfway across (the Narrows). When I first saw the steamer I think she was inside Chain Rock. When I first saw her three lights I was rather to the southward of her. After I saw her I continued on my southerly course, heading towards Freshwater Bay, Fort Amherst light bearing broad off my starboard bow.
>
> My starboard light was visible to her all the time. She did not go out of the Narrows in a straight line, for she turned so far to the southward that I could see Chain Rock shore to the north of her...The steamer kept too close to the south shore of the Narrows altogether and I was keeping my course, because I relied that a steamer coming out would keep a steamer's course through the middle of the

Photo courtesy Peter Cook and Marine Archives

The two hundred forty-six net ton *Elizabeth Fearn*, built in Placentia in 1917, grounded at five am on February 12, 1921, on the north side of Quidi Vidi harbour. Captain Vatcher and his eight crew later reported to owners Campbell & McKay of St. John's that it was impossible to see the St. John's Narrows entrance in the blinding northeasterly blizzard.

Elizabeth Fearn, a well-built tern schooner and classed A1 with Lloyd's insurance, lies with her port rail under water and her bowsprit in over the sand and rocks. Her jumbo, mizzen and foresail are gone; the jumbo boom and topmasts broken off. A few hours after this photo was taken the harbour tug *D.P. Ingraham* attempted to tow the unlucky ship to St. John's, but *Elizabeth Fearn* sank en route.

> Narrows by the leading lights.
>
> ...Immediately afterwards the steamer struck my vessel, her starboard bow striking my starboard quarter abaft of the main rigging.

A little over a hundred years ago one of Newfoundland's most tragic sea collisions happened near the high traffic seaway of St. John's Narrows. *Maggie*'s crew and passengers who disappeared in the wreck were residents of Lethbridge and Brooklyn, Bonavista Bay and the loss of fourteen residents dealt the small towns a severe blow in both human and economic terms.

Chapter 35

Phoebe: Wrecked at St. John's Narrows

St. John's Narrows, Random Sound

An example of what crews of small ships had to go through to escape the grip of the sea near St. John's harbour entrance happened on November 13, 1909. The schooner *Phoebe*, commanded by R.J. Strange and his crew of Sam and Nathaniel Mugford and George Bursey, left St. John's harbour en route to Random Sound. Random Sound lies south of Random Island with its inlets, North West Arm and South West Arm. As the crow flies, Random Sound is about eighty kilometres northeast of St. John's, but Strange and his crew had sailed no farther than St. John's harbour entrance when disaster struck.

While beating out through the narrows in a gale of wind, she mis-stayed and ran into a little inlet known as Pilot's Cove, under Fort Amherst. *Phoebe* stranded a few yards from shore.

High seas were running up over the treacherous ledges and cliffs. Strange and his crew could see no choice but take to the small boat in order to save their lives. Since there was no way to get out to sea in the adverse winds and waves, they had to attempt a landing on the rocks in Pilot's Cove. Breakers, one after another, rolled in and as soon as the little boat touched a shoal, they jumped into the surf. Two of the four

Author's collection

While good pictures of wrecks of schooners like *Phoebe* are rare, this photo shows a government coastal boat turning around in St. John's harbour in the 1960s. The "Narrows" — Signal Hill on the left and the South Side Hills on the right — loom in the background.

Over the years the constricted entrance proved to be a nemesis to many ships, including the following: Western boat *Paradise* 1811, brig *Avalon* 1848, S.S. *Dauntless*; schooner *Phoco* 1870, bark *Maggie* 1896, schooner *Dauntless* 1907, schooner *Luetta* 1921, British steamer *Marsland* 1932 and schooner *Ethel Collett* 1934 are some of the "Narrows" victims.

Above, *Nedrill*, one of first ocean oil drilling rigs, enters St. John's harbour.

men went under water, but somehow held on to the boulders.

Drenched and frozen with cold water, the crew of *Phoebe* set foot on solid land and climbed up to the Fort Amherst lighthouse. On the way they turned occasionally to catch a final glimpse of their schooner. Combers continuously passed over the craft and they realized that had they stayed on *Phoebe* another minute they would have been washed overboard and drowned.

Within ten minutes the vessel was beaten to matchwood and became a total wreck. By the time a correspondent from *The Evening Telegram* reached the scene, only the mainmast was intact. Debris floated along the shore.

Phoebe, fully outfitted for the spring fishery, was owned by E. Hampton of Chapel Street in St. John's and was insured for seven hundred dollars under the Brigus Insurance plan. Except for the wet clothes they wore, the crew lost all other personal belongings. One man had just purchased a new suit of clothes valued at twenty-two dollars.

Chapter 36

Red Gauntlet Goes Down

St. John's, Port aux Basques

Not only did the overseas trade cause the demise of many large, foreign-going terns, but smaller schooners and their five-six man crews paid a price as well. Not designed for the dead weight cargoes of salt and the tremendous seas of mid-Atlantic, scores of Newfoundland vessels went to the bottom while delivering fish to Europe or returning with salt for Newfoundland. The following table lists Newfoundland vessels which disappeared with crew in the winter of 1912.

Vessel	Net Ton	Bound	Date Posted Missing
Arkansas	98	E.	February 14, 1912
Dorothy Louise	125	W.	May 22, 1912
Reliance	96	W.	May 22, 1912
Beatrice	89	W.	May 22, 1912
Grace	129	W.	May 22, 1912
**Erna*	-	E.	May 22, 1912
Pearl Eveline	99	E.	April 30, 1912

* S.S. *Erna* disappeared on a voyage from Glasgow, Scotland to St. John's with fifty-one persons on board, including survivors of the schooner *Aureola*, abandoned at sea a short time previous.

Not all Newfoundland ships on transatlantic voyages were as unfortunate, but one schooner that came close to being classed as "Lost with crew" was the two-masted *Red Gauntlet*, owned by E. Pike of Port aux Basques. At fifty-nine ton she was one of the smallest in the Atlantic trade and, in addition, *Red Gauntlet* was well past the average age for a schooner having been built in 1876 at Jersey in the Channel Islands.

Red Gauntlet left Lisbon, on November 9, 1908, bound for St. John's with seventy ton of salt. All went well until November 26 when a succession of mid-Atlantic storms followed and continued in increasing fury until December twentieth.

Mountainous seas raged and battered the fifty-nine ton schooner so severely, she began to take on great quantities of water and the pumps had to be kept going day and night. Eventually the seawater reached the salt in the holds. Much of the salt melted or formed brine until there was only about thirty ton left.

That evening someone in *Red Gauntlet*'s crew discovered the stern of the schooner was gradually breaking away from the rest of the hull. The heavy bolts in the iron knees and in the sides were working loose from the beating the little craft took in the wild seas. Every hour the amount of water coming in through the seams was increasing. Soundings showed that *Red Gauntlet* gained ten inches of water in her hold in one hour.

Prospects looked gloomy and the crew — Captain Hoeberg, Patrick Murphy, Samuel Stanley, Herbert Evans and M. Palfrey — realized the helplessness of their situation. To launch a small dory in the mad seas was certain death; to stay aboard a disintegrating ship was to face a watery grave.

On December twenty-first, the next day, Hoeberg saw a steamer in the distance toward the east. Realizing that it would be too much of a risk to let her pass without signalling and, fearing that *Red Gauntlet* would sink before another vessel came in sight, the men asked the captain to hoist a distress signal.

Soon the ship was seen to change her course a little and bear directly down on the Newfoundland schooner. When the liner, which was S.S. *Louisiana* bound from New York to Havre, France, came near enough that several crewmen launched a lifeboat from the davits and rowed over to the sinking *Red Gauntlet*. Hoeberg and his four men climbed aboard the lifeboat. Before he left the schooner Captain Hoeberg set fire to her, so that she would not be a menace to other ocean craft.

By this time *Red Gauntlet* was four hundred miles east of the Newfoundland coast in latitude 47.48 North, longitude 39.39 West. *Louisiana*, crewed by French sailors, arrived at Havre on the twenty-ninth of December. The shipwrecked mariners stayed a day at Havre; then travelled to Southampton, England, where they remained another day before taking the steamer for Liverpool.

In Liverpool they were cared for by the Board of Trade and within two days joined the Allen Line *Grampian* for Halifax. Joining the S.S. *Rosalind* in Halifax bound for Newfoundland, they arrived in St. John's on January 15, 1909.

Hoeberg and his crew had left Lisbon en route to St. John's in their little schooner and completed the voyage two months later on the Red Cross liner *Rosalind*.

During the Great War several Newfoundland vessels disappeared their fate supposedly due to enemy action; others were recorded as torpedoed or shelled by German submarines. In most attacks the German sub commanders allowed the crews ample time to get provisions and to launch a lifeboat. Such was the case of one hundred ten ton *Percy Roy*, a two-masted schooner owned by Smith and Company of St. John's and crewed by Captain William J. Dawe, mate Philip Hynes, cook James Rogers, seamen George Eldridge, Azariah French and Daniel Bursey, all of St. John's and area. *Percy Roy* was originally owned in Grand Bank by Foote's business.

On February 13, 1917, while en route to Naples, Italy, *Percy Roy* was stopped by an enemy sub in the Gulf of Lyons off France, shelled and sunk. Dawe and his crew rowed into Paloma, Spain, and according to the March 26, 1917, edition of the *New York Times*, they arrived back in North America, in New York, on that date aboard a French steamship.

Chapter 37

Abandonment of the Ruby W

St. John's

In early December 1921, a storm swept across Newfoundland which sank or wrecked several schooners and claimed many lives: *Passport* out of Greenspond, lost near Caplin Cove with seven people aboard (see Chapter 19 "Loss of the Nerette"); *Jean and Mary* struck the Penguin Island with the loss of six men. Along the northeast coast several other schooners were wrecked; many of which were laden with winter's supply of food and provisions for families.

On December 5, during the height of the storm, other vessels wrecked were the St. John's harbour tug *D.P. Ingraham* which had been towing *Jean and Mary*; three ships lost at Bay de Verde, *Gordon W*, P. Johnson of Seldom Come By, *A. Hardy* and *Dianthus*; *Galatea*, E. Sturge of Goose Cove, wrecked at Grate's Cove; *W.S. Monroe* at Little Bay Islands; *Drummer's Tax* at Bonavista; *Pansy*, William Frost, wrecked at Lower Island Cove and *Theresa Stone* driven ashore near Bauline. Estimates of property damage along the northeast coast reached two hundred and fifty thousand dollars.

Not all destruction was confined to the shores and water near the island, but the storm extended some distance out to sea and affected the foreign-going fleet. On December seventh, the Ministry of Shipping in St. John's received a wireless via Cape Race from the Danish steamer *Gudrun Maersk* which read:

> "Dec. 7th, latitude 40.08 N. longitude 56.02 W. steamer *Gudrun Maersk* from Philadelphia to Genoa, rescued the crew from the derelict three-masted schooner *Ruby W.* of St. John's. Wreck afire and dangerous to navigation. Captain suffering with broken arm, one sailor with bruised knee, others all well."

Built in 1917, *Ruby W*, the first tern schooner constructed by the Nova Scotia Shipbuilding and Transportation Co. at Liverpool, Nova Scotia, was fitted with a one hundred horsepower auxiliary engine and netted two hundred ninety-six ton.

Owners Baine Johnston and Company of St. John's put Captain Charles Forward of Carbonear in charge of *Ruby W.* Forward had selected his crew from the experienced seamen of Carbonear — mate William Janes, Thomas Lawrence, Jim Thoms, William Pike, Nathan Penney, William St. Croix and Stanley Bryant.

Captain Forward, after he arrived back in Newfoundland after his ordeal on the high seas, wrote a letter to the *Daily News* describing what had happened: *Ruby W* left St. John's November fifth with a cargo of fish bound for Pernambuco in northeastern Brazil arriving there in good time with beautiful sailing weather. After discharging their cargo they left Pernambuco in sand ballast for their return trip to St. John's, but *Ruby W* never reached port.

On November 29, four hundred miles south of Newfoundland, Captain Forward and his crew encountered a fierce storm which so disabled the tern that they were forced to abandon ship. First the flying jib and foresail were carried away and the mainsail ripped. Two days later, as winds diminished, this was repaired, but on December third another storm forced Forward to shorten and reef the sails. This storm intensified to a West Southwest hurricane with high seas.

Courtesy Seamen's Museum

Banking schooner *Neva Belle*, owned at one time by Arthur Samson of Flat Islands, Bonavista Bay, waits for cargo destined for the northeast coast. The windlass used to raise the anchor can be seen in centre; the deck engine (left) was used to raise cargo from the holds.

Neva Belle is tied up in front of A. H. Murray's premises in St. John's. As a young man at the turn of the century, Alexander Hamilton Murray began supplying the Labrador fishing fleet and dealing in salt, coal and general provisions. In 1908 A.H. Murray & Company was incorporated and the Murray premises near Beck's Cove and Bishop's Cove expanded. During the Depression years, A.H. Murray accepted lumber in lieu of money and this arrangement helped establish his building supplies division. In 1989 the business closed. Today the Murray Premises is a fish-and-trade historic site and a shopping centre.

About ten-thirty that night what Captain Forward described as a "tidal wave" broke over the stern, smashed the life boat to pieces, carried away the rails and stanchions, the binnacle, compass, companion doors, skylight and part of the rudder. He wrote of the injuries to himself and others in the crew:

> The wave...drove myself through the door into the cabin, flooding it and breaking my right arm. Thomas Lawrence, who was at the wheel, was crushed in the leg and pinned him under the wheel, where when chance offered, he was released by his shipmates and carried to my room.
>
> It was then that the stern was opened and the ship leaked badly and the pumps had to be kept going. In this condition we were drifting helplessly about until December seventh when the Danish steamer "Gudrun Maersk", seeing our signals, came to our aid at midnight.

Before Forward and his crew abandoned ship, the mate set *Ruby W* afire to keep the derelict from being a menace to navigation. Owing to the heavy seas and the injuries to two of the schooner's crew, it took two hours to make the transfer from the sinking ship to the Danish steamer.

Incidentally Forward and his crew landed in Genoa on Christmas Eve, 1922. Five days later they left for America via the S.S. *Arabic* en route to Boston and transferred to another ship bound for Newfoundland. Forward concluded his letter by thanking three people in particular: crewman William St. Croix, who had a course in first aid; mate Janes who took over the ship after Forward was injured; and train conductor Lee of the Newfoundland railway for dropping the crew off near their Carbonear homes. Captain Forward himself lived on the Carbonear's South Side.

They had left Pernambuco November fifth and arrived home in Carbonear February third, three months later.

Ruby W was the second vessel Baine Johnston had lost within a few days. Auxiliary schooner *June,* Captain Marshall, was wrecked at Port Mahone, Minorea Islands in the Mediterranean on November thirtieth.

Chapter 38

Disastrous Voyage of the Kinsman

St. John's

By the early twenties, the end of the era of tern schooners was evident. Owners operated their vessels year round, bucking winds and vicious storms of the mid-Atlantic to carry fish to Europe and to return with salt. Wages were low, work was tough and ship-board comforts were few. The story of A.E. Hickman's tern schooner *Kinsman* represents just one of many sea stories of Newfoundland ships and seamen pitted against the treacherous sea —forty-four days battling hardship and danger.

Captain Martin Picco, mate Noah Blake, bosun Alf Payne, cook J. Yarn, seamen Joseph Picco, Jack Mullins and Philip Cheeseman left Battle Harbour on November 19, 1921, en route to Gibraltar with eight thousand quintals of Labrador codfish. Fine weather was the order of the day until *Kinsman* was eight hundred miles southeast of Newfoundland.

Then a heavy northwest gale roared around them. For two days the storm raged badly buffeting the gallant schooner. *Kinsman*'s decks were continuously swept with high seas causing her to leak so much the crew was compelled to pump in constant shifts.

Courtesy Marine Archives, Harry Roberts' Collection

Kinsman (above), a three hundred ton tern built in 1919 at Charlottetown, became a victim of heavy cargoes, strained seams, harsh weather and damage inflicted by a would-be rescue ship. Captain Martin Picco, a veteran seaman and captain, had, some years earlier been captain of Hickman's *Olive Moore*.

Although they worked day and night, water began to gain steadily in the holds. Captain Picco decided, seeing a moderation in the weather on November 28, to get the vessel to nearest land, the Azores. Picco believed that with continual pumping it was quite possible to get there. He ordered up all canvas which gave the wallowing *Kinsman* fairly good speed.

Two days later the S.S. *Guild Rosa,* bound from Jamaica to Harve, France, bore down on the troubled Newfoundland tern. Captain Picco lowered his sails, signalled to obtain his correct position and, since *Kinsman* was hove to, mate Noah Blake and one or two others rowed over to the steamer. Blake would talk to *Guild Rosa*'s officers to obtain accurate position.

Unfortunately, while waiting for the mate to return both ships drifted closer together. *Guild Rosa,* an iron ship towering above the bobbing wooden schooner below, fell across *Kinsman*'s bows tearing away the headgear, smashing off the bowsprit and doing other minor damage.

After the crews cleared the wreckage, the captain of the steamer asked Picco to abandon ship. This the intrepid captain and his crew refused to do for Picco still believed he could make land. *Guild Rosa*'s captain bade farewell after promising to report *Kinsman*'s condition and position by wireless.

Kinsman, a wallowing, sinking wreck with considerable damage inflicted by a would-be rescuer, was still three hundred fifty miles southwest of the Azores. Yet, to her captain and crew, everything still looked hopeful until the evening of December second when another gale pounded the Newfoundland schooner.

The badly strained vessel leaked more copiously and on sounding it was found that there was four and a half feet of water in the holds. There was no respite for the labouring men who were exhausted from constant pumping. *Kinsman* was settling slowly by the head, but the crew never lost hope and on December 3 the purple smudge of Santa Maria, part of the Azores group, was sighted. It was thirty-five miles distant.

Quite possibly the crew could have made land but the wind turned against them. At five pm December fourth, with the vessel still a considerable distance from the shore and threatening every minute to go under, the Portuguese steamer *Gilannes* happened along.

Captain Picco, seeing that all efforts to save his vessel and her valuable cargo of dried fish were in vain, decided to abandon ship. *Kinsman* sank from view at latitude 38 North, longitude 30 West.

Picco and his crew received excellent treatment on board *Gilannes* and were taken to the Maderia islands, Portuguese-owned islands three hundred fifty miles off Morocco, and afterward they found transportation to Lisbon. There they joined a steamer bound for Liverpool, England, and connected with the liner *Minnedosa*. *Minnedosa* landed *Kinsman*'s sailors in St. John, New Brunswick. From there they travelled to Sydney, Nova Scotia, crossed the Gulf and joined the eastbound train at Port aux Basques. Also on the train was the crew of the Harbour Buffett schooner *Amy B. Silver*, abandoned at sea on December 12, 1921.

If, at this point, *Kinsman*'s crew thought their troubles were over they were mistaken. The train carrying them through Newfoundland was wrecked at Rapid Pond, about eleven miles east of Curling. During blizzard conditions, sections of the train were derailed in a snowslide as it rounded Rapid Pond. Two baggage cars, a diner and the second class passenger cars, in which Captain Picco and the seamen were located, were pushed completely off the track. Captain Picco was hurtled through a side window and into the snow. He had his forehead badly cut requiring four stitches to close the wound and received minor scratches. Other passengers were bruised, but otherwise had no serious injuries.

Without any further incident *Kinsman*'s shipwrecked (and train wrecked) crew, as well as the crew of *Amy B. Silver*, arrived in St. John's on January 3, 1922. All in all a remarkable tale of hardship and endurance which serves to demonstrate the perseverance and trials of Newfoundland seamen.

Chapter 39

Evelyn: Lost with Crew

St. John's

When reports filtered into St. John's that the wreckage of missing tern schooner *Evelyn* had been located, newspapers of the day listed her crew. *Evelyn*'s Captain Nilson hailed from Denmark, but her crew came from various Newfoundland towns: mate Frederick Hollett from Spencer's Cove, a town near Harbour Buffett on Long Island, Placentia Bay; John Yarn, was born in or resided at English Harbour West or Coomb's Cove on the Connaigre Peninsula; Peter Mullett, Wesleyville on the North East Coast; Donald Burton, Central Street, St. John's, and Ernest Pilgrim, Carbonear. Also sailing on *Evelyn* was Captain Nilson's wife and another sailor from Denmark, Khristian Jensen, making eight lives — five from Newfoundland — lost in another disaster of the sea.

Evelyn had been built for Job Brothers in 1907 by A.D. Mills and Sons at Granville, Nova Scotia. Registered in Bridgetown, Barbados, she netted two hundred eighty-seven ton and measured over one hundred forty foot long. This was the second tern schooner bearing that name registered in Newfoundland; the previous *Evelyn* was wrecked in 1913 at Ferryland. (See Chapter 42 "Evelyn: Fearless Men of Ferryland")

The tern had recently been purchased by the St. John's business Monroe Export Company and was making her first voyage for that company. On February 25, 1924, she left St. John's bound for Pernambuco laden with fish. Previously in her career *Evelyn* had made several voyages to the European and Brazilian markets.

Eighty days passed and Monroe's had heard no word or received a telegram stating that their schooner had reached any port. Then on May 20, nearly three months after the missing schooner left Newfoundland, the schooner *John W. Miller* reached Barbados with grave news of *Evelyn*.

While en route to Barbados, Captain Cyril Horwood of *John W. Miller* sighted wreckage a distance away. Since the seas were relatively smooth, Horwood decided to have a closer look in his vessel's dory. Going near the derelict, which was located at latitude 41.19 North, longitude 58.09 West, Captain Horwood discovered that the debris was of the port quarter of a large schooner painted white and bearing on the stern timbers the words "Bridgetown, Barbados" in full. Above that on the broken bulwarks were two letters "**EV**".

The wreckage was floating in an upright position with a portion of the stern and port bulwark out of water. A large section of the poop was attached with the rudder, stern post and after rail intact. Some of the rigging was still attached to the wreck. None of the forward section of the schooner could be seen.

Horwood and the crew of *John W. Miller* were sure from the size, colour and the lettering on the debris it was of the missing tern *Evelyn*.

How her missing crew died, and the manner and time when she met her end was a mystery. Many were of the opinion she was run down by a large steamer for the location of the wreckage was a few hundred miles from the coast of Nova Scotia and in the lane of trans-Atlantic shipping.

In his fine and informative book *Newfoundland Ships and Men*, (1971) author Andrew Horwood related the story of one crewman, Wallace Smith, later Captain Wallace Smith, who had been engaged to sign on *Evelyn* as a sailor. Smith refused to sail and claimed his life was saved by a squeaking fender — a device used to protect a schooner from rubbing against the wooden wharf pilings. As Horwood tells it:

> Smith was left as a watchman on board (*Evelyn*) for the afternoon. Perhaps he was lonely.
>
> The wind died out to a dead calm but a small undertow in the harbour caused the ship to rise and fall by the wharf. Every time this would happen the fender would squeak. It seemed to Smith that the fender was saying something. He noticed two syllables — daw gaw and again daw gaw. Why they are saying "Don't go." He stayed aboard till the captain came. "Captain," he said, "I'm not going." Captain Nilsen was annoyed but Wallace Smith stuck to his decision.
>
> He (Smith) was not surprised when the *Evelyn* was posted missing.

Courtesy George Buffett

Harry and Verna, above, a two hundred fifty-seven ton tern schooner built in the United States in 1919, flies the Hickman flag. Captain Fred Hollett (bearing the same name as the young man lost on *Evelyn*) of Burin made twenty-four trips across to Europe in eight years in *Harry and Verna*.

On April 7, 1919, another of Hickman's fleet was lost; this one, *Jennie E. Ritcey*, went ashore in Sicily, never to be refloated.

Six years later *John W. Miller* was abandoned at sea. She was owned by the Crosbie business of St. John's and left Newfoundland in November 1930 for South America with a cargo of drummed fish. When a storm forced open her seams, *Miller* was abandoned and Captain Cyril Horwood and his crew was taken off by the German ship S.S. *Wido*.

Chapter 40

Captain Abe Kean's Ships: Cecil, Jr., Little Stephano

St. John's, Flower's Island

Newfoundland's most successful seal hunter, Captain Abram Kean (1855-1945) was born on Flowers Island, Bonavista Bay. In the 1879 he moved to Brookfield and began his successful career as a sealing vessel captain. He continued as master of sealing ships like *Wolf, Florizel* and *Terra Nova* (with stints as captain of government coastal vessels) almost continuously through to 1934-35 until he had brought to St. John's a million seal pelts. In the spring of 1934 Kean became a seal pelt "millionaire", having brought in a million seal skins. He was presented with a model of a sealing steamer *Terra Nova* and a silk flag.

Captain Kean had also set up a mercantile business at Brookfield, Bonavista Bay, which he left mainly in charge of his sons when Kean moved to St. John's. In the war years when fish prices rose and many businesses acquired tern schooners to transport their product overseas, Kean had two tern schooners built in Nova Scotia and with his sons formed the Little Stephano Company in 1917.

That year McGill's yard at Shelburne built *Little Stephano* for Captain Abram Kean and within the next year *Cecil, Jr.*

was launched at the Shelburne Shipbuilders yards. Both schooners plied the Atlantic on their foreign-going voyages for Kean until 1926 when both were abandoned at sea a little less than two months apart. Capt. Abe Kean's decline in fortunes in the fish exporting trade rests in the story of his schooners. He had already lost the foreign-going tern *Little Princess* in mid-ocean on December 1, 1923.

Cecil, Jr., a two hundred net ton wooden schooner, measured one hundred and fifteen feet long. She set sail prior to November 18, 1925, for Seville, Spain, with a cargo of fish and arrived there on January sixth.

Her crew — experienced Carbonear seamen Captain George Burden, mate Malcolm Penny, William Butt, Samuel Cole and Nicholas Shanahan — sailed from Herring Neck around November 18, 1925, for Seville, Spain, with a cargo of fish. They arrived January sixth, discharged the vessel and sailed from Seville in ballast for St. John's on February twenty-eighth.

A mid-Atlantic gale with adverse winds buffeted the tern schooner from March thirteenth until the twenty second. Gales increased in intensity. *Cecil, Jr.*'s stern began to leak; then, the pounding of the sea opened seams and the tern filled with water. Realizing it was only a matter of hours before the Atlantic claimed another victim, the five crew tried to launch the lifeboat, but it was smashed in the heavy seas.

When the oil tanker *War Divan* came upon the wallowing *Cecil, Jr.* at latitude 41.04 North, longitude 37.46 West, she saw distress signals raised to the masthead. In the height of the gale, the five Carbonear seamen were taken off. Before he stepped off his tern schooner, Captain Burden set fire to *Cecil, Jr.* to prevent her from becoming a menace to navigation.

On March 24, a few hours after the rescue, *War Divan* sent a message to Newfoundland that the crew was well and on the way to Lisbon, Portugal. From there Captain Burden and his hardy Carbonear crew made their way to Southampton, England, where they secured a passage to Halifax.

Courtesy Marine Archives, Harry Roberts' Collection

Cecil, Jr. (above), netted one hundred twenty-five ton with an overall length of ninety-nine foot, was one of three tern schooners including *Little Stephano* and *Little Princess* owned by Captain Abe Kean. Kean became a successful sealer who ventured into the foreign trade and fish exporting business. He died in 1945.

While Kean commanded Bowring's sealing vessel *Stephano* in 1914, he was involved in the infamous "Death on the Ice" controversy (he was later exonerated in an enquiry) when seventy-eight sealers from the S.S. *Newfoundland* froze to death on the ice floes. The steel-hulled *Stephano* was a successful sealing vessel for Kean; thus, when he had his a wooden tern built, he christened it *Little Stephano*.

In January 1923 *Little Stephano* went through a battle with the sea, but with the grit and determination of a dedicated captain came through virtually unscathed. Fred Collett of Harbour Buffett was put in command of Kean's *Little Stephano,* his first trip as captain. Well-experienced as a seaman, Fred Collett — and his brothers, Bill and Ernest — had seen, helped load and eventually sailed on the foreign-going schooners frequenting the salt-dry fish producing port of Harbour Buffett, Placentia Bay.

Collett sailed from Twillingate on January 8, 1922, en route to Greece laden with dried fish collected by Kean's company along the northeast coast. The eastward journey was rough and *Little Stephano* sustained considerable damage to her bulwarks and spars.

On the westward voyage a piece of the rudder was swept away by the heavy seas putting the tern schooner in a helpless condition. Without proper steering gear, *Little Stephano* drove broadside to the waves with heavy seas pounding her planking. If the schooner could not be brought around or was kept too long under those circumstances she would soon break up or would have to be abandoned.

A less caring or dedicated master than Collett would have abandoned ship, but the experienced Placentia Bay master was not daunted by the demanding sea nor the difficult task ahead of him. He had his crew move as much gear and cargo forward as was necessary causing *Little Stephano*'s head to dip and the stern to lift out of water.

Collett, working over the stern and just above the tossing seas, secured a temporary section on the rudder and with that crude device in place the vessel made port without undue stress. While in port he acquired another piece for the smashed rudder and, with the help of his crew, put it on. After the repaired rudder was in place Collett striped himself of his clothes and dived down to make sure everything was all right.

When *Little Stephano* reached St. John's Captain Kean arranged for a thorough examination of Collett's work. Afterward, Kean commended his captain highly for his pluck and seamanship placing him in command again.

Collett's second foreign-going voyage, which began October 19, 1923, destined for Seville, was again long and difficult. As with the previous voyage, on the westward trip he bucked adverse winds and high seas. Many of the large ocean liners out in the same storm suffered severe damage, but Collett reported his schooner did not break a single rope. From port back to port — Seville to St. John's — the voyage lasted two months and twenty-seven days. Captain Collett brought *Little Stephano* through the narrows without the help of the harbour tug.

Around the early 1920s when sinking and stranding were frequent, insurance premiums on foreign-going terns had risen substantially. Often companies would refuse to insure schooners at all. Ship owners like Kean knew that with the declining markets and high costs only seaworthy vessels like *Little Stephano,* commanded by reliable and determined captains like Collett, could make the exporting business a paying investment.

But despite the most gallant attempts of captains and sailors many aging tern schooners foundered in the North Atlantic. In 1926 *Little Stephano*'s end came when she was abandoned off the Azores. By this time Captain Collett had moved on to another venture and Captain Joseph Lake commanded the tern schooner.

Captain Lake and his sailors John Lake, Thomas Pike, Alfonse Bonia, Fred Dooley and Joseph Ingram abandoned the sinking tern and were picked up by the French steamer *Carmia.*

Little Stephano had been at sea forty-five days, fourteen of them without a rudder and eight days with no provisions. After drifting rudderless with sails blown away and the schooner leaking badly, Captain Lake, despite every attempt to keep afloat, decided that the best course of action to save himself and his crew was to take to the boats. *Little Stephano,* representing Captain Abe Kean's declining endeavours, went down in mid-Atlantic on April 20, 1926 — fifty-one days after the loss of *Cecil, Jr.*

The roster of tern schooners abandoned in mid-Atlantic in the first few months of 1926 continued to grow. Some of the Newfoundland-owned terns lost were: *General Smuts, General Maude, Max Horton, Myrtle Piercey, Gordon T. Tibbo, Novelty, Spencer Lake,* and *Retraction.*

The latter vessel, *Retraction,* was owned by Philip Templeton of Catalina. Captain John Sinclair and his brother mate Max Sinclair hailed from St. John's while the rest of her crew were from Bonavista Bay and area: bosun Maxwell House

Courtesy PANL

This is the two hundred sixty-six ton Novelty, built in LaHave, Nova Scotia, and later sold to A.S. Rendell and G.M. Barr of St. John's. Like several other Newfoundland terns in the mid-1920s, she was abandoned in a sinking condition two hundred miles northwest of the Azores on February 12, 1926, when the S.S. *Vindermore* came by.

Her crew all from Carbonear — Captain George Winsor, mate Thomas Pike, bosun Robert Penney, cook Thomas (or John) Butt, seamen Thomas Lawrence, Arthur Winsor, Ralph Crocker and Sidney Clarke — were taken to Manchester, England, where arrangements were made for their return home.

and cook Simon Stead of Catalina, Abner Brenson, Bonavista and Harry White of Harcourt, Trinity Bay.

Retraction sailed from Cadiz, Spain, on New Year's Eve of 1925, but as January of the new year progressed, the tern encountered a tremendous southwesterly gale. In the wild seas her deck heaved, opened the seams and *Retraction* filled with water that no amount of pumping could keep out.

On February fifth a tanker, *El Oso* bound for Curacao in the Dutch West Indies, rescued the crew. The crew, except Simon Stead who had joined another vessel in New York, arrived in St. John's March 14.

Chapter 41

Cape Freels Burns

Southeast of St. John's

In 1934, when Responsible Government in Newfoundland was replaced with the Commission of Government, a Department of Natural Resources was formed primarily to monitor offshore fish stocks. Considerable research and investigation was carried out in the Bay Bulls Research station. Trawler *Cape Agulhas* (the same vessel which searched unsuccessfully for the missing *Stanley Parsons* in 1932) was used to survey fish stocks until 1935.

After a developmental lull in the early 1940s, off-shore research on cod and other groundfish resumed in 1946 with the launching of the eighty-two foot *Investigator II* at Clarenville. Within another twenty to thirty years vessels like *Marinus, Gadus Atlantica, A.T. Cameron* searched for new fish stocks and observed the operations of foreign fleets off Newfoundland.

In 1976 one Fisheries Research vessel operating off Newfoundland was the seven hundred forty-nine ton *Cape Freels* under the command of Captain Doug Skinner and his twenty-two crew:

Carbonear
Captain Skinner

St. John's
First officer William Hewitt

Second Officer James Martin

Third engineer Willis Organ
Steward Thomas Dicks
Seaman Thomas A. Lawlor
Seaman Henry Lake
Oiler Nat Norman

English Harbour West
Third Officer Raymond J. Bartlett
Cook Richard Price

Grand Bank
Seaman Leslie Buffett
Seaman Cyril Hillier
Waiter Morgan Green

Rushoon
First engineer James Emberley

Fox Harbour
Waiter James Baker

Marysvale
Second engineer David W. Smith

Lark Harbour
Fourth engineer Walter Childs

Carmanville
Seaman R. Boyd Cull

Arnold's Cove
Ernest L. Penney

Baine Harbour
Oiler George Clarke

Bay L'Argent
Oiler Ed Walters

Grand Falls
Fisheries Officer David Aylward

Musgrave Harbour
Seaman Clarence Bannister

About two am on February 12, 1976, while *Cape Freels* was on a routine mission off Newfoundland a flash fire broke erupted in the engine room. The fire, fuelled by fumes and oil, quickly went out of control. After about twelve minutes, power and lights went out.

The only message transmitted was to marine radio in St. John's advising them of a fire, but no "Mayday" or distress call as such was sent. As soon as the watch reported the fire to Captain Skinner, the captain rushed to the engine room to find the fire out of control and spreading fast.

Courtesy H. Stone collection, Marine Archives

Cape Freels (above), a fisheries patrol vessel with a gun mounted on her bow, caught fire and burned off Newfoundland March 12, 1976.

Making his way back to the bridge through thick smoke, the captain sent alarms to the rest of the crew and ordered his officers to assemble the men at the fire stations and to prepare to abandon ship. Moments after he radioed the ship's position — about one hundred fifty miles southeast of St. John's — the power went out and the radio failed.

By this time two life rafts, holding seven or eight men each, and the lifeboat were in the water. Ship engineers wearing breathing apparatus had fought the fire, but without success.

Cape Freels had a built-in compressed carbon monoxide fire-fighting system which was set off, but it failed to put out all the fire. When flames began shooting out of the ventilators and up through the deck, Skinner and his crew got off the ship.

The lifeboat and dinghies were brought around to the stern, now about eight feet above the water line and, in single file, the men jumped in as the little craft rose and fell with the swells.

It was the intention to remain near the burning *Cape Freels* using a two hundred foot painter to allow both craft to drift together. When the painter (rope) became entangled in the rigging and gear on *Cape Freels* the three boats were cut free for fear of capsizing. According to second mate Jim Martin:

> Smoke was so thick by the time the captain and I jumped, we could only see the outline of the lifeboats. We jumped and hoped she was there. One of the crew had already fallen between the ship and the lifeboat, but the rest of the boys grabbed him when his head came above water.

A choppy sea and moderate winds made the fourteen hours on the high seas anything but comfortable for the shipwrecked crew. Within a few minutes all three boats had drifted out of sight of *Cape Freels*. One of the rubber life rafts was partially deflated and had taken on water; so she was tied to the back of the lifeboat. Waves breaking over the side of the boats kept everyone busy bailing using anything they could get their hands on — a hard hat, rubbers and blankets to soak water.

When daylight finally broke about five hours later, *Cape Freels* was nowhere in sight. The seas were even rougher and heavy freezing rain was falling.

Some of the men began to wonder if and when rescue would come. Captain Skinner assured them radio contact had been made and with improved visibility planes would be out. As he recalled:

> I told them a search was definitely started. Normally emergency provisions were not touched until after the first twenty-four hours, but I broke open a package of hard candy to give the men encouragement.

Despite the captain's assurances, the morning soon passed and it was early afternoon before one of the crew saw an airplane. Fourteen hours had passed since the abandonment of *Cape Freels* and the men hurriedly lit two flares to get the attention of the plane. As Skinner put it, "There's no worse feeling than seeing a rescue plane and then thinking it didn't see you." However the plane circled back, banked its wings and dropped a package.

The crew of the plane put a note (saying how good it was to see them) in a box of assorted juices, attached the box to a small parachute containing a float and dropped it to *Cape Freels* men. The note also said the rescue ship *Hudson* was about a hour and a half away and to wave four oars if all hands were accounted for and to wave two oars if anyone was lost.

Only after the men were aboard *Hudson* and the fourteen hour ordeal was over, did the danger of the situation sink in. As *Hudson* steamed up to find them, the weather was getting progressively stormy. The men in the lifeboat were the worse off; they had all they could do to keep the tiny craft into the wind. If snow had come or visibility been reduced, there was no telling how long it would have taken to find the shipwrecked men.

For the forty-eight year old chief engineer, James Emberley of Rushoon, it was the third time he had been in a similar situation: he had been on another ship that caught fire and on one that was crushed in Arctic ice. Emberley said he was asleep when the fire broke out and when he looked down all he could see was smoke and flames in the engine room. He said:

> After that I helped out the crew and captain, helped get the engines shut down and isolated the engine room to see if self-contained extinguishers would put out the fire. When the order came to abandon ship the deck was burning through and the only thing we could do was get away for fear of an explosion.
>
> After we took to the lifeboats I was pretty sure we were going to be rescued. You don't panic when such a situation

develops. If you do, you're lost. We had a very disciplined crew.

By doing what they could, assessing with clear minds the best plan of action, so it was the disciplined men of St. John's, Grand Bank, Carbonear, English Harbour West and the other Newfoundland towns survived. The following is the chronological record of the burning and sinking of the Fisheries Patrol vessel *Cape Freels*:

Friday March 12, 1976:

2:00 am — Fire breaks out in the engine room, 120 miles southeast of St. John's
2:12 am — Power failure on board interrupts radio message
2:45 am — Abandon ship order given. Crew evacuate *Cape Freels* in two life rafts and one life boat
5:42 am — Tracker aircraft leaves Torbay
6:55 am — *Cape Freels* spotted by Tracker
7:30 am — Research vessel *Hudson* instructed to join search along with CCGS *John Cabot*, CCGS *Sir Humphrey Gilbert*, three trawlers and a freighter
12:00 am — Weather moderates slightly in search area
2:00 pm — Buffalo aircraft spots raft and boat, drops rafts and supplies. Confirms by means of dropped message and waving from *Cape Freels* crew that all are present
5:15 pm — *Hudson* rescues first survivor
5:32 pm — Last survivor picked up
8:40 pm — *Cape Freels* sinks slowly while under tow by *John Cabot*

Chapter 42

Evelyn: Fearless Men of Ferryland

Ferryland

News of the wreck of the schooner *Evelyn* near Ferryland had been sent to St. John's on January 9, 1913, by the Ferryland lighthouse keeper and by Police Constable Murphy stationed in Ferryland at that time. Both had wired St. John's —located thirty-two miles north of Ferryland by sea — to say the vessel was stranded and all aboard her had been rescued, but made no mention of the crew's narrow escape from drowning nor of the heroic efforts of several Ferryland men in saving the lives of *Evelyn*'s seven mariners.

For a day only the following information was available to concerned owners and relatives in St. John's: *Evelyn*, a large schooner, painted white, with three masts, had broken up on Isle aux Bois (Bois Island) off Ferryland. Curiously, although the name means woody island, today it is grass covered. Ninety-seven feet high at its highest peak, Bois Island is the outermost of a treacherous chain of rocks, reefs and small islands near Ferryland Head and is a buffer for the winter northeasterlies. The entrance to Ferryland's superb harbour lies between the island and Ferryland Head.

Crosbie and Company put Captain Edgar Burke of Carbonear in command of *Evelyn*. His crew of C.G. Edgecombe, James Rendell, George Wright, William Collins, Alex Keefe,

Courtesy of Marine Archives, Harry Roberts' collection

At one hundred sixty-seven ton and one hundred seven foot long, *Evelyn* was built in 1899 at Shelburne, Nova Scotia, for John A. McGowan and Captain Charles Nicholls of Nova Scotia. In 1903 Crosbie and Company, a fish exporting business based in St. John's and founded in 1882, purchased *Evelyn* for the foreign trade registering her to Bridgetown, Barbados.

Three flags fly from the mastheads: on the foremast, Crosbie's red C on a white background; mainmast, the ship's name and on the mizzenmast the British flag.

and James Healey were experienced seamen. *Evelyn* had sailed from Newfoundland to Pernambuco late in 1912, discharged her cargo of salt fish and headed home. Up to late December, she had a fine time along but in the northern latitudes the weather took a turn for the worst.

A few days into January of 1913, *Evelyn* was thirty days out from Brazil, off Newfoundland and bound up to St. John's. On January eighth she was sighted by the crew of the steamship *Bellaventure* about five miles east by north of Bay Bulls.

Bellaventure, a relatively new steel steamer, was one of three ironclad ships especially constructed for the seal hunt and built for A.J. Harvey of St. John's. *Bellaventure,* the largest of the trio (the other two were *Adventure* and *Bonaventure*), was in command of Captain Cross.

Evelyn had distress signals flying from the masthead and *Bellaventure* bore down on her. In the heavy seas, Captain Cross manoeuvred down to within hailing distance. He could see the tern was in trouble — she was scudding along under bare poles with all canvas gone, most of the foresail was in tatters. Cross thought the tern was unmanageable and perhaps it would be best to transfer the crew to his own vessel.

In the brief exchange through the megaphones Captain Burke asked to be towed into Bay Bulls. Cross, realizing the impossibility of transferring *Evelyn*'s crew of seven to his own vessel when both ships were so close to land, offered to stand by the disabled tern and to render whatever assistance he could.

Bellaventure's crew prepared hawsers to pass to the distressed vessel. One end of a heaving line was attached to the hawser and the other to a cask which was thrown overboard in the hope it might drift to *Evelyn* and be taken aboard.

However, in the middle of preparations the weather cleared. Goose Island, off Ferryland and a little distance north of Bois Island, was sighted and Captain Cross thought *Evelyn* would get into Cape Broyle or Ferryland under the sheltered lee of the island without assistance.

Once again weather played a trick; as *Bellaventure* backed off a thick snow storm came on. Seeing his steamer was near land in a perilous position, Captain Cross altered his course and bore up for St. John's. There he would alert authorities to the plight of *Evelyn*.

By the next morning *Evelyn*'s captain, seeing he could not clear the land, ran his vessel in Capelin Bay on Bois Island. Outside the small bay both anchors were let go and for a while the vessel stopped. Soon the port chain broke under the heavy strain and the starboard anchor dragged. That evening *Evelyn* drifted in on Bois Island striking stern first on a cobblestone beach. The tide was low and for awhile the crew was safe. *Evelyn* partially filled with water with freezing spray going over the vessel and crew.

Bellaventure's men, while endeavouring to give assistance, endured intense frost and constant soaking from the cold seas while working on deck. According to the report given by *Bellaventure*, those on *Evelyn* fared much worse.

As Captain Burke described the ordeal later, the schooner was constantly swept by white seas breaking across her deck, the temperature was below freezing and the crew could only work on deck at the risk of their lives. Sea and spray flying over the vessel froze on impact coating the hull, deck and rigging with several inches of ice.

With high cliffs surrounding them, there was no likelihood the crew would save themselves by land. The possibility of launching the ship's boat into the angry seas was courting death. It seemed only a matter of time before high tide crept over the stranded schooner and it would only be a matter of time before they died of exposure or drowned.

But the fishermen of Ferryland had seen the plight of *Evelyn*'s weary crew and immediately took matters into their own hands. With no regard for personal safety several Ferryland men — Jim Barnable, his brothers Jack and Bill, William Furlong, Michael White, Michael and Jno. Devereaux, James Walsh and Howard Morry —launched a skiff and rowed to the island navigating through a narrow gap or opening which was termed locally, the "Y of the gaps." Seas breaking over the shoal drenched the men who had to manoeuvre the boat into position without upsetting her, but they made land on the south side of the island. In fact the boat struck a rock puncturing a hole in the side which fortunately was small and just above the water line.

High winds prevented a rope from being dropped to the stranded men trapped on a ledge below the cliff. Will Furlong, a slight man, was lowered down over the cliff and he assisted the shipwrecked crew. Each man was pulled to safety. Kind hands supported them, helped them cross the island, and into the damaged skiff. With constant bailing, they managed to keep the skiff free of water until all reached shore without mishap.

When *Evelyn*'s crew landed, they were taken in by various families including the Morry family, given dry clothes, warm food and a bed for the night. Father Vereker, the Parish Priest, stood by the shipwrecked men making sure they were well-lodged and cared for.

When the message from the Ferryland light keeper (as well as the one from Constable Murphy at Ferryland) arrived in St. John's, Inspector General Sullivan and Goodridge, the Deputy Minister of Marine Affairs, arranged for a tug to tow the stranded vessel off. Harbour tug *D.P. Ingraham* was at Greenspond and unavailable; tug *John Green* was busy with harbour shipping and could not be sent. By this time *Bellaventure* had also arrived in port to report her version of *Evelyn*'s difficulties.

J.(John) C.(Chalker) Crosbie, manager of the company and at that time a Member of the House of Assembly, received a message from Captain Burke which cancelled any plans for sending assistance for the wrecked *Evelyn*. The wire stated the ship was ashore with the bottom torn out, filled with water, but the spars were still standing. It was expected she would break up during the night.

In conclusion, the message stated, congratulations had to be given to the Ferryland people who had efficiently saved the lives of seven seamen.

Meanwhile, at one pm on Friday, *Evelyn*'s crew left for St. John's, but reached only as far as Cape Broyle where they stayed at Mrs. Sculley's home for the night. On January 13 when they finally reached the city, their ordeal with the sea was over. Captain Burke had left all his navigating instruments on the wrecked schooner, but he knew certain items had been saved from the wreckage by the Ferryland people and figured some of his property was in safe hands.

Tragedy at Stone Island, Calvert

Twenty-three years after the wreck of *Evelyn*, a more tragic shipwreck happened in the same general locale, a little north of Ferryland. On the night of December 4-5, 1934, the twenty-three ton schooner *Gertie*, owned and commanded by Thomas Devereaux of Trepassey, headed for St. John's. *Gertie* was manned by three men of Trepassey — Captain Devereaux and his brother George, and Michael Curtis — all unmarried.

The first indication of the wreck reported to St. John's was that wreckage had been located at North Gut, Calvert on the morning of December fifth. The debris consisted of fifteen empty oil drums, part of a ship's cabin, a bag of wool, a man's cap, and piece of wood with the name "Gertie" painted on it.

By December 6 a second missive, this one from M. J. White, the Wreck Commissioner at Calvert, confirmed the report: a lot of wreckage was floating about, crew of the vessel had been lost, but no bodies had been recovered. Dr. Giovanetti, the Magistrate at Calvert, wrote:

> "Schr. *Gertie* believed lost last night (Tuesday) with all crew on Stone's Island. Picked up board with name "Gertie," various parts of hull, gasoline drums, men's clothing, spars and broken-up dory. No bodies found; too rough to go out and search."

Subsequently a coat rack marked Thomas Devereaux and a bag of yarn owned by a Mrs. Corrigan were located. With the identity of the wreck determined, the owner and his home town were contacted and the vessel's final journey traced: *Gertie* had landed a cargo of fish at the premises of James Baird Ltd. about a week previously, returned to Trepassey and was once again sailing to St. John's with a cargo of about four hundred and fifty quintals of dry fish for the Tor's Cove Trading Company. As far as could be concluded she was caught in a snow storm and hit Stone's Island with tragic results.

Chapter 43

No Survivors from President Coaker

Cappahayden, Port Union, Catalina

Tern schooner *President Coaker* was built for and named after Sir William F. Coaker, founder and president of Fishermen's Protective Union (F.P.U.) in Newfoundland. Beginning in November 1908 and for a period of approximately ten years, William Coaker unionized fishermen in many northwestern Newfoundland communities. Basically the union deplored the powerlessness of the fishermen under the credit system and decried the control of the merchant to determine both the price of fish and the supplies credited to fishermen.

Coaker attempted to regulate the grading, pricing and exporting of salt-dry cod to foreign markets and set up his headquarters in Port Union, a town situated on eastern side of the Bonavista Peninsula. Scores of local branch organizations were scattered around Newfoundland's coast. Remnants of his once-powerful union existed until the 1930s.

To export fish produced by the unionized fishermen of the north east coast, Coaker had foreign-going vessels built which operated through the Union Trading Company. Several tern schooners were built in Port Union: in 1918 the three hundred fifty-five ton *Nina L.C.* and the smaller *Fisherman;* 1919, *President Coaker*; 1920, the one hundred forty-one ton C.

Bryant and in 1921 *Port Union*. The latter vessel lasted less than two years.

On January 1, 1923, *Port Union* burned to the water's edge in Port Union, the harbour after which she was named. At the time she was tied on the company's wharf with no one aboard and was awaiting the remainder of a cargo of barrelled herring destined for Jamaica. Fire broke out in the forward part of the vessel, and despite a team of volunteers and men from the F.P.U. premises who gathered to fight the blaze, flames enveloped the hull. *Port Union* burned until she sank.

Thirteen years later another of the F.P.U.'s foreign-going fleet was destroyed, this time with devastating results: *President Coaker*, built in 1919 at Port Union was owned and managed by Coaker. Netted one hundred sixty ton, she measured one hundred fifteen foot long, twenty-nine foot wide and eleven foot deep. Considered the flagship, the

Courtesy Marine Archives, Harry Stone Collection

Tern schooner *President Coaker* (above), built in Port Union in 1919 by the Ship Building Company affiliated with the FPU and incorporated under the laws of Newfoundland. In 1924, her debris was located near Cappahayden.

pride of Coaker's concept of a foreign-going fleet, *President Coaker* was crewed by men from the Port Union area: Captain Norman Sheppard, his brother Harold Sheppard, mate, Alfred Sheppard, bosun, and George House, cook, all of Port Union and Catalina; John Kelly of Ireland's Eye and Israel Downey, a resident of Port Rexton.

Three years previously Norman Sheppard captained the one hundred ton *Mintie,* built in 1918 in Trinity Bay for Coaker's enterprise. On January 10, 1921, she was abandoned at sea; Sheppard and his crew were taken off safely.

In October 1923, *President Coaker* left Port Union for Pernambuco (today named Recife), Brazil, with four thousand six hundred seven quintals of dry codfish. A round voyage that took two or three months to complete, *President Coaker* was not due back until the latter part of January or early February. She was slated to return to Port Union in ballast, that is, with a cargo of sand or rocks for weight. From Port Union *President Coaker* was due to take another load of fish to South America.

Representatives of the F.P.U., General Manager Hazen A. Russell, in Port Union and Martin Finney in St. John's, knew their tern had arrived in Pernambuco after a routine voyage of thirty-two days. On December 10, *President Coaker* left for Newfoundland. Nothing more was heard of the ship until early February 1924 and the news on that date was surrounded by uncertainty.

The scene of the fate of *President Coaker* shifts to Shoe Cove near the towns of Cappahayden and Renews. Six years previously, on the night of February 23-24, 1918, the rocks near Cappahayden had claimed the S.S. *Florizel,* bound from Newfoundland to New York. Shortly after *Florizel* left St. John's, faulty navigation and poor weather set the steamer off course and she grounded full speed upon the offshore reefs northeast of Cappahayden. Only forty-four of her one hundred thirty-eight crew and passengers survived the wreck. The little craft and dories of Cappahayden and surrounding towns played a key role in guiding larger rescue ships or helping survivors reach the shore safely.

Now six years later, concerned citizens of the Cappahayden shoreline again helped search for bodies or survivors, this time at Shoe Cove. Shoe Cove, located six miles from Cappahayden and nine miles west of Cape Race, is a remote, uninhabited spot and one of the loneliest on Newfoundland's rugged southeast corner. The cove, over two miles long containing three smaller coves, is over a quarter mile from the road which in 1924 meandered near the shoreline from Cappahayden to Chance Cove.

Author's collection

Disaster at sea takes many forms in remote places far from home. William Bishop, a director of Bishop Brothers of Burin, one of leading outport merchant houses in Newfoundland, booked a passage to Halifax on the ill-fated S.S. *Florizel*. His stone stands in the Collin's Cove (Burin) cemetery.

On February first the local mail man, a man named Brazil, and his son walked along the road carrying mail to the various communities. For some unknown reason, Brazil asked his son to continue along the road with the mail while he walked seaward toward Shoe Cove.

On the shoreline which is bordered by huge cliffs and in the central section, numerous breaking rocks, Brazil saw wreckage of an unknown ship. Later that day he contacted the Custom's sub-collector at Renews who wired this information to authorities in St. John's: "Mail courier Brazil reports wreckage in Shoe Cove, near Cape Ballard. Leaving to investigate. Will wire particulars later. Arthur O'Leary, Sub-collector."

President Coaker was due back from Brazil and was perhaps off that coast on this date; fears surfaced that this may be the shipwrecked vessel. There was some speculation the wreckage might have belonged to *Annie M. Parker,* a two-masted schooner reported overdue. By that date though, and unknown by her Newfoundland owners, Gabriel Hollett of Great Burin, Captain Joseph Hollett and his crew had been picked off the sinking vessel and carried to Rotterdam, Holland. *Parker*'s crew had developed smallpox, one had died on the sea voyage and the rest of the crew were detained in hospital in Holland; thus, delaying considerably the news of their safety.

Three groups of searchers anxious to discover the name of wreck in Shoe Cove set out for the Cape Ballard area: O'Leary with a group of men from the surrounding localities; Martin Finney, an agent of the Union Trading Company, left St. John's for the southern shore by horse and slide. A tug, S.S. *Walker* — owned by Cashin & Company and captained by W. Dalton — was harboured at Renews and left for the area.

As ominous as it was, the first news back to Port Union and St. John's came from O'Leary's group of men who had descended the cliffs to the beach. Two messages, received by H.W. LeMessurier Deputy Minister of Customs, read:

> Just arrived at Shoe Cove. Picked up a sailor's clothes bag, marked George House, Catalina, Newfoundland. Wreckage broken in matchwood. Would judge vessel lost about 100 tons. (Second Message) Have found nothing further to identify name of wreck. She was evidently a three-masted vessel and ashore for sometime.

Thomas Perry of Catalina wired custom's officials in St. John's saying that George House, of Catalina, was one of the crew of *President Coaker* and that the schooner was fifty-three days out from Pernambuco to Port Union. The information was confirmed by Russell at Port Union and seemed to indicate the tern had been lost with crew.

By late evening, February second, there was little doubt

the wreckage strewn around Shoe Cove was that of *President Coaker*. That day another clothes bag was found marked Harold Sheppard, but there was no sign of bodies. Captain Dalton of S.S. *Walker* had searched coves and the sea up the coast to Cape Race and had found no other traces of the wreck on offshore rocks or islands.

A land search located *President Coaker's* chains and anchors between Western Cove and Chance Cove Head which formed the south-western side of Shoe Cove; her rigging and small portions of her hull were found entangled around the rocks or among the cliffs. Imbedded in the sandy beach of Western Cove, about one quarter of a mile beyond where the chains and anchors were located, was a thirty foot section of the vessel's keel and portions of her timbers. This indicated

WELL-KNOWN F. P. U. FISH CARRIER FEARED LOST WITH CREW

"President Coaker," Capt. Norman Sheppard was due on Coast From Pernambuco.

Clothes Bag Bearing Name of Member of Crew Picked Up

Mr. H. W. LeMessurier, C.M.G., Deputy Minister of Customs and others in the city, have received further information regarding the wreck, reported by mail carrier Brazil at Shoe Cove near Cape Ballow. LeMessurier. Thos. Perry of Catalina wired the following:—

"George House, Catalina, is one of the crew of the schooner 'President Coaker,' which is 53 days out from Pernambuco to Port Union."

Newspapers of the day carry headlines of the loss of *President Coaker*.

the vessel was swept from Sandy Cove Rocks and shattered in pieces over the shores of Shoe Cove.

One remarkable feature of the wreckage was that there was no sign of the ship's boat or dory and this gave rise to the belief that the men may not have been aboard when she struck. A small piece of an oar, broken slantwise, was picked up at Chance Cove, south of Chance Cove Head. Questions remained unanswered: Did the captain and crew leave *President Coaker* in a lifeboat? Was the vessel becalmed and later thrown on rocks by heavy seas? Was she impaled on the Sandy Cove Rocks and broken up?

Martin Finney, in his report to Sir William Coaker the man after whom the vessel was named, claimed the wreck was surely *President Coaker*; pieces of wreckage bore her

Courtesy Decks Awash

S.S. *Illex* near the shore in Port Kirwin. Owned by A. Wareham & Sons, Harbour Buffett and captained by Alex Rodway, the six hundred ninety-four ton *Illex* was en route to south coast ports to complete a salt fish cargo destined for Jamaica. On a stopover in Fermeuse on October 27, 1949, she caught fire, completely burned inside and was grounded at Blow Me Down, Near Port Kirwan. Wareham's had bought her the previous year from the U.S. Maritime Commission.

Residents of the area — Patrick Hogan of Kingmans, Cecil Walsh, Martin Walsh, George Walsh, Victor and Kevin Reddy, Cyril Brennan, Felix O'Shaughnessey, all of Fermeuse —salvaged salt fish and ship materials from the burning steamer.

registry numbers and tonnage. Coaker arranged for the search for bodies to continue.

The tragedy at Shoe Cove was further heightened by an accident that had happened a year and a half previously in the summer of 1922 when three brothers named Sheppard, relatives of the missing Norman, Harold and Alfred Sheppard, lost their lives by drowning.

Chapter 44

A.B. Barteau's Ordeal by Ice

Off Cape Race

In the era of sail there were hundreds of Newfoundland-owned ships that left European or Canadian ports deeply laden with cargo destined for our island. Not all of them made it; some simply disappeared, others were more fortunate and crews were rescued. One of the most unusual stories of survival —an experience of shipwreck and hardship probably unsurpassed in the history of Newfoundland shipping, happened to these Carbonear seamen:

Captain Thomas Janes	mate Leonard Dale
cook John Hynes	Moses Janes
John Vatcher	Walter and Gordon Parrott

The seven were crew of the tern schooner *A.B. Barteau* reportedly overdue after leaving Perth Amboy, New York, with a cargo of coal for the Gas Company of St. John's. The two hundred sixty-eight ton schooner left early February; by mid-month she was slated to arrive at St. John's.

Fears were expressed for *A.B. Barteau*'s safety although she was considered an able vessel and one of the largest of Newfoundland's fleet. Built in 1909 at Canning, Nova Scotia, her registry later passed to A.S. Rendell & Company of St. John's. She measured one hundred fifty-three foot in overall length, thirty-five foot wide.

Late winter of 1923 was an unusual one for Newfoundland shipping for ice practically surrounded the island. Arctic ice rarely drifts along Newfoundland's South Coast, but that year pans of ice filled the ocean for a hundred miles or so southwest of Cape Race, into St. Mary's Bay, Placentia Bay and Fortune Bay. It lasted from February to mid-March.

In the spring of 1923, several Newfoundland vessels had been sunk, damaged by ice or delayed in reaching port. Rendell & Company, knowing *A.B. Barteau* was heavily laden, asked other ships to keep a lookout for her.

Captain Janes sailed from New York on February 5 and for the first few days weather was fair. A week into the voyage *A.B. Barteau* encountered the ice field off Cape Race. For some days Janes edged the tern through the small bergs, large pans of ice and slob.

On February 20, about seventy-five miles southwest of Cape Race, *A.B. Barteau* seemed to be settling by the bow. Captain Janes went into the forecastle to see for himself. Then, to be doubly sure, he crawled out onto the bowsprit to check the schooner's depth in the water. Suspicions confirmed, he hastily called all hands to the deck for he knew then *Barteau* was sinking fast. Apparently, he told them, a pan of ice had stove in the bow; the vessel had to be abandoned immediately.

While the crew was cutting the lashings from the lifeboat and getting her to the side for launching, the heavily burdened tern went under. Without time to get extra clothes, oilskins or provisions, the seven seamen jumped into the boat. Captain Janes was the last to leave and in doing so fell into the slob ice up to his waist. Others had their boots filled with water.

A.B. Barteau's men were stranded in zero degree weather amid a vast field of ice in an open boat. They had no food, fuel or extra clothes, but with great determination headed toward land. For the most part they were on solid ice, but in case they reached open water the men dragged their boat behind them.

Pulling the boat slowed them down and sometime after the first day it was left behind. In the event the boat would be found later, the men attached a note to it which read:

> "Schooner *A.B. Barteau,* foundered February 20th, 1923. Crew left ship on the ice and are hoping to reach land. Finder of the boat, communicate with British Consul or A.S. Rendell & Co., St. John's."

When darkness came the men stopped to rest. Janes suffered the most for his pants and boots were frozen on him. At night some men were frozen onto the ice and had to be cut out. For three days and nights the exhausted men plodded on; each hour the need for food and warm drink became more intense. They used every means to cheer each others spirits and to keep warm. At night they had only one oil coat to lie on.

On the third night they rested behind a pinnacle of ice and stacked smaller pieces to make a crude windbreak. Mate Leonard Dale had a vision or harbinger of rescue. He felt they couldn't survive another day and stayed alert all night watching and praying.

At three am on February 23, his persistence paid off for he saw in the distance the lights of a vessel. He roused the others, propped up the oilskin, and set it afire.

For anxious relatives and owners in Newfoundland, the first word that *A.B. Barteau*'s crew had been saved came on March 6, thirteen days after rescue. Survival came in the form of a Norwegian steamer.

When Captain Mitchell on the Red Cross liner *Silvia* docked in St. John's on March 6, he told the story of the S.S. *Hauk*. Mitchell had been asked, while he steamed from the mainland to Newfoundland, to keep a lookout for the overdue *Barteau*. What Mitchell sighted on four pm on March fifth was the Norwegian steamer *Hauk* also bound, like *A.B. Barteau* had been, to St. John's with coal.

Hauk was south of Cape Race, slowed practically to a stop amid a sea of ice. The chief officer went aboard *Silvia* to ascertain position and to ask about ice conditions. While aboard he related the rescue of seven men stranded on the ice. Captain Mitchell offered to take them aboard *Silvia,* which was able to steam through the ice field, and transport the men to St. John's. But they were badly frostbitten and were too ill to be transferred from one ship to another.

Hauk had butted through ice until February 23 when she saw the flare of a fire indicating distress. As *Hauk*'s crew gathered on deck for a look, they could make out several men huddled on a pan of ice with a flare on a pole. Occasionally one or two of the men would stumble only to be picked up by the others.

For five hours the captain of the Norwegian vessel pushed through dangerous ice before the ship reached the ice pan holding *A.B. Barteau*'s crew. Another six ice-bound days passed before she reached St. John's on March sixth. *Barteau*'s crew had been eleven days suffering and frostbitten before they received proper medical treatment.

In the meantime as *Hauk* steamed for St. John's, everything possible was done by *Hauk*'s crew to relieve suffering. They cut off clothes which was frozen onto the shipwrecked men and gave them hot drink and food. Frostbitten hands and legs were rubbed with snow to draw out the frost.

When Captain Janes, mate Dale and the other crew arrived in St. John's two doctors — Carnell and Knight — met them. Cook Hynes, Vatcher and Captain Janes, who had the worst injuries, were sent to the General Hospital. Walter Parrott, not so badly frost bitten, was hospitalized at the Sudbury Hospital. Dale, who had a toe frostbitten, was sent home while Moses Janes and Gordon Parrott were put up in the Kitchener Hotel. They were the only two who escaped the wreck of *A.B. Barteau* and the three days stranded on ice floes unscathed.

Captain Janes, despite the best of care and treatment aboard *Hauk* and at the General Hospital, had to have both legs amputated. All in all the crew were fortunate to escape from such uncompromising circumstances; only the captain had serious injuries.

Unusual Rescue off Cape Race

It has been said that practically anything that could happen has happened to a Newfoundland schooner and, with several hundreds lost that were registered to island owners, the statement may be valid. Over the years, many of our seamen were plucked off sinking schooners, were taken from rocky ledges near shore, pulled from wreckage, or were snatched, like those men of *A.B. Barteau*, from an icy world where death from exposure stared them in the face.

In June 1941, another unusual rescue took place off Cape Race when the tern schooner *Chesley R* came upon five stranded men. But these castaways were not seamen, but airmen from a downed plane.

Built in 1905 in Denmark and named *Maagan* (Danish for seagull and she had a seagull carved on her stern), the one hundred and twenty three ton schooner was bought by Forward and Tibbo of Grand Bank in 1929 and renamed *Chesley R*. Her square topsails were converted into fore and aft rigging and, in 1937, an engine was installed. For many years she went across to Europe without incident; then, during the war years, she carried lumber, oil, food, fish, and supplies from various ports: Halifax, Sydney, Grand Bank and St. John's. On June 22, 1941, *Chesley R*, under the command of Heber Keeping and mate Walter Keeping, was off Cape Race heading for home from St. John's.

That same day, a Douglas "Digby" Bomber #752 based in Newfoundland was returning from a routine submarine patrol mission out over the Atlantic when it ran short of fuel. The pilot had to make a forced landing in the ocean off Cape Race.

The bomber's five-man crew spotted a schooner in the distance and landed ahead of it. Captain Keeping, in the unwritten understanding of mutual aid on the ocean, manoeuvred *Chesley R* nearby. Soon the airmen clambered

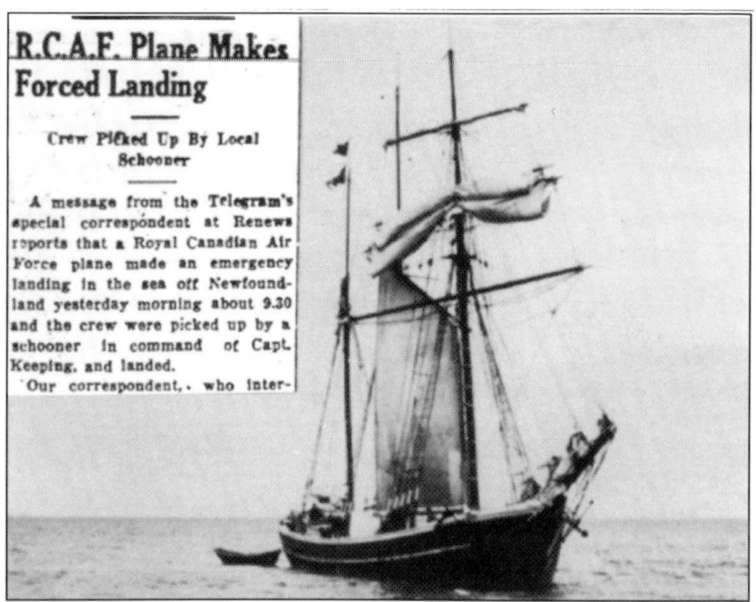
R.C.A.F. Plane Makes Forced Landing

Crew Picked Up By Local Schooner

A message from the Telegram's special correspondent at Renews reports that a Royal Canadian Air Force plane made an emergency landing in the sea off Newfoundland yesterday morning about 9.30 and the crew were picked up by a schooner in command of Capt. Keeping, and landed.

Our correspondent, who inter-

aboard the tern and, within a few hours, Keeping had landed the airmen at Renews. A naval tug was sent to tow in the plane which remained afloat for some time, but the ditched bomber sank a short distance from Cape Race. Except for a wetting and a few minor injuries, the bomber's crew were none the worse for the experience.

Chesley R's fate was intertwined with Cape Race and the southern Avalon Peninsula: she had run aground at Latine Point, near Argentia, in November of 1936 and was refloated after several weeks of work by Thomas Duke of Ship Harbour. Then, thirteen months from the day of rescue of the downed airplane, *Chesley R* ran aground at Mistaken Point, a point a few miles west of Cape Race and eventually went to pieces. Her crew: Captain Heber Keeping, his brother Walter, Don Baker, George Lee and another unidentified seamen rowed safely to Cape Race.

Chapter 45

Loss of the *Fond Return*

Trepassey, Bay Bulls

In the era of sail-driven vessels and limited communication, winter storms brought many casualties with the schooner fleet and 1910 was no exception. Three men of Trepassey, Captain Gus James and his two men Joe Perry and Tom Finlay, were sailing to St. John's when they encountered a typical December storm near Gull Island, off Bay Bulls.

Their schooner was *Fond Return,* owned by Captain James, laden with five hundred thirty-four quintals of fish, all but twenty quintals or so owned by Monroe and Company of St. John's. Neither James nor Monroe carried insurance on the vessel or the cargo which was valued at $3500.

According to James' story, while he and his crew were off Gull Island about two or three am they found the schooner settling in the water. James knew *Fond Return* was seaworthy and water tight when she left port. In the heavy weather James assumed planks at the butt head had "started" or worked loose below the water line.

James, Perry and Finlay put the pumps in action immediately. Although the pumps worked well, they knew within a few minutes that pumping could not keep up with inflow. Water was gaining rapidly. They grabbed their belongings and while they were launching the dory, seawater ran over the deck.

Finlay performed a daring act just before the men left their vessel. He saw Perry's watch hanging on the wall in the forecastle. By this time water was three feet high above the forecastle floor and the table was under water. Finlay jumped from the deck into the forecastle, saved the watch at great risk to himself and joined the other two in the dory.

As they were steadying the dory — within a minute after they had let go of the railing — *Fond Return* heeled over and sank taking down with her a season's earnings for the Trepassey men. But they had no time to think about lost income for the prospects of saving their lives seemed remote.

The wind was blowing a gale from the southwest accompanied by a heavy cross sea. As soon as the three Trepassey men straightened out for the land the dory half filled with water. They were three miles off Bay Bulls in the darkness of four o'clock in the morning and, with thick snow and heavy seas, the shipwrecked men could not see a dory length ahead. But courage and determination were in the very fibre of their souls and lesser men might have daunted or been fainthearted at the expectation of reaching safety.

In a row toward land lasting four hours that under normal conditions might have taken thirty minutes, they dodged seas and squalls. Each whitecap threatened to upset the dory. Whenever a heavy squall came down with a big swell, James, Perry and Finlay turned away from their course for the shore and ran the dory before the wind. Only by watching the "lulls" or calmer wind breaks, they pulled with all their strength. Both sets of oars were out; the third man constantly bailed water to keep the dory afloat until they rounded point of land and reached the safety of Bay Bulls.

From Bay Bulls they were taken to St. John's in a carriage driven by J. Williams. With no money or means of travel the crew of *Fond Return* called on the city's Poor Commissioner who made arrangements to transport them to their Trepassey home.

Joe Perry was no stranger to shipwreck and marine misadventure. Three years prior to his narrow escape from *Fond Return*, he was lowered down over the cliffs in Drook and rescued twenty-two men stranded from the wreck of the steamer *Tolsby*. (See Chapter 46 "S.S. Tolsby's Wreck at Drook")

Nor was the loss of *Fond Return* the only shipwreck Perry and Captain James had gone through. While on a voyage from St. John's to Trepassey, they were driven to sea two hundred eighty-six miles in a schooner called *Fanny Belle*. Relatives had them given up as lost when they arrived in another port; eventually reports came to Trepassey that the schooner and men had been located.

The same gale that sank *Fond Return* wrecked the schooner *Ada E. Young* at Tinker's Island, approximately forty kilometres east of Rigolet, Labrador. Charles Young and his crew were sailing in ballast when the gale overturned the vessel. Young and his crew of six left in a small boat. They spent the night on the island and made land the next morning without incident.

In 1919 another vessel of Trepassey was wrecked at Baker's Head on the west side of Trepassey Bay. While laden with fish and oil, *Golden Hope*, owned and manned by Michael Tobin and his brothers of Trepassey, struck the rocks and sank within ten minutes. After they reached land Tobin and his crew claimed dense fog and an error in navigation caused the wreck.

Chapter 46

S.S. Tolsby's Wreck at Drook

Drook, Portugal Cove South, Trepassey Bay

Portugal Cove South, about ten kilometres west of Trepassey on the Southern Avalon Peninsula, was once regarded as a superior fishing berth despite the area's exposure to gales and proximity to dangerous shoals. In 1921 Portugal Cove South had one hundred sixty-one inhabitants with a few families of Perry and St. Croix living in a nearby settlement called The Drook. One or two families occupied Little Seal Cove. It was on this rugged shoreline, with seas roiled by a wild storm, an American ship stranded — the crew was saved by the hardy fishermen along the coast.

S.S. *Tolsby*, bound from Galveston, Texas, to France with a load of cotton, was caught in a mid-January snowstorm of 1908 off the coast of Newfoundland. At twelve thirty pm on January 13, snow was so thick it was impossible to see the length of the ship ahead. Captain Payne heard the fog whistle on Powell's Head, off Trepassey harbour, and not knowing anything about any whistle nearby other than that on Cape Race, thought he was a safe distance off Cape Race.

Without warning *Tolsby* struck head on the jagged ledges off Freshwater Point near Little Seal Cove, caught on the rocks for a minute and swung around broadside to the surf that was running at a tremendous rate.

The twenty-five crew, who for the most part were from southern United States, were trapped. When *Tolsby*'s officers got a glimpse of land through the thick snow that was falling, they saw a nearly vertical cliff looming about five hundred feet above them. At first there was hope of staying aboard the doomed ship, but soon, as the weather deteriorated, she began to break up in the pounding surf.

Captain Payne ordered all hands to look out for themselves and to save their own lives if possible. *Tolsby*'s boats were lowered but as fast they were put out, each was swamped or was broken up on the side of the ship.

One lifeboat containing five men eventually made it out to sea. The remaining crew made several attempts to reach the narrow cobblestone beach at the foot of the cliff in another small boat carrying a line from the steamer with them. The small craft hit a rock and swamped, but the men swam and tumbled through the surf to reach the beach safely.

Using the life line, the marooned crew made the shore without loss of life. In January temperatures with a snowstorm swirling around them, twenty of S.S. *Tolsby*'s men, wet and cold, huddled on the rocks on a narrow beach with the tide rising. Meanwhile five men in the boat that put to sea came back to *Tolsby* at four pm, climbed aboard, but decided not to stay long as their steamer was fast going to pieces.

It was no easy task getting back aboard the lifeboat as heavy seas threw it against the side of the ship several times. Within a few minutes however they joined the rest of the crew on the beach.

All twenty-five were in more danger. Cold spray dashed against them every few seconds as the tide rose higher and they realized all would be drowned if they stayed there throughout the coming night.

The bosun, a Swede named Alexander Windberg, volunteered to climb the cliff with the aid of a marlin spike, a pointed tool of iron or wood used to splice ship's rope or cable. Within an hour he had succeeded; three others followed him, but by this time the tide had risen so that the others could not get to the place where the climbers had begun their ascent.

The remaining twenty-one crew spent the night of January 13-14 in abject weariness and hopelessness. Although they built a fire from driftwood and wreckage, the sea and wind put it out. High tide and breakers forced the men back to the extreme end of the cove. Snow fell steadily all night. Occasionally rocks tumbled from the cliff and the stranded men didn't know at what minute one would hit them.

In this predicament the shipwrecked crew stayed until eleven am on January 14 when salvation came unexpectedly. The fishermen of Seal Cove and Drook, small communities near Portugal Cove South, saw the bedraggled group of men in the cove and took immediate steps to save them.

In the meantime, the four men who had scaled the cliff returned. They had wandered on the shore all night seeking human habitation, but found none except an empty shack where they stayed until daylight.

When the men of Drook realized the situation, they obtained a rope. Joseph Perry volunteered to have it tied around his waist. He descended the cliff to the beach, tied the rope around the men one by one and they were pulled up by the fishermen of Drook and Seal Cove. *Tolsby*'s crew were taken to Drook where they were fed and sheltered.

St. John's harbour tug *D.P. Ingraham*, Captain L. Young, arrived in St. John's at one pm on January 18 with the shipwrecked American seamen aboard (Appendix D lists the crew).

F.H. Osborne, chief engineer of *Tolsby* who with his captain and several other officers stayed in the Crosbie Hotel, told his version of Joe Perry's feat this way:

> Finally, when we were beginning to feel uncomfortable, a fisherman was seen coming down the cliff with a line made fast around his body. The fishermen on the cliff belonging to Seal Cove were lowering him down. As he descended we noticed him every now and then clearing away large portions of the rocks and other stuff from the cliff to make

for us a passageway up the cliff as feasible as possible...

The fisherman was Joseph Perry and I might say that he is worth a medal for his bravery. He worked to get us safely landed as I never witnessed a man working before. When we were all landed the inhabitants came and took us to their homes and made us as comfortable as possible.

The coat that I have on my back was given to me by a fishermen. I saved nothing except my watch and chain. I would like to thank these fine men who were the means under Providence in saving our lives. Too much praise cannot be given to them.

Chapter 47

Jennie Barno Disappears

Trepassey

By the 1960s, many Newfoundland coastal towns were connected by road and highway and its people no longer had to depend solely on sea transportation to bring necessary supplies. The TransCanada highway from Port aux Basques to St. John's was finally completed in 1965 and the slogan "We'll finish the drive in sixty-five" became a reality. Although an improved road system connected many formerly remote communities, coastal trading ships still plied the sea lanes to Newfoundland's offshore islands as they had for years. The wooden schooner, once the vital link between towns, had virtually disappeared and modern steel hulled vessels which had replaced them carried goods into the more inaccessible places.

The steel vessel *Jennie Barno*, owned by E.F. Barnes, was fifty foot long and equipped with modern navigational equipment: ship to shore radio and radar. She left Trepassey on August 14, 1960, headed for St. Lawrence and the French island of St. Pierre to pick up freight. Other sources claim she was bound for St. John's; however, it is known that *Jennie Barno* was crewed by three: Captain Richard Penney, his twelve year-old-son Richard (Jr.) and Frank Marks. Captain Penney and his wife were former residents of Bell Island.

Two days later *Jennie Barno* had not reported. The first evidence that the vessel and its crew had met an untimely end came when the body of Frank Marks was found off Cape Race. Then a trawler located the body of the captain's son. Apart from an empty oil barrel and a dory with oars and a bucket inside drifting off Cape Race, there was little other debris. Of the steel freighter itself, there was no sign.

Search and Rescue, the RCAF and the United States Coast Guard and Naval Base at Argentia co-ordinated a massive hunt which covered over ten thousand square miles off southeastern Newfoundland. Several ships including the RCMP craft *Irving* made a surface search.

The vessel's all-steel construction would leave little or no floating debris. The two victims gave some clue to *Jennie Barno*'s fate. Marks' body had a life preserver as did the boy's whose preserver was properly fitted and tied.

Authorities and relatives could only speculate. The vessel must have been rammed by another ship or had struck a submerged rock. There may not have been time to send a

Courtesy Marine Archives, Captain Harry Stone Collection

Employees of E.F. Barnes with the company's small trader *Jennie Barno* moored in the background.

SOS, but the crew could have prepared to board *Jennie Barno*'s dory, which had been located some time after the coaster was reported missing. Possibly *Jennie Barno* sank before they could get into the dory.

Despite the extensive air/sea search and a request to fishermen in the Cape Race, Trepassey, and St. Shott's area to report or recover any objects found along the shore, the exact cause of *Jennie Barno*'s disappearance was never determined.

Chapter 48

Finally Located: S.S. Morien

Placentia, St. Bride's

Much has been written and told about mysterious disappearances of many ships in the Atlantic Ocean. It is claimed, whether through folklore or through research, that the "Devil's (or Bermuda) Triangle" between Bermuda, Florida, and Puerto Rico has swallowed tankers, warships, wooden sailing ships, pleasure craft, even airplanes without a trace or without a word of communication indicating the missing vessels were in difficulty.

As far as Newfoundland is concerned, perhaps the "Devil's Triangle" — especially in the era between 1910 and 1930 — was the area where island schooners, as well as others, sailed to and from the European ports. Scores of local schooners vanished in the North Atlantic with entire crews. Most losses were attributed to violent ocean storms which battered the wooden craft into fatal submission. For example five schooners associated with the town of Burin disappeared virtually without a trace within three decades: *Mina Swim*, 1917; *Susan Inkpen*, 1917; *Herbert & Ruby*, 1917; *Ada D. Bishop*, 1918 and *Wilson T*, 1931.

These staggering totals were duplicated over and over in towns like Fortune, Grand Bank, Burgeo, Trinity, St. John's, Twillingate, Harbour Grace, or Carbonear. Each town had a fleet of wooden vessels which regularly plied coastal or trans-atlantic routes in all seasons and each town knew the pangs of sorrow in the toll of human lives.

Although the locale of following event is not the mid-Atlantic, it has the elements of tragedy coupled with an unusual disappearance and re-discovery and could be likened to looking down into the bottom depths of a Devil's Triangle to view missing ships.

The story begins in Nova Scotia in mid-November 1912. Newspapers of the day, the Nova Scotian *Morning Chronicle* and *Sydney Post*, speculated on the whereabouts of the Nova Scotian collier S.S. *Morien* which had left Louisbourg for Placentia on November sixteenth, 1912. Newfoundland's newspaper *Daily News* on December 3, 1912, had a column headed **The Missing Morien** which stated, "There is still no news of the missing steamer *Morien* which has not been heard of since she left Louisbourg for Placentia."

It was a voyage of two days duration, but seventeen days after she sailed, *Morien*, carrying a thousand ton of coal destined for the Reid Newfoundland Company railway terminus at Placentia, was declared "lost at sea" with Captain Charles M. Burchell and his seventeen crew. A steamer of eight hundred thirty-four ton, she was owned by Sydney interests.

Reasoned theory, wild speculation and rumours of her whereabouts ran rampant. While people speculated, ships scoured the adjacent seas for a month after *Morien* disappeared; yet, relatives of the missing crew decried the futile efforts of search parties. *Lady Laurier* and *D.H Thomas*, two Nova Scotian vessels, searched the seas off the Atlantic seaboard for the steamer without sighting any wreckage.

On December third, several veteran sea captains gave their opinion of *Morien*'s fate. Captain Morgan of the steamer *Kamouraska*, which left Sydney the same night as *Morien*, reported having encountered a heavy storm outside the harbour and had a difficult time weathering it. Morgan thought Captain Burchell and *Morien* would have been caught in the same gale and probably went down off Nova Scotia.

One of *Morien*'s owners, John A. Young, declared publicly that he was confident the missing steamer was riding safely southward somewhere on the Atlantic and gave reasons for his statement. According to Young, the northwest gale combined with a strong southerly current pushed the storm-disabled steamer well south. Young's confidence was reinforced by the knowledge that *Morien* had weathered all sorts of conditions in all seasons since going into the coal trade. Captain Burchell was one of the best at adapting his vessel to adverse conditions.

Captain E. Wallace Hickey of North Sydney, who resigned command of *Beatrice* a few months before, was to have taken charge of *Morien* after her return to Nova Scotia from Placentia. He thought it was only remotely possible she was still drifting about disabled. Most likely, he claimed, she struck the "Keys," a well-known navigational hazard off St. Mary's Bay.

This latter opinion was shared by a veteran Newfoundland master mariner, Captain Thomas Fitzpatrick of Placentia, who knew every inch of the coast in Placentia Bay. Possibly *Morien* had foundered on the lance-like Keys off St. Mary's Bay or had struck on the "Nests." Located about four miles west of Distress Cove near St.Brides in Placentia Bay, the Nests lie about nine feet under water and the sea generally breaks over the treacherous reef.

In those years, especially from 1900 to 1930, several ships met their end on Newfoundland's southern Avalon shore, and on December 20, 1912, another shipwreck, S.S. *Florence* occurred near the community of St. Shott's. This latest disaster — more visible and with survivors who told the horrifying details — drew public attention away from the missing *Morien*.

In the same month as relatives went to church to pray for the lost souls aboard *Morien*, S.S. *Florence* struck the cliffs in Mariner's Cove, east of *Morien*'s intended destination. Out of

Florence's total compliment of twenty-five, only five crew made it safely to shore. The wreck commissioner from St. John's and search parties from St. Shott's and other nearby towns combed the area off Southern Newfoundland, but found no sign of the sunken *Florence* nor any bodies. Bits and pieces of the crew's clothing and assorted wreckage driven up on remote beaches was all that remained of two thousand four hundred ton British steamer.

Thus, with other tragic wrecks occurring around Newfoundland's shores, the disappearance of *Morien* was forgotten and the fate of the coal carrier remained a mystery of the sea. Authorities in Nova Scotia released the names of her lost crew: Captain Burchell, Sydney; first mate D.J. MacDonald; second mate P. Grandy; third mate John Bagnell, chief engineer F.W. Hickey; second engineer Louis Frazer; cook Charles Clemens; stewart Charles Earl; donkeyman J. Hazelhurst; seamen W. Mosher; Peter McMullin; E. Wood; C. Wood; J. Fleming and R. Martin. *Morien* also carried three firemen who names were not given in the local papers. Most of the crew belonged to Nova Scotia and resided in Halifax, Pictou, Sydney, or Louisbourg; many had young families.

"**After ten years the mystery was solved**," declared the *Daily News* headlines on October 2, 1922. The Newfoundland paper went on to say that "After being an unsolved mystery of the deep for nearly ten years, the fate of the ill-fated S.S. *Morien*... has recently been cleared up."

Edward, Edmund and Philip Keefe, three fishermen of the town of Big Barachoix, a fishing community near St. Bride's, were fishing in the vicinity of the "Nests" in early October 1922 when they made a remarkable find. All three had had their fishing lines fouled in what they knew was the rigging of a submerged ship. On another occasion another man in his small vessel brought up part of a steamer's hawser which was attached to the wreck, but the hawser could not be salvaged.

On a clear day when the water around the Nests was calm, it was possible to see the outline of the vessel lying on the bottom. Although no official dive search was conducted nor was the wreck site ever investigated by marine authorities, local people could see a steamer's shape and knew it was the missing *Morien*. Possibly locals had pulled up identifiable items from the wreck, but were reluctant to admit it.

Fishermen of St. Bride's, Placentia, and Big Barachoix claimed the heavily-laden vessel struck the rocks in the night during the mid-November storm of ten years previous, filled with water and slid off into deeper water taking her crew with her. The dire prediction of Placentia's Captain Fitzpatrick had proven correct.

Remarkably, with *Morien* in such close proximity to land and inhabited harbours, no wreckage of any description and no bodies ever came ashore. Even more extraordinary was the underwater view of the missing *Morien* on the bottom near St. Bride's — a decade after she disappeared.

Chapter 49

Clintonia's Captain: Ordeal in Water and Fire

Placentia, St. John's

Owned by Campbell & McKay's business of St. John's, the schooner *Clintonia* left Placentia on Friday, October 28, 1921, bound for Oporto with thirty four hundred quintals of fish for Harvey and Company. Captain W.H. Bradbury was in command. A two-masted vessel, *Clintonia* was launched from the John Bishop yards in Vincent's Cove, Gloucester, in 1907 bought by Newfoundland interests eight years later. Built as a banker and netting ninety-seven ton, she was not designed or structured for the severe winter conditions of the overseas trade.

While sailing out through Placentia Bay the weather was favourable, but within hours the vessel found itself in the teeth of a raging gale. *Clintonia* was forced to seek shelter near Cape St. Mary's, but during the night, with the storm at its full power, the anchor stock broke and *Clintonia* was forced to run before the gale all day Saturday. At sea, the schooner "hove to" with mountainous seas running.

On Sunday conditions looked serious for the high winds threatened to damage *Clintonia*'s spars and masts. Bradbury again was forced to "run before the wind" which drove his vessel farther and farther from land and relative shelter. All Sunday night the crew wondered if the schooner could remain afloat.

Shortly after six am Monday, both masts broke off near the deck. Immediately the crew set about clearing away the wreckage and tangle of ropes, lines and rigging. They did what they had to do and simply viewed it as "Making the best of a bad job" .

By now, *Clintonia* was two hundred eighty miles south southwest of Cape Race with still no sign of the storm moderating. For four days the little schooner had been knocked about at the mercy of wind and waves. Then seemingly the crew's life would be spared. On Tuesday night a red-funnelled steamer eastward bound passed within one and a half miles of the dismasted schooner. Despite signal flares, which the crew figured could be easily seen by the passing crew, the steamer continued on her way. Again on Wednesday night another steamship hove in sight, steamed around the disabled *Clintonia* which was displaying flares and distress fires and then continued its journey.

Eventually and ironically, after being passed by large, international steamers, it was a Newfoundland schooner which saw the distressed *Clintonia* and stopped to rescue the crew. On Thursday night, November third, Captain Jerry Petite in the tern schooner *Jean Wakely,* twenty-one days out from Turk's Island to St. John's laden with salt. Built in 1920 at Essex, Massachusetts, the two hundred sixty-three ton *Jean Wakely* was first owned by Thomas Wakely of Harbour Buffett. Captain Jerry Petite's father, Jeremiah Petite of English Harbour West purchased the schooner when Wakely closed his business. It was during one of her many runs to the West Indies that the foreign-going *Jean Wakely* happened upon the sinking *Clintonia*.

With *Jean Wakely* standing by, at midnight and after nearly a week of battering by the storm Captain Bradbury and his crew prepared to abandon ship. First, as was the custom of Newfoundland skippers leaving a derelict schoo-

Courtesy PANL

Tern schooner *Jean Wakely* moored in St. John's harbour (with the Southside Hills in the background) in the early 1920s, probably just after rescuing the crew of *Clintonia*. The loss of *Jean Wakely* is obscure, but according to local tradition she was sold to foreign interests and her final fate is unknown.

This was not the only sea rescue Capt. Jerry Petite had experienced. On April 25, 1936, while fishing on the Grand Banks in his newly-built banker *Ethel M. Petite*, Petite rescued seven crew of the Marystown schooner *J.R. Rogers* under the command of Captain Walsh.

Built in 1910 for James Rogers of Marystown, the twenty-three ton *J.R. Rogers*, while fishing at latitude 44.52, longitude 50.35, sprang a leak and had to be abandoned. Petite saw the plight of the crew, steamed over and transferred the crew to his schooner. They remained aboard Petite's schooner until the baiting (or voyage) was over and he returned to Harbour Breton on May first.

ner on the high seas, the wallowing vessel was to be set afire so as it would not become a menace to navigation.

Bradbury sprinkled the cabin with gasoline. The cabin lamp was still burning and within seconds, as fumes from the gas reached the flame in the lamp, a flash explosion knocked Captain Bradbury down. The captain was badly burned about the face and hands; the cook, Arthur Kelly, near the cabin at the time, received slight burns. Both men, who barely escaped death from fire, kept their clothing from catching afire.

Rescue complete, Captain Petite and the crew of *Jean Wakely* did everything possible to comfort the captain and cook. On their arrival in St. John's on November fifth, Brad-

Photo courtesy Neil Piercey

The fate of many a Newfoundland wooden vessel, pulled up on a shore to die like a beached whale. Once owned by Pius Power, the forty-four foot long *Anna F & Mary P* (in 1995) lies derelict at South East Bight, Placentia Bay. She was built in the now abandoned community of Clattice Harbour, Placentia Bay, in 1949 and re-built in South East Bight in 1974.

bury was taken to hospital where he spent two weeks recovering from his burns. *Clintonia* carried a crew of seven as well as a Portuguese stowaway who was returning to Oporto.

This *Clintonia* was the second of her name to be shipwrecked: in mid-January 1923 *Clintonia,* built in Lunenburg in 1908 and owned by Harvey and Company of St. John's and operated out of Belleoram by Kearleys, was abandoned at sea. Kearley Brothers of Belleoram had shares in *Clintonia;* thus, she operated out of Belleoram. After his two-masted schooner took battering by mid-Atlantic storms which opened her seams, Captain Aaron Kearley of Belleoram and his five-man crew were plucked off the sinking schooner by *Empress of Scotland* about one hundred miles south of Sable Island.

Chapter 50

Beatrice K, Sunk by a Derelict

Red Island, Burin

One of the greatest threats to sailing ships travelling by night in open water is the danger of striking a partly-submerged object. The impact of hitting debris while sailing at eight to twelve knots causes severe structural damage to wooden vessels. Planking is jarred, seams open and water pours in. As the crewmen pump, every effort is made to get to port to have the damage checked and repaired.

According to the United States Hydrographic Office in a bulletin issued in 1921, an average of eight vessels a year were wrecked or damaged in the North Atlantic by collision with derelicts. By the 1920s the office estimated no less than thirty derelicts drifted somewhere in the ocean.

A derelict is a wreck that does not sink at once. Such a vessel, if loaded with lumber or other buoyant cargo could remain afloat for weeks even months. Often wooden ships abandoned in mid-ocean were set afire; thus, the hulk could lose all top structure and so be rendered almost invisible. Derelicts were such a menace that sailors dreaded them more than icebergs, fogs or storms. Shipping records log many unusual stories of abandoned hulls: such was *Taurans*, a Norwegian barque, which was sighted eighteen times before she was finally sought out and destroyed. Two ships actually collided with her, but without receiving serious damage.

One day in 1914 a settler living on a small bay in New Caledonia in the Pacific, woke early in the morning to see a large sailing vessel in the bay. She was veering about in an odd manner and did not seem to be under control. Taking his boat, the man pulled out to find that there was not a soul aboard her. It was the British barque *Dumfrieshire*, a vessel of one thousand one hundred fifty ton with a cargo valued at a hundred thousand dollars.

The explanation came later. Sailing from New Zealand to New Caledonia, the barque had struck a reef and as she seemed to be sinking her crew abandoned her and rowed ashore. But she was not so badly holed as the crew thought and eventually drifted into the bay, where the lucky settler picked her up. His claim to salvage was considerable.

Unusual stories of derelicts near Newfoundland abound. *Dunmore,* an eight thousand-ton Cardiff steamer abandoned off the Newfoundland coast early in 1906, drifted around the Atlantic for more than two months before she was officially located and booked. Owned in Grand Bank, the two-masted schooner *Nordica,* with her sails set and in sound condition, was found drifting and abandoned in mid-Atlantic in 1921. She was towed to Boston where it was determined that *Nordica* had a damaged steering apparatus. Her crew, thinking she was unmanageable in the gale, left in the lifeboat and was later picked up by a liner bound for New York. Patten and Forsey's business of Grand Bank paid the salvage claim and re-acquired their schooner.

On December 16, 1924, a south coast schooner became the victim of a partly-submerged derelict. *Beatrice K,* en route to St. John's from a Burin Peninsula port, was seven miles off Red Island in Placentia Bay when she collided with wreckage in the form of a sunken hulk of another boat.

Beatrice K, built in Sable River in 1905, was first christened *Bella G* and was owned by William Goddock's business of Burin. After Goddock sold his forty-three ton schooner she was renamed *Beatrice K* and put under the command of George Rodway. Rodway claimed *Beatrice K* collided with a

In February 1924 the American liner *Huronian* reported the derelict *Roy Bruce*, a tern schooner owned by Hollett's business of Burin. Sections of her hull floated in shipping lanes and according to *Huronian*'s crew, she had been cut down.

Her crew disappeared, never to be seen again: Captain Robert F. Hollett, his son Morgan, Max Adams, all of Burin; and three seamen of Fortune, Steven Batten, Berkley Morris and Cecil Strong. (Note: some names on this crew list were omitted or mis-identified in *Lost at Sea Vol I*, 1991).

sunken wreck which he believed still had her two masts attached. So damaged was *Beatrice K* that despite every effort of the crew to save their schooner, they were finally forced to take to the lifeboat.

With a wild sea raging and the temperatures well below zero, Rodway and his men had a trying voyage while covering a distance of merely seven miles. At five-thirty in the morning, exhausted and cold, they pulled into Red Island harbour.

Police Constable Ryan of Red Island, after making arrangements to get Rodway and his crew back to the Burin Peninsula, wired the Marine and Fisheries Department to say *Beatrice K* was abandoned and stated the cause of accident. He then made plans to find the spars of the unidentified sunken wreck in order to destroy this potential menace to Placentia Bay transportation. Subsequent reports do not state if he was successful or if the derelict was identified.

Courtesy Seamen's Museum

Herbert L. Rawding, the largest schooner owned in Newfoundland, made its home port in Harbour Buffett, a once-thriving town on Long Island, Placentia Bay, but now-abandoned. A four-masted, one thousand one hundred nine net ton schooner owned by Freeman Wareham, *Rawding* was built in the United States. In June 1947 while on a salt-laden voyage from Cadiz to Newfoundland she sank. Her crew were rescued by a passing ship: Captain Alex Rodway, cook Wallace Dicks, second mate George Upshall, of Harbour Buffett; mate Thomas Ashford, Harbour Breton; engineer George Pomeroy, Bay Roberts; Freeman Gilbert, Calvin Gilbert, Lewis Pauls, Haystack, Long Island; Ted Porter, Nova Scotia; William Follett, John Flynn, Presque; Isaac Peach, Spencer's Cove, all Placentia Bay seamen except Ashford, Pomeroy and Porter.

Chapter 51

Nineteen Hour Struggle: Joan Ellamae

Burin

A grim nineteen hour struggle against a furious sea ended May 2, 1957, for nine Newfoundland and Nova Scotian seamen when their wallowing wind-battered dories were spotted by a passing freighter.

The men were the crew of the abandoned *Joan Ellamac,* a schooner owned by Hollett and Sons of Burin, on her way from Halifax to Newfoundland. Her crew: Captain Edward Owen Grandy, Captain George W. Loveless, who was serving as mate on *Joan Ellamae* (both were former Newfoundlanders residing in Halifax); engineer Giles Reeves and Andrew Brushett, Burin; cook Richard Farrell, Little Bay near Marystown; Robert Jensen of Garnish and two other seamen.

A freak May blizzard had ravaged the coast of Newfoundland and Nova Scotia practically bringing transportation to a halt: five ships in a sixty-mile-wide belt were trapped in ice off the northern tip of Cape Breton; jagged-topped ice stalled the liner *Nova Scotia* off Cape Race delaying her arrival at Halifax; destroyed hundreds of lobster pots stacked on shore in Pictou county, Nova Scotia and dumped several inches of snow throughout the Atlantic Region. Ship-to-

Photo courtesy Marine Archives, Capt. H. Stone collection

Joan Ellamae, seen here moored at the Irving Oil premises in Halifax, was en route from Halifax to Burin when she sank in May, 1957. At fifty-three net ton, she was built in Creston with help from the shipbuilding bounty legislated in 1934-35 by the Commission of Government.

In the Second World War, during the building and staffing of the Argentia Naval Base when many Newfoundland men found ready work and cash, *Joan Ellamae*, under Captain Freeman Boyd, served as a ferry. Five dollars a head one way was the rate between Burin and Argentia. An old saying about her then was "If you can't get over on the *Home*, you can always go on the *Joan*." In peak times, over a hundred men jammed her holds and passenger areas.

Other local men who captained the schooner when she fished the Grand Banks were Wallace Murley, Epworth; Abel Moulton, Lewin's Cove; Ab Joyce, Don Moulton, Tom Bartlett, and Arch Broydell.

shore radio communication with the car ferry *Cabot Strait* and the CNR freighters *Burgeo* and *Random* was cut off for several hours.

Captain Michael Tobin of the ferry *William Carson* said in ship-to-shore reports that his ship had battered its way through ice and was heading for Argentia. Of all the damage and delays in shipping, only one vessel sank: *Joan Ellamae*.

Winds, blasting up to fifty miles an hour, tossed the schooner's dories until the freighter *Roonagh Head* picked up the nine weary men — nineteen hours after *Joan Ellamae* was abandoned! *Roonagh Head* had responded to radio messages from Captain Loveless pleading for "immediate assistance."

A second SOS said the men were abandoning the schooner as she was taking in water through a leak in her side.

Roonagh Head, heading for Montreal, located the dories fifteen miles south of St. Pierre. Four planes and five ships — including St. Pierre schooner *Miquelon*, M.V. *Bonavista* and the United States cutter *Bibb* — took part in a criss-cross search for the crew of *Joan Ellamae*.

In Halifax, where the families of Captain Loveless and Grandy resided, relief was evident. Mrs. Loveless, who waited through the third shipping accident in her husband's life, said she "got through it only by my faith in God."

Captain Loveless, age fifty-eight, while commanding his own ship, was torpedoed off Nova Scotia during the war and survived. In 1952 another vessel on which he sailed was ripped by fire and heavily damaged. For the relatives of Grandy, who resided at 23 Prescott Street, Halifax, news of rescue was the best news they had heard. Captain Grandy, originally from Garnish and age forty, captained a vessel designated for ammunition transportation during World War II, but had not been involved in a close encounter with the demanding ocean.

During the voyage aboard the rescue freighter, the crew had transferred to the RCMP cutter *McBrian* which carried them to Burin.

Two years previous to the loss of coaster *Joan Ellamae*, another well-known coasting schooner went to the bottom off St. Pierre. Skippered and owned by John Blackwood of St. John's, *Mont Murray* was bound for Glovertown with three hundred ton of coal when she sprang a leak. On September 20, 1955, *Mont Murray* was caught in a storm about fifty-eight miles off St. Pierre.

Captain Blackwood sent a SOS confirming that water had reached the engines and *Mont Murray* lay helpless in the eye of the storm. His emergency call was picked by up the Gloucester dragger *Red Diamond IV* fishing on the St. Pierre Bank about twenty-eight miles from the sinking coaster.

Courtesy Seamen's Museum

In 1942 a plant for fresh frozen fish was constructed by Fishery Products Ltd. in Burin North, the first of its kind in Newfoundland. Seeing that the hook and line dory fishing was costly and inefficient, plant owners adopted newer technology at the time when the salt fish industry was phasing out.

Built in 1948 in Maine *Zerda* (above), a one hundred three net ton wooden dragger, was one of the earliest, along with the dragger *Mustang*, to use an otter trawl in Newfoundland's deep sea fishery. For many years she was skippered by Victor Adams of Burin; *Zerda* was later re-sold back to the United States.

Four hours later Captain Blackwood and his eight crewmen were on the dragger and had managed to save all their belongings. *Red Diamond* was about to resume fishing when the forecast warned of hurricane Ione and she harboured in St. Pierre.

Captain Baxter Blackwood, *Blue Spray*, brought his dragger to the mouth of St. Pierre harbour to transfer the shipwrecked crew of *Mont Murray* onto his vessel. On September 23 *Blue Spray* landed the crew at St. John's.

Chapter 52

Steamship Rescues Six

St. Lawrence, Burin

When the steamship *Solway* arrived in St. John's on December 19, 1912, she not only brought a full freight for the Reid Railway Company, but also landed the shipwrecked crew of the schooner *Minnie Pearl*, plucked off their sinking schooner by the steamer.

The surnames of *Minnie Pearl*'s crew — Hollett, Farrell, Drake, Burfitt, Davis — were typical Placentia Bay names and the last ports the schooner left were Lamaline and St. Lawrence. Thus, although the place of residence for the Newfoundland men are not recorded, it is likely they were seamen from the eastern side of the Burin Peninsula.

Owned by James Burgess of Burin, the ninety-six ton *Minnie Pearl* had been built in Mahone Bay, Nova Scotia, 1904. Burgess, a Nova Scotian by birth, bought a business in Burin on a site now occupied by the old Bank of Nova Scotia (part of the Heritage House complex). When Burgess retired, he sold out to William and Thomas Hollett, pioneers in the bank fishing industry.

Minnie Pearl left Twillingate in the latter part of November 1912, laden with over two thousand quintals of fish destined for Halifax. Her crew: Captain Michael Davis, a Newfoundlander who resided in Sydney; mate Bernard Burfitt, seamen Samuel Hollett, Edward Farrell, Michael Drake and Samuel Anthony. From the onset of her voyage *Minnie Pearl* met the worst of winter weather. As she crossed Trinity Bay a storm carried away all her head gear and she had to run into St. John's for repairs.

Captain Davis departed St. John's Monday, December 2, to continue his three day voyage to Halifax, but again a terrific snowstorm engulfed *Minnie Pearl*. She had to shelter in Trepassey on Tuesday and anchored there two days. As she crossed St. Mary's Bay on Thursday three of her crew narrowly escaped a watery grave.

In the southerly gale and snow storm, a mountainous sea ran and that night one sea broke over the vessel sweeping everything moveable off the deck. Edward Farrell was carried over the quarter but he managed, although immersed to the shoulders, to grab the peak halyards. After a desperate struggle Farrell swung himself over the rail and back onto the deck. Burfitt, who was also on deck, was up to his neck in water and kept himself from going over the side by clinging to the fore sheet. Another seaman grabbed the lashings of the life boat tied to the deck.

During all this time Captain Davis was lashed to the wheel. To stand on the deck without being tied to lifelines was to run the risk of being swept into the ocean. *Minnie Pearl* took a severe beating until Saturday morning when she made the mouth of Lamaline harbour. But a northwest wind with thick snow prevented her from safely navigating the shallow and rocky harbour.

Forced to run back to St. Lawrence's more sheltered harbour, Captain Davis decided to remain there until Wednesday, December 11. After leaving that port the schooner was five hours on the open sea when again, due to high winds, she had to return. Three times Davis tried to leave port. On the third attempt, when Davis swung around again to return to St. Lawrence, he only made port under great difficulty.

Courtesy Y. Andrieux, St. Pierre

Venturing near the French islands of St. Pierre-Miquelon was no guarantee of safety for the battered *Minnie Pearl*. The islands greet all comers with hazards: thick fog, Atlantic gales and hidden shoals.

According to a 1967 *National Geographic* magazine article, St. Pierre is a grave to over six hundred ships. Rich fishing banks near the islands attracted many victims; others grounded as they ventured near the archipelago en route to Canada's coast and the Gulf of St. Lawrence. Above is the lumber-laden Norwegian *Inger* aground at Langlade, near St.Pierre, in 1916.

On October 24, 1922, the schooner *Mariner*, jointly owned by Clem Hann's business at Lamaline and J.J. Miller of Wabana, was a total wreck at Langlade. *Mariner*'s Newfoundland crew were rescued and brought to Lamaline by the schooner *Excelda*. *Mariner* was bound to Sydney from Bell Island with a cargo of scrap iron.

The frost was so intense that over six inches of ice formed on the hull and decks. In order to let the anchor go, ice had to chopped from the anchor and chains. In this weather the jumbo was torn into shreds and the captain had to buy a new one at St. Lawrence.

Finally, on December 16, *Minnie Pearl* left St. Lawrence for Halifax and was off St. Pierre at dusk. Since it still looked threatening, Captain Davis thought of stopping in St. Pierre. Within a short while the wind veered and he tried to get out over St. Pierre Bank as soon as possible. On Tuesday morning, the seventeenth of December, *Minnie Pearl* was a hundred miles off St. Pierre and about forty miles from Flint Island on the Cape Breton Coast when a gale from the north northwest with thick snow set in.

Minnie Pearl was hove to under a double reefed foresail but this was soon split in two by the hurricane. The gaff was whipped off the foremast and the heavy seas caused the vessel to labour badly while sea after sea broke on board.

Minnie Pearl was now in danger of foundering. Captain Davis gave orders to jettison the cargo to lighten the schooner. Driving full before the gale, with her canvas virtually gone, the schooner shipped a sea which smashed the life boat to pieces.

Opening the hatches to get at the cargo would have been disastrous; thus, the crew set to work cutting into the hold through the forecastle bulkhead. Two hundred quintals of fish were carried to the deck and tossed overboard. This lightened *Minnie Pearl* considerably by the head and put her into a better trim.

As the fish was being dumped, seaman Samuel Hollett went on deck to take his turn at the pumps. At the moment he stepped on deck, a sea swept the schooner and Hollett was washed aft to the quarter deck. He clung to the monkey rail to save himself from being hurled into the roiled ocean!

On Tuesday night, with *Minnie Pearl* completely at the mercy of the pounding ocean, seas smashed the cabin door and poured tons of water into the cabin saturating everything. Clothes, trunks, boxes floated about the compartment. The stove was partly underwater; denying the crew of the simple act of getting a refreshing cup of tea or of cooking food.

Wet and freezing in the low temperatures, six men were in suspense wondering what minute *Minnie Pearl* would take her final plunge. By this time it was impossible to stand on the listing and icy deck. All had to take refuge below while two men stood watch at the companionway to view the sea and to watch the weather. As each monstrous wave rolled across the hapless vessel they quickly closed the door of the companionway to prevent more water from getting below deck.

Early Wednesday morning Captain Davis discovered *Minnie Pearl* was taking water at an alarming rate through strained seams. When the pumps were sounded there was four feet of water in the hold. Despite incessant pumping the crew could not keep the schooner free of water. But pump they must! Davis gave the order, "Pump for your lives."

At eight-thirty that morning the hull of a steamer could be seen coming straight for them. Someone ran for the Union Jack and hoisted it upside down to the peak, a universal signal for distress. Within an hour the steamer stood by; it proved to be S.S. *Solway,* Captain Parsons bound from Sydney.

A eight hundred thirty-six ton vessel built by Barclay and Curie of Glasgow in 1881, *Solway* was once employed as a Russian cattle carrier and later was registered to R.G. Reid, Reid Newfoundland Railway Company. Re-named *Meigle,* she was later sold to the Shaw Steamship Company. In 1947 she was lost off St. Shott's, Captain Billy Windsor.

Solway ranged nearby preparing to transfer the beleaguered crew from the sinking schooner which had settled to the rail in the water. Seemingly no life boat could operate in the mad seas, but three of *Solway*'s men volunteered — mate Burge, seaman Power and a fireman.

From the time *Solway*'s boat left her side until the transfer was made, two hours had elapsed — once the boat went half a mile adrift. In the attempt to get the six rescued Newfoundlanders on board, *Solway* rolled over on the small boat and almost capsized her. The men's duffel bags and clothes were swept out and disappeared; Captain Davis lost all his clothing, personal effects and nautical instruments valued at one hundred dollars.

All the while the small life craft was bobbing below them, the crew of the steamer stood at the rail with life belts ready to throw in case the rescuers and rescued were thrown into the sea. *Solway*'s side ports were opened; each man had to jump into them grabbing life ropes as they did.

Before Captain Davis left *Minnie Pearl* he saturated the cabin with kerosene and set her afire. As *Solway* left the scene,

Photo courtesy Jack Keeping

Derelict *Catherine Mary Hann*, built by Jack Hann, was the last western boat built in Merasheen (1926). At sixty-three foot, one inch in length and thirty-five gross ton, *Catherine Mary Hann* was once owned by John E. Best of Tack's Beach and later registered to Gerald J. Hann and Michael J. Hann of Petite Forte.

Like many aging Newfoundland vessels, she was left behind by changing technology and eventually beached; in this case, near the Canning Bridge, Marystown. Eventually her rotted hull was burned by the town council, but kelp-festooned remains can still be seen today at low tide.

the burning schooner made her final dip and sank from sight. It was Wednesday December 18.

It had taken the steamer fifty-three hours to make the voyage from Sydney to St. John's including her three hour stop off Cape Race to rescue Hollett, Farrell, Drake, Burfitt, Anthony and Davis. The six seamen boarded at Mrs. Poole's on Adelaide Street while awaiting transportation to their homes. Captain Davis owned part shares and had both hull and cargo insured.

Chapter 53

Ontario: Death at Lawn

Lawn, St. Lawrence

Well over one hundred years ago two ships crashed ashore at Lawn Point — one with disastrous results. On October 25-27, 1881, a wild gale roared over the Burin Peninsula. The schooner *Mary Ann Louis*, owned in Halifax, Nova Scotia, left Halifax on October 25 with Captain Fadden in command. Fadden was bound for Cape North, but stopped in Isaac's Harbour, Nova Scotia. After he left the latter port on October 26, a gale carried away *Mary Ann Louis'* sails and damaged the steering gear.

Fadden and his crew were pushed across the ocean to a point off the Burin Peninsula and were driven unto land at Lawn Point. All the crew reached shore in an exhausted condition and were cared for by residents of Lawn.

The second vessel driven ashore at Lawn in the same time frame was not so fortunate. The schooner *Ontario* left St. John's in command of Captain McAuley and five other crew members: two Norwegians Ole Saurenson and Thor Nicholson, the latter aged twenty and a cousin to Saurenson. Three others, presumably Canadians, made up *Ontario*'s crew.

Ontario had delivered Cape Breton coal to Newfoundland three times between July and October of 1881; now she was travelling in ballast back to Nova Scotia. McAuley

Sandy Cove near Lawn. The point on the right is Lord's Cove Point; Middle and Gull Islands are centre. It was in this general area the Canadian vessel *Ontario* was wrecked with one survivor.

hoisted sail on Monday, October 24 and everything went well until Wednesday morning at ten o'clock. By then the schooner was several miles off Newfoundland's South Coast.

The wind suddenly veered from south east to west and increased in intensity. McAuley hove the schooner to, reefed the foresail and staysail and hoped to ride out the storm. Sailor Nicholson wrote of what happened after that:

> We were headed north northwest. I did not know whereabouts where we were as we had not seen land since Monday night after leaving St. John's. During the night wind increased to a heavy gale with a dreadful sea running.
>
> The captain thought we had plenty of sea room and had no idea that we could be so near land which we made out two am Thursday.

Straining their eyes landward, the crew of *Ontario* could make out breakers not too far distant. With her rudder and sailing gear damaged by the pounding she took from the

Author's collection

A frequent visitor to Newfoundland's south coast, *Delawanna II*, an ten-dory Nova Scotian schooner employed men of Burin and Marystown. John Joe Mallay and his brother James sailed with Captain Douglas Mosher to the fishing grounds. In the late 1950s she was owned by Pearce Fudge of Corner Brook and for a short while was in command of George Lace, who later lived in Harbour Breton.

In this photo *Delawanna II* lies a sunken wreck off some unidentified coast. She had been launched from the Smith and Rhuland yards in Lunenburg in 1925.

westerly gale, the schooner became unmanageable. *Ontario* drifted fast toward land, but Captain McAuley, Nicholson and the other crew members were powerless to prevent the ship from striking the rocks. Although the crew did not know it at the time, the land was Lawn Point. As Nicholson recalled:

> At four am she struck the rocks heavily and filled almost immediately, every sea sweeping clean over her. We saw no chance of escape, and awaited anxiously our fate.
>
> In about ten minutes after striking the rocks, a heavy sea swept four of the crew overboard. The captain and I remained clinging fast to the windward rigging right close to each other. The next sea carried us overboard. Captain McAuley held on to my reefer for a few moments when in the water.
>
> A wave carried me some distance on the rocks and again back into the water; in another instant I was cast well in on the shore, uninjured.

Cold and wet, Nicholson remained in the general area until daylight. He searched the rocks and shoreline for other shipmates who like himself may have been flung ashore onto the rocks. He saw no one; not even a piece of the wreck remained visible. The sea had dragged the hulk farther from shore where it sank. The lone surviving mariner concluded his epic:

> Seeing that I was left alone I set out to try to reach some habitation along the coast, and after travelling five or six hours, I reached the harbour of St. Lawrence where I received great kindness from the inhabitants.

So ended the wreck of the Nova Scotian schooner *Ontario,* wrecked on Lawn Point in October 1881 with only one survivor who told his tale to residents of St. Lawrence.

Chapter 54

Two Fishermen of Fortune

Fortune

When the steamer *A.W. Perry* arrived in Halifax from Boston in mid-April, she had among her passengers two bank fishermen from Fortune, George Perry, age twenty-two and Samuel Forsey, seventeen. From Halifax both men were to be transported as "distressed seamen" to Newfoundland. In the meantime both were housed in the Sailors' Home — an institute which cared for foreign seamen — and from there told their tale of near disaster on the high seas.

Both had been in an open dory for over two days — from early morning April seventh until mid-day on April ninth —(unfortunately the account does not give the year, but in all likelihood it was 1911) without food or water and were near death when rescued. Sam Forsey related the following story:

On Friday morning at five am, he and Perry left the Fortune schooner *Hubert Mack* for the morning's fishing. *Hubert Mack,* a banking schooner originally built by and owned by John E. Lake business of Fortune and later registered to Johnny Paul and William Keeping, fished the Quero Banks about one hundred seventy-five miles from St. Pierre.

Both dorymates were a bit late getting under way for their day's work and, since the sea was calm with signs of a beautiful day, they neglected to take the morning's provi-

Hubert Mack, the cutwater schooner that Perry and Forsey left on a Friday morning in April and did not see again until a month or so later when both men arrived back in Fortune.

Built in Fortune in 1908, the fifty-six net ton *Hubert Mack* was wrecked on October 26, 1925 when, during a storm, she parted her lines and drifted out of Fortune harbour. She broke up near High Bank, east of Fortune.

sions. As a general rule, banking dories carried a sealed tin of water and/or dried hard tack, but in this case Perry and Forsey did not have even that meagre sustenance.

About eleven am, after five or six hours of hauling and re-baiting hundreds of fathoms of trawling gear, they put out the two sets of oars and prepared to return to *Hubert Mack*.

However, as is so often the case on the fog-enshrouded fishing banks, a dense fog had settled in so quickly Perry and Forsey could hardly see two boat lengths ahead. They rowed in the direction of the schooner and about noon heard the schooner's small swivel gun being fired. Sound plays tricks over water and in the grey world of fog enclosing them, they could not locate their mother ship.

Although tired and hungry from a day's work, Perry and Forsey did not and could not rest. All afternoon the dory-mates rowed around in the general vicinity, but without luck.

Friday night a heavy rainstorm accompanied by choppy winds, thunder and lightning, tossed the little dory around.

During the night Forsey's feet became soaked. "The darkest hour is just before dawn" as the old maxim goes, but that time is also the coldest and with the dip in temperature to below zero, Forsey's feet froze.

Without food or water, both Fortune men suffered from exposure, but their hardships were not so great as what they experienced on Saturday and Sunday. There was plenty of fish aboard, but no way to cook it. In desperation on Saturday evening, using the splitting knives, they cut out codfish sound bones and gnawed on these. Sam Forsey also had a few peanuts in his pocket which he willingly shared with Perry and both men, being very hungry by this time, ate them shells and all.

By Sunday morning they were weak from hunger, thirst and exposure. When the sun came up they saw a schooner's sail in the distance —just how many miles away they had no way of determining. The sight of possible salvation gave Forsey and Perry renewed strength, but somehow in the heaving and tossing the dory went through, one oar of the two pair was lost allowing only one man at a time to row.

That morning when they saw the schooner so far away, both men made a near-fatal mistake. Their mouths were so parched with thirst, they moistened their lips and mouth with salt water. This had the opposite effect making them worse. Overcome with delirium, they scooped up handfuls of salt water and drank it.

By this time over two and a half days had elapsed since they had strayed from *Hubert Mack*. Forsey suffered more from frozen feet and legs and his strength gave out. He collapsed to the bottom of the dory in a semi-coma.

Perry, as he related to Forsey later, kept rowing until he was within a mile or so of the ship; then, out of sheer exhaustion, aroused Forsey and told him to take the oars for a while. But it was no use, after a few strokes Sam Forsey slumped and again fell to the bottom of the boat.

Fortunately, by then they were so near the ship they were seen and rescuers came to their aid. It proved to be the

Fortune (facing west) about the time of salt fish trade. The large white building (centre) once stood where the Royal Canadian Legion building stands today.

American fishing schooner *Monitor* out of Gloucester, Massachusetts.

Forsey, near death, had to be hoisted over the side and carried below. It was two weeks before he was able to walk and get up on deck of *Monitor*. After her trip was over, *Monitor* set sail for Portland, Maine, and arrived there in mid-April. Forsey and Perry were transported to Boston and thence to Halifax, on the steamer *A.W. Perry*.

That particular voyage on *Hubert Mack* was Forsey's first experiences as a seaman — and his last. Vowing he would never to go to sea again, Sam Forsey joined the Newfoundland Constabulary, served until his retirement and died in Toronto in the 1950s.

In time, the Gloucesterman *Monitor* had a Newfoundland connection: in the fall of 1916 she was sold to Philip Templeman of Bonavista for $14,000. Her end came on April 25, 1917, when she was shelled by a German sub in the Mediterranean. Captain Joseph Legge and his crew of seven survived.

Chapter 55

Workman, Cut Down off Spain

Grand Bank, St. John's

Another tern schooner, owned and operated in St. John's, became a casualty of the hungry Atlantic when A.E. Hickman's *Workman* went down in February, 1923. Captain George Anstey, master of the tern schooner *Workman* was born in Grand Bank, one of seven sons of John Samuel Anstey. One of Captain George Anstey's brothers was John Ben who, in later years, recalled the following story of George's sea exploits.

The father, John Sam, was born in Fortune, a much-frequented seaport and fishing town located on the toe of the Burin Peninsula. He lived on the west side of Fortune harbour and as a young man worked for merchant John P. Lake. In later years Samuel Anstey moved to Grand Bank.

Several of George's brothers were seamen; some, like Aaron, rose to the rank of captain. In his early years George Anstey was a bank fishermen; in 1914 he was a crewman on the Grand Bank schooner *Nina Lee*, then worked as a seaman on the government mail/passenger boat and later honed his seamanship skills in the foreign trade on voyages to Europe with Captain Leslie Tibbo of Grand Bank.

In St. John's, after he had completed his training and qualifications as a navigator, business magnate Albert E.

Hickman hired him as master of *Florence Swyers*. In 1920 Anstey was given command of the newly completed tern schooner *Workman*.

Workman had been built in 1920 under the supervision of Arch Chaulk in Charlottetown, Bonavista Bay. Hickman, who owned and managed several foreign-going vessels engaged in his fish exporting enterprise, knew Anstey well — both were born in Grand Bank. George's brother, Charles who later became a captain as well, was mate on *Workman*.

On January 5, 1923, while under charter to the Spanish-owned business Juan Lazo & Company, *Workman* left Newfoundland bound for Seville in Spain with a full cargo of salt-dry cod. Captain Anstey, age twenty-nine, who lived on 36 Colonial Street, St. John's carried the following crew with him: mate Charles, age eighteen who resided on 23 Boncloddy Street; Michael Sutton, twenty-three and John White, twenty-three, were both of Catalina and William Ellis, twenty, St. John's. Cook Joachim de Jesus hailed from Portugal.

On February 6, the night was calm and clear. *Workman* was within several miles of the coast of Europe when Captain Anstey and his crew saw a large steamer headed straight for them. It later proved to be the steamer *Maryland*, outward bound from Wales to the Panama Canal. She was carrying ten thousand ton of Cardiff coal and plowed through the Atlantic at full speed.

Anstey could see the large ship was making no effort to turn out of his path and ordered his crew to set up flares, but the ship didn't alter course or slacken speed. Oddly enough, a flare came up from the fast-approaching *Maryland* indicating she saw the schooner.

Seeing an imminent collision and knowing there was no time to put the life boat over the side, Captain Anstey ordered his men to climb to the topmasts. When *Maryland* hit *Workman*, the topmasts and rigging of the latter dragged along the side of the larger ship. Anstey and his crew jumped or dropped down onto the deck of the still-speeding steamer.

Photos courtesy of Kurt Krantz collection, Marine Archives

Debris and wreckage float away from a schooner cut down by an ocean-going steamer. These photos was taken from the deck of Belgian liner *Jean Jadot* on June 17, 1937, when she sliced into the Jersey Harbour fishing schooner *Pauline Lohnes* and sent her to the bottom. Her crew was rescued and carried to New York by *Jean Jadot*. Some crew are known: Captain Michael Augot, Pius Augot, Albert Stoodley, Philip Day, Tom Smith, Mike Ridgely, Stanley Bungay and William Miles, all from the Harbour Breton/Jersey Harbour area.

In the left photo the schooner dips forward by the bow as movable gear and fishing equipment float off the deck. Moments before the craft takes her final plunge, trapped air (the grey cloud left) spouts from seams. Fish tubs and crates drift away.

The steel hull of *Maryland* easily sliced into the wooden hull of *Workman* and dragged her along for a few hundred feet. This gave the crew time to get to the steamer's deck without losing a man or incurring serious injury. Hickman's fine tern schooner was soon left behind, torn apart and sinking.

Captain Anstey strode into the bridge demanding an explanation from the man at the wheel. *Maryland*'s young helmsman and his watch on the bridge had seen *Workman*, set off the flares, but received no orders from superior officers to change course. Apparently they had been below socializing and had not known or noticed that a collision had occurred. When Anstey barged into the stateroom, interrupting a game of poker, *Maryland*'s captain asked where he had come from. "I, and my crew," Anstey replied in no uncertain terms, "are just resurrected from the **grave."

The ramming happened off the Spanish coast and *Maryland* landed the Newfoundland crew at Madeira, Spain; from there they went to Gibraltar, a British protectorate. On one of the many British ships passing through the Straits of Gibraltar Anstey and his crew secured a passage to England.

In time Captain George Anstey and his crew had to appear in England's Admiralty Court to determine who was at fault in the collision of two ships under British registry. There in the ancient courthouse of Old Bailey in London, British judges and retired admirals with white powdered wigs heard evidence from the Newfoundland crew who were pitted against the lawyers and representatives of *Maryland*'s owners.

During the course of the hearing, a table was brought into court with model ships placed upon it aligned in their relative positions leading up the time of the collision. George's brother, Charles, who was up in the masts of *Workman* when the larger ship plowed into them, knew the law of the sea and disagreed with the ships' positions on the table. In no uncertain terms he told the British Admiralty and Lords of the Sea exactly what he thought of the layout, "Do you think my brother is a God-damned fool? That's not the way it was!"

Mate Charles Anstey strode up to the table and changed the arrangement of the ships. "This is the proper position," he roared. While the Admiralty Court could tolerate someone losing his temper, they would allow no profanity. Charles was ejected from Old Bailey and immediately sent back to Newfoundland.

Before all was settled, it was six months before Captain Anstey finally arrived back in Newfoundland, but in the end his knowledge of the sea had served him well for the court ruled in his favour. A.E. Hickman received compensation for *Workman* and George Anstey's value as a loyal captain to the Hickman business rose.

Each crewman, including mate Charles Anstey, was given five hundred dollars for the loss of his clothes and personal possessions. In addition, George was paid a thousand dollars for his navigation instruments which now lay on the bottom somewhere off Spain.

In time George Anstey became the St. John's harbour pilot guiding ocean going liners, large and small, through the St. John's Narrows. For thirty years until he retired in 1961 he did his job without mishap. One of his most memorable events was in late January 1941 when he piloted the American troopship *Edmund B. Alexander* bringing soldiers and supplies to Newfoundland for the military base to be established at Fort Pepperell. At twenty-one thousand ton, she was the largest ship to enter St. John's up to that time.

On January 28, the troopship arrived off St, John's, but with the stormy weather and tide conditions, entrance into the harbour was delayed. Laden with stores of explosives and ammunition, the American commander and officials discussed how she could be safely docked. *Edmund B. Alexander* eventually anchored in Bay Bulls where many troops disembarked. Harbour pilot Anstey, who knew the tides and channels, brought her into St. John's at five am on January 29. In the morning when city newspaper reporters arrived at the

Courtesy Seamen's Museum

Two dory mates row over to *Freda M.* — On October 7, 1961, another Grand Bank captain had his schooner rammed and sunk: the 154-ton *Freda M*, owned by G & A Buffett, was struck by British freighter *Merchant Royal* off Newfoundland's South Coast. Captain George Follett, mate George Keeping, Ches Keeping, Edgar Bonnell, Jim May, Martin Parrott and George Parrott escaped in dories and were picked up by schooner *Nina W. Corkum*, Captain Harvey Banfield.

waterfront to record the grand entrance, the ship was already docked.

When she was ready to depart, he took her out as well, but *Alexander*'s departure was delayed an extra day until Anstey was available. Anstey, who loved the land as well as the sea and enjoyed hunting, was in the country and had to be located before the American ship left.

George was married to Ethel Edgecombe of Catalina and had two sons. He died in 1980.

Chapter 56

When Two Ships Collide: Flirt, Marshall Frank

South Coast/Halifax

Looming out of the blackness of a night laced with patches of coastal fog, the one hundred ton engine-driven schooner *Marshall Frank* knifed through the fishing vessel *Flirt* and, in a matter of minutes, the latter was on the bottom. Of the six fishermen aboard *Flirt*, all but two escaped with their lives. Captain Jake Weymouth and Lance Locke disappeared with the sunken vessel.

In the darkest hour of four thirty am on Monday, March 15, 1937, as little fishing vessel *Flirt* lay to near Halifax harbour, she was struck a little aft of the main rigging. *Marshall Frank* was proceeding at a speed of eight and a half knots, rammed the Halifax fishing vessel throwing most of *Flirt*'s crew into the water. *Flirt* was stopped in the harbour fairway just inside Chebucto Head preparing for a day of fishing.

Most of the six man crew of *Flirt* stood on the deck of their small vessel baiting trawls and were thrown from the vessel into the sea. The last glimpse the four survivors had of Captain Weymouth was when he was trying to move his craft to avert disaster. He was still at the wheel of *Flirt* when last seen. Locke, cook on the vessel, was below deck.

Captain Jake Weymouth, age forty-one, was born in Molliers, a small town about five or six miles east of Grand Bank. It was settled in the 1800s by those pursuing the inshore fishery in Fortune Bay —families of Bennett, Hatcher, Grant and Weymouth lived there. By the 1960s, however, most families had left Molliers to settle in Grand Bank. Weymouth, after his wife died in the 1930s, chose to make a living in Halifax and found employment on *Flirt*, owned by Bentley and Flemming Limited of Halifax. He lived aboard the fishing vessel. *Flirt* was previously owned by Captain Edward O'Neill of Halifax.

Lance Locke, hailed from Trinity, Newfoundland, and had lived in Halifax for eleven years. He had been employed on the Halifax-based trawler *Viernoe* and joined *Flirt* as cook two years previously. His brother Richard, employed as a shoemaker, lived on Chebucto Road in Halifax and another brother Levi sailed on the cableship *Lord Kelvin.* Locke's sister, Mrs. Freeman Butler, resided on Monaghan Lane, Halifax.

Flirt's other four crew were rescued: John Hanlon and David O'Hearn of Canso, Nova Scotia. Jerome Farrell, the son of John Farrell, once resided "across the brook" in Bay de Nord, Fortune Bay; Joseph Savoury belonged to Parsons Harbour, a resettled community once located at the mouth of Rencontre Bay.

The impact of *Marshall Frank* was so heavy and direct the fishing vessel was smashed to pieces and moments after the crash all that remained was drifting wreckage. Shrill cries of men pleading for help filled the blackness of the night. The search for the whereabouts of survivors was hampered by patches of fog. Lights flashing from the Lunenburg banker revealed tragic scenes of men fighting to keep afloat in the harbour water strewn with broken planks, trawl tubs, dories and oars.

The work of rescue was directed by Captain Frank Risser of *Marshall Frank,* one of the best known of Lunenburg's fishing skippers. Risser was in the wheelhouse when the collision occurred as *Marshall Frank*, owned and based in Lunenburg, was inbound from the offshore fishing banks off Halifax harbour. "I saw no lights and did not know the *Flirt* was on our course until we struck," Captain Risser asserted. The helmsman, Carl Wagner of Lunenburg, also said there were no lights showing from the sunken vessel.

In their reports to local papers survivors told tales of narrow escapes from drowning. John Hanlon related:

> I could not swim a stroke. I went under water. It seemed a long time and I gave up hope. Then I came to the surface. There was some wreckage by me and I managed to take a hold and keep afloat until I was picked up in a dory.

Savoury and Farrell were rescued in a like manner. Both said they would have quickly sunk to the bottom, weighted down by heavy sea boots and oilskins, but for wreckage which kept them afloat.

Only one of *Flirt*'s crew, David O'Hearn, succeeded in climbing over *Marshall Frank*'s rail. As he remembered it:

> When the crash came, I leaped and grasped the rail and tried to pull myself over it. There was some wreckage being carried along by the schooner's bow and I clung to that. The wreckage began slipping astern and I kept trying to crawl aboard. Then hands grasped me from the deck and helped me reach the schooner's deck.

One of the dories which was put over *Marshall Frank*'s side was manned by Ronald Mossman, P. Smith and Lepine Mosher. The second was manned by helmsman Carl Wagner, Russell Hirtic and Willis Mosher. Rescuers leaped from their bunk below deck when they learned of the ramming and raced topside. The first dory rescued John Hanlon and the second pulled Joseph Savoury from the water.

Marshall Frank's engines were reversed immediately after impact and dories were ordered over the side instantly. Ten minutes later the last of those rescued was taken aboard.

On February 17, 1949, *Marshall Frank*, a 144-ton banker owned by James Petite of Halifax, stranded on Marie Joseph Shoals off Nova Scotia during a severe winter storm. She had been built in Nova Scotia in 1926.

Despite a long and thorough search no trace was found of Weymouth and Locke.

When *Marshall Frank* docked at Halifax Fisheries Company its flag flew half-mast, signalling the end of an unfortunate trip for the big schooner. She also had only fifty-five thousand pounds of fish to show for a week out on the banks.

The name *Marshall Frank* was certainly a familiar one to south coast seamen. Many men from places like Harbour Breton, Belleoram, Wreck Cove, Mose Ambrose and other Connaigre Peninsula towns found employment on the productive banker; however, her name sends a chill of dread and sadness to others. In the episode with *Flirt* two south coast seamen met a tragic end and when *Marshall Frank* stranded and broke up twelve years later at Frambroise Cove, Nova Scotia, five of her Newfoundland crew were lost: Leo and Conrad Blagdon of Boxey, Garfield Greene and Norman Ball of Rencontre West and John Blagdon of Coomb's Cove.

The Loss of William S. McDonald

When the British tanker *San Manuel,* from Cardiff, Wales, laden with a cargo of oil put into New York on October 24, 1923, she had on board seven members of the crew of the tern schooner *William S. MacDonald.*

Built at Dayspring, Nova Scotia in 1920 and netted two hundred fifty-two ton, *William S. MacDonald* was owned in Nova Scotia. In the fall of 1923 she was commanded by two Nova Scotians, Captain Maurice H. Randall of La Have and Captain E. Coates of Annapolis, who was supercargo on the ship; the other five crew men were from Newfoundland's South Coast: mate Hughie Grandy of Grand Bank, cook John R. Harris, Jerry Bungay, Charles S. Skinner and James M. Keeping.

San Manuel sighted the tern in the morning, first flying distress signals and a little later with flames and smoke flying from her. *William S. MacDonald* was carrying a cargo of liquor, but had fought a gale of wind for two days while sailing off the American coast and was leaking badly. Seeing a potential

Courtesy of Jack Keeping

Awaiting her load of coal at the North Sydney coal depot, this is *Eva U. Colp*, a schooner similar to *Marshall Frank*. On June 13, 1942, *Eva U. Colp*, owned by Forward and Tibbo of Grand Bank, was cut down by a convoy ship. *Colp*'s crew, all of Grand Bank —Captain Will Thornhill, Sammy White, Jim Penwell, Charles House and John Keeping — were rescued by the vessel which rammed them.

In 1941, a similar fate nearly happened to the schooner *Metamora*, owned at that time by Southern Fisheries of Bay Bulls. While under the command of Captain Mike Augot, with mate Pius Augot, Phil Augot of Harbour Breton, engineer Leo Hackett of English Harbour East and three other crew, *Metamora* left Halifax for St. John's. She had been converted to a coasting vessel and carried ammunition and explosives.

Off Cape Race, when *Metamora* encountered a convoy bound overseas, Augot, in his effort to avoid the speeding steel vessels, ordered her two dories overboard. Three men in each of the dories slacked astern. Engineer Hackett volunteered to stay aboard and fire a gun should a convoy ship come too close. Luckily the large steamers missed *Metamora* and the dories.

In time *Metamora* was sold to Thomas Garland of Gaultois and on August 16, 1953, she was lost at Point Riche while carrying barrelled oil for South Coast ports.

rescue vessel standing by, Captain Randall decided to abandon the leaking ship, but before he and his crew left they set fire to the tern schooner.

In New York American custom officials told Captain Randall *William S. MacDonald* was on their suspect list. Since he was operating outside American territorial limits and could not be apprehended, Randall told them he had sailed

Courtesy Postcard from Hotel Robert, St. Pierre

During the American Prohibition, "speed boats" low vessels designed for quick getaways, off loaded cargoes of illegal liquor to smaller boats which took the goods to willing buyers on shore. In this photo crewmen off load sacks or small wooden boxes of whisky or rum to a customer.

Nova Scotian schooner *William S. McDonald* would have waited in "Rum Row" for such a small boat to appear to take care of her illegal cargo.

from Havana bound to Nova Scotia on August thirteenth with about 3400 cases of whisky on board. When he reached Lahave, Nova Scotia, he was told to return to 'Rum Row' —off the American east coast — and to unload his cargo to a certain vessel. This had been partly done when the storm of October 23-24 hit the tern schooner.

According to Randall's story given to the *New York Times, MacDonald*'s anchors would not hold, most of the canvas was blown away and the massive waves broke over the schooner smashing her planking and opening seams. Drifting before the gale and leaking, Randall and his men manned the pumps for forty-eight hours without letup. By then *William S. MacDonald,* almost filled with water, had drifted one hundred and fifty miles to a point near Long Beach, New Jersey. When Randall sighted the British tanker, the sinking schooner was set fire and abandoned.

Insurance to the value of ten thousand dollars was carried on *William S. MacDonald*'s hull. On last report she was afire sixteen miles east of Sandy Hook, New Jersey, in an area off the U.S. coast known as "Rum Row." During the American Prohibition (1919-1933) the shipping lane was renown for schooners carrying illegal liquor connecting with smaller vessels hired to transport the cargo to shore.

Chapter 57

February Storms

Off Newfoundland and Nova Scotia

For several days in late February 1967, air-sea search and rescue units — four RCAF Argus aircraft, two Albatross planes and two Neptune patrol planes of the United States Air Force — scoured the seas off Newfoundland and Nova Scotia and eventually located some debris of a missing ship. But the wreckage probably belonged to *Maureen and Michael*, a schooner which went down off St. Pierre after her crew had been rescued by the United States Coast Guard.

Maureen and Michael's Captain Max Fiander, Halifax, formerly of English Harbour West; Isaac and Seward Bartlett, Coomb's Cove and later a resident of Grand Bank; William Hardiman and William Dominaux, Bay L'Argent; John Ben Strowbridge, Harbour Breton formerly of Jersey Harbour; John Tom Tibbo of Harbour Breton, who resided in Liscomb, Nova Scotia and Conrad Mills of Louisbourg were rescued by the U.S. Coast Guard cutter *Castle Rock*.

Lockeport vessel *Polly and Robbie*, an eighty-five ton longliner owned by Captain Edwin Brewer, which had steamed to help *Maureen and Michael* was not so fortunate. The forty-eight ton *Polly and Robbie*, only two years old, went down with all her seven crew: Captain Brewer, his brother Randell, both born in Epworth on the Burin Peninsula and

Nova Scotian fishing vessel *Maureen and Michael*, sinking stern first in the cold seas off Newfoundland, was caught in a storm of February 21-23, 1967, which claimed three ships with full crew: *Polly and Robbie*, *Iceland II* and *Cape Bonnie*.

Two American coastguard personnel of *Castle Rock* had to don wetsuits and take a rubber raft over to the side of *Maureen and Michael* to ensure the safety of all. Rescuer Pettek said, "The stern was going down as we got there. One guy jumped aboard the raft...the raft drifted away and we had to pull it back to get the other man. We were only about fifty yards away in the raft when the ship sank."

living in Lockeport; Isaac Wells of Grand Bank who in 1965 was cook on the halibut fishing vessel *Marjorie and Dorothy* and had signed on *Polly and Robbie* a short while previously. The other four crewmen were from Nova Scotia: James White, Lockeport; twin brothers Currie and Harold Harnish, and Reid Jollymore of Mill Cove.

According to the last transmitted message from *Pollie and Robbie*, when she was about one hundred miles south of Cape Race, a sea (estimated that night to be forty foot waves) hit her which probably ripped off the cabin and stove in the sides. Winds, as measured by Newfoundland weather stations to be in excess of one hundred miles an hour, pushed up seas so mountainous that no ship of any size could turn broadside to them and hope to survive.

The week of sea disasters began on a Tuesday morning, February 21, when trawler *Cape Bonnie*, racing to make Halifax harbour in the storm, grounded on a ledge off Woody Island one mile from the shore of Pennant Bay. In the raging storm *Cape Bonnie*, was off course and was carried into the waters near Sambro ledges, one of the most treacherous coastlines on the Atlantic coast located twelve miles west of Halifax harbour.

According to investigators, the crew may have believed they had struck the Sisters Ledge and they left the trawler quickly in lifeboats. All eighteen of her crew were lost. Built in Britain in 1952, *Cape Bonnie* carried direction-finding, echo-sounding, radar and radio-telephone equipment, but possibly the ship's radar may have failed. Throughout the four-five day storm *Cape Bonnie*, a four hundred ton trawler laden with 70,000 pounds of fish for National Sea Products of Halifax, was still partly afloat, but searchers and rescue units were unable to reach the wreck.

Captain Peter Hickey, a forty-two year old native of Harbour Breton who had lived in Grand La Pierre and Halifax; mate Bernard Hepditch, St. Pierre-Miquelon; Howard Gastie of West Bay Centre were three of *Cape Bonnie*'s crew with Newfoundland connections while the remaining fifteen belonged to Nova Scotia.

Many of *Cape Bonnie*'s victims were found along the shoreline which led investigators to conclude that her two large lifeboats had been put over the side, but both upset in the turbulent seas.

But *Cape Bonnie* was not the last victim. Throughout the storm, authorities on shore knew another ship — the ninety-one foot stern trawler *Iceland II* — was in difficulty off Cape Breton. The lack of word from the vessel was ominous; then, on Saturday, February 26, seventeen year-old Brian MacKay, out walking on beach near his home at Forchu saw the wrecked trawler, a derelict near the shore. Her fate was similar to that of *Cape Bonnie*. Apparently she was trying to make Louisbourg, Nova Scotia, in the storm and grounded at high speed, probably with her crew not knowing she was off course. No radio calls since Thursday, two days before she course. No radio calls since Thursday, two days before she was discovered, had been received from the distressed vessel.

Two smashed dories and an empty life raft indicated the crew had not lasted long in the freezing waters once they launched the dories to escape the grounded wreck. There

Photos courtesy Jack Keeping

Two views of *Iceland II*, grounded near Pennant Bay, Nova Scotia, on February 21, 1967. Eighteen crew lost their lives.

Courtesy Randell Pope

Sometimes the rocky shores of Newfoundland were more kind to stranded vessels. In 1966 dragger *Rubert Brand II* went ashore in Kelly's Cove, a little east of Grand Bank. She was later refloated, but today is a rusted derelict in Jersey Harbour.

were no survivors. On charter to Eastern Fisheries of Souris, P.E.I., *Iceland II* carried ten crew: Captain Thomas Hodder and Reginald Foote both hailed from Burin; mate Leslie MacDonald; chief engineer Albert MacDonald; James Carter; Clarence Malone; Lee Jenkins, David O'Hanley and John Hendsbee, all of Souris, P.E.I. and Clovis Gallant, Rustico, P.E.I.

By Saturday, February 25, 1967, when the storm abated, the toll of the sea was one of the worst in the history of the Atlantic seaboard — four ships with thirty-five crew lost in three of them:

Vessel	Date Lost	Number of Crew
Cape Bonnie	Feb. 21	Eighteen
Polly and Robbie	Feb. 21-23	Seven (missing at sea)
Iceland II	Feb. 22-23	Ten
Maureen and Michael	Feb. 23	Eight (all rescued)

Chapter 58

Vogue: One Ship and One Life

English Harbour West/St. John's

The last voyage of *Vogue* began at Quirpon, a town located on the tip of the Northern Peninsula, when she sailed for Gibraltar with a full load of dry fish. *Vogue* left Quirpon on Saturday, November 12, 1921; the crew arrived in St. John's December 1 with their vessel on the bottom one hundred fifty miles from St. John's.

Built in Lunenburg, Nova Scotia, four years previously at G.A. Cox yards, the one hundred ninety-six net ton *Vogue* measured one hundred eight foot long, twenty-eight foot wide and was 10.7 foot deep. In 1918 A.E. Hickman's business bought the tern (or three master as they were called locally) for $48,000 and Captain Frank Pine was assigned as her first master.

Eventually Pine and his crew changed ship to be succeeded by other South Coast sailors: Captain George Yarn, mate Joseph Emberley, cook Thomas Yarn, seamen Bert Power, James Dolimount, Ephriam Yarn and Allan Barrett. With the exception of Barrett, who belonged to St. John's and Emberley of Harbour Breton, the rest of the crew were residents of English Harbour West.

On her final voyage *Vogue* was hardly out of sight of land when she ran into the teeth of a vicious northeasterly gale. All day of November 13, Sunday, the wind continued in violence and to add to the troubles of the captain and his crew a blinding snowstorm engulfed the vessel.

Before Captain Yarn could prevent it, the ship's canvas began to tear. Heavy seas swept the deck of heavily laden *Vogue*, but in the teeth of the gale, Power, Emberley, Barrett and Dolimount managed to get out on the bowsprit to bend, or tie on, a new jib.

Just as they were about to return to the deck a giant sea struck the crippled craft carrying Dolimount into the sea. According to the other seamen who saw him go over the side, but were powerless to help, not a sound came from the young sailor as he struggled in the water.

Captain Yarn quickly brought the schooner around and the seamen were willing to launch a dory into the angry seas, at great risk to their own lives, but Dolimount disappeared forever from view. This tragic event happened about sixty miles off Cape Bauld. James Dolimount was twenty-one years old, lived with his parents at English Harbour West, and had an aunt, Mrs. Stephen Smith, living on Gannon Road in North Sydney.

With difficulty the disheartened crew secured the dory and were about to resume their normal duties when it was discovered the ship was leaking badly. As the crew prepared and primed the pumps the fury of the sea increased and throughout the night not one of the six closed an eye.

Next day *Vogue* had no canvas left save a few straggling remnants left swinging to their fastenings. Both lifeboats were either smashed into small pieces or washed away. Hope of rescue from a passing ship seemed impossible; they were well north and completely out of shipping lanes.

For four days and nights the men laboured at their toil of keeping the tern afloat to which there was no letup. With not a stitch of workable canvas and the sea water constantly rising in the hold, sleep and rest were out of the question. As one of the crew later told the newspaper *North Sydney Herald*:

> We prayed day and night for deliverance, and as the day began to fade away in the hours of evening on Thursday, the 17th, we finally resigned ourselves to our God, expecting every minute our end would come, when, like a phantom in the night, the dark outlines of a ship away off on our lee, hove in sight.

Heartened by the sight of a ship, the fatigued men — and who but sturdy Newfoundland toilers of the sea could stand such a nerve-wracking experience — gave vent to their feelings with a whoop of joy and thanksgiving. The ship was bearing down on the doomed schooner.

This was about four in the afternoon of November 17, but the sea was so mad that the steamer, which proved to be the Norwegian steamer *Ella Clausen* on her way from Manchester, England, to Boston, was unable to launch a lifeboat. However the captain remained in the vicinity until around nine o'clock that night when a full moon came out from behind ominous clouds.

Courtesy William Chapman

Banking schooner *Progressive II*, moored in English Harbour West, the home of Captain Yarn and James Dolimount. Her riding sail and foresail are lashed down. The dory tied on just below the wheelhouse is well down in the water.

In 1948 *Progressive II* caught fire and burned near Belleoram harbour.

Ella Clausen's men launched a boat in which were seven seamen willing to risk their lives for their fellow man. It was no easy task, but after a desperate battle with the elements, Captain Yarn and his surviving crew were taken off and landed on board *Ella Clausen* bound for Boston. The Newfoundland tern schooner was abandoned and soon slipped beneath the waves.

Bert Power recalled the kindness of the steamer's crew:

> Such treatment as we received on board the *Ella Clausen* could not be exceeded by the hands of man. The officers, all Norwegians, the remainder of the crew being German, did everything humanly possible for us, even giving us their beds.

Courtesy Rev. Vernon Cluett

Sparkling Glance, two hundred seventeen ton foreign-going tern managed by Benjamin Keeping of Belleoram, tied up at Harvey and Company premises in Belleoram. Her jib, jumbo and balloon sail lie on the bowsprit.

On February 9, 1921, while en route to Europe, the Shelburne-built *Sparkling Glance* took a severe battered from winter storms and sank about six hundred fifty miles southeast of St. John's. Her Belleoram crew — Captain Reginald Keeping, navigator Harold Baker, James Buffett, William Cluett, Samuel Poole, Stanley Bond and Henry Carter — was rescued by a passing freighter.

Most likely one of the first questions *Vogue*'s crew asked was how and why the steamer arrived in the vicinity of their sinking ship. How had their prayers been answered? *Ella Clausen* was out in the same storm that wrecked the tern schooner had been driven two hundred miles off her course and was seven days overdue at Boston. Fortunately for the six Newfoundlanders on a sinking ship, the vessel drifted north and within a mile or two of *Vogue*. It was then the lookout on *Ella Clausen* saw them or their names would have been added to the toll of the ocean.

Early in December the beleaguered crew of *Vogue* arrived in St. John's and thence made their way to their homes — those headed to English Harbour West had to retell the tale of the loss of the tern schooner and the death of their friend and crew mate.

Chapter 59

Florence Swyers, Victim of the Deeps

English Harbour West

In his later years Captain Frank Pine, the first master of *Vogue*, became a renowned master of vessels, especially in those of A.E. Hickman's extensive foreign-going fleet. As a young man in English Harbour West, he learned the lore of the sea, worked his way up through the ranks and commanded several tern schooners. He had lost one: the ninety-nine ton *Adriatic*, stranded near St. Lawrence harbour in September, 1918.

After the Burgeo schooner *A. Moulton* was detained at Key West in 1922 for infractions of the United States Marine laws, she was later bought by Newfoundland parties. Captain Frank Pine renamed the vessel *Mount Pearl* which was later changed to *Cape Bonavista*. *Cape Bonavista* was abandoned off Newfoundland on January 31, 1946, when she developed a bad leak.

When Captain George Anstey turned over the command of the tern schooner *Florence Swyers* early in 1922, Pine was asked by the joint owners, A.E. Hickman and J.T. Swyers, to take over. Built in 1918 by Arch Chaulk of Charlottetown, Bonavista Bay, *Florence Swyers* netted a hundred fifty-seven ton and measured one hundred and one feet long. She left Newfoundland on May 7, 1925, and despite adverse weather in which some of her canvas was blown away, Captain Pine reached Oporto after seventeen days.

On May 26, 1925, Pine left Alicante, Spain, and two days later a terrific west southwest gale engulfed the schooner off Cape St. Vincent, Spain. *Florence Swyers* was blown back to within forty-five miles of the European coast. In the meantime while the crew tried to keep the beleaguered tern off the land, she sprang a leak.

Pine ordered his crew — mate A. Morey, cook W. Turpin, bosun James Penney, seamen Nicholas Gill and W. Hodder — to the pumps around the clock. From four pm May 28 until eleven pm May 30, pumps were kept going without letup.

Seeing no hope of saving his vessel, Pine abandoned ship. The holds were full of water and, for an hour and a half before the crew left, *Florence Swyers* was unmanageable and sinking. She went down ten minutes after the small boat pushed away. Captain Pine took a compass, charts and sextant with him, but lost his expensive navigation instruments. The crew saved noting but the clothes they stood in.

The six Newfoundlanders set their backs into a forty-five mile row back to the coast of Spain; this was the first leg in a series of seven or eight legs or modes of transportation in their attempt to reach home.

After rowing all night, the crew was picked up by a small Spanish boat engaged in catching tuna. The tuna fish plant, managed by a woman, was located in a small port called Rota and was the chief industry of the town. The proprietress made sure the crew were lodged, fed and treated well by the citizens of the remote town.

From Rota, Captain Pine and crew secured a passage to Cadiz and from there to Gibraltar. Many British ships passed through the straits and the shipwrecked men of *Florence Swyers* soon obtained a passage on the Australian\Oriental line *Orama* headed for England. *Orama* dropped off the crew at Tilbury Docks on the Thames River; then they took a train to London and switched trains to reach Liverpool.

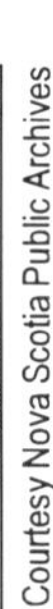

Margaret K. Smith, a Nova Scotian built schooner owned and operated by Kearley Brothers of Belleoram, disappeared off Canada's east coast in August 1943. Lost with the vessel were Captain Horatio Kearley, age 26; Eric Bond, 27; Charles Dominaux, 24; Silas Savoury, 65 and his son Charles, age 18 all of Belleoram. Cook Herbert Sheppard, 35, of Rencontre East and Charles Blagdon, 47, hailed from Coomb's Cove.

At least two of *Smith*'s crew had been involved in marine mishaps previously: Captain Kearley survived the abandoning of *Elsie* in 1935. Silas Savoury was a crewman with Captain Jack Lavey on the thirty-four ton schooner *Jessie Beatrice*, owned by Petites. In 1942 storm conditions in the Gulf of St. Lawrence pounded the rudder case open and *Jessie Beatrice* was abandoned. The crew was rescued by a Canadian Coast Guard vessel. *Jessie Beatrice* was built in 1935 by John Cluett of Frenchman's Cove for Thomas Pierce of Fortune.

From Liverpool they joined the S.S *Newfoundland* headed for St. John's. Despite the fatiguing rounds of travel and stops in foreign ports, the six were in good health as once again they made the final voyage to their Newfoundland homes — they finally reached St. John's on the twenty-seventh day of July, nearly three months after they left Newfoundland.

Undaunted by his close encounters with disaster and death on the high seas, Captain Frank Pine bought the tern schooner *Isobel Moore* and he later commanded *Isobel*'s sister ship, *Olive Moore*. In the twilight of his career he was master of a government vessel.

Chapter 60

Fire on the Jean and Mona

Boxey, Connaigre Peninsula

When Captain Abe Myles and his twenty-one crew arrived in North Sydney on September 13, 1951, they told a harrowing tale of fire at sea — a fire, which enveloped *Jean and Mona* so suddenly that her engines could not be shut off, completely consumed the schooner until she sank.

Built in Garnish in 1935 as part of Commission government's shipbuilding scheme, *Jean and Mona* landed her catches of halibut at Halifax and had left that port on September sixth to begin another trip. One week into her trip, at nine o'clock in the morning, while about one hundred and twenty eight miles east of Sydney a fire broke out in the engine room which could not be contained. It burned with such intensity that the four men aboard ship — Captain Myles, engineer Chelsey Myles, cook George S. Myles and Edward Bennett — had no choice but abandon ship. They had two or three minutes to grab the belongings of ten crewmen stored in the forecastle while all personal possessions kept aft were lost. *Jean and Mona*'s eight dories were out fishing when the fire broke out. The men rowed up, but nothing could be done but watch a sheet of flame consume the schooner. The engines were still running; thus *Jean and Mona* went around in wide circles for nine hours until fire destroyed the engines and then what was left of the vessel sank.

Seen here sailing out of Lahave, Nova Scotia, with her white wings spread to catch the wind, Jean and Mona measured ninety-six feet long. Captain Tom Grandy of Garnish skippered this schooner for several years. Later in her career *Jean and Mona*'s owners had two 100 horsepower engines installed and her registered tonnage was one hundred and two. At the time of her loss she was valued at $40,000.

Captain Myles had already sent one or two of his dories to the nearest vessel for help. Captain Arch Evans in *L.A. Dunton*, fishing about three or four miles away, steamed over and picked up the entire personnel of the burning craft.

Captain Myles, and his son Chelsey, both natives of Boxey on the Connaigre Peninsula, resided in Halifax. Most of his crew were the hardy fishermen of the Connaigre Peninsula and other towns along Newfoundland's south coast:

Boxey
Captain Myles
Chelsey Myles, age 31
cook George S. Myles, 60
Edwin Myles, 36 (captain's brother)
Richard Price, 27
William Stoodley, 20

Coomb's Cove
Edward Blagdon, 48

English Harbour West
John Evans, 25

Jerry Blagdon, 22
Onslow Blagdon, 22
Charles Sheppard, 23
Simeon Keeping, 21

Brunette Island
John Douglas, 20

Dawson's Cove
Edward Bennett, 33

English Harbour East
George Saunders, 38
John Clarke, 24

Belleoram
Freeman Poole, 27

Terrenceville

Andrew Hynes, 36

Hermitage
George Short, 43

Rencontre West
Budd Beauchamp, 41

Miller's Passage
Aloysius Quann, 45
Thomas Smith, 39

Courtesy George S. Spencer

Palfrey, (above) was built in Placentia in 1924. By the 1950s she was a coal carrier delivering coal to every lighthouse on the south coast from Channel Head to Merasheen, including the Penguin Islands off Cape La Hune. In this photo *Palfrey* is docked at Ramea discharging coal; her crew: Captain Charles "B" Thornhill, George S. Spencer, Tom Spencer, Eli Thornhill and Arch Thornhill, all of Fortune. When *Palfrey* was put into the passenger trade between St. Pierre and Fortune she was renamed *Spencer II*.

Ramea's eastern Passage is in the background. On the left is the beach area of Ramea Island. In recent years a government wharf was built along the point on the left. Big (Great) Island, centre; and Middle Island on the right. Bags of coal which *Palfrey* delivered to South Coast lighthouses and islands are stacked on the after quarter up almost to the level of the wheelhouse windows.

For Captain Abe Myles, a veteran of the sea who had been going to the banks for forty-one years, it was his second shipwreck in two years and third in his lifetime. He and five of the crew of *Jean and Mona* — Edwin Myles, Richard Price, Simeon Keeping, Charles Sheppard and Jerry Blagdon — had survived the stranding of *Marshall Frank* on February 17, 1949. (See Chapter 56 "When Two Ships Collide")

Chapter 61

Inez G of Burgeo Capsizes

Burgeo, Lingan, N.S.

Caught in a violent September gale, Captain Joseph Vatcher and his crew had valiantly tried to reach North Sydney. Three miles from port, while off Lingan, Nova Scotia, *Inez G* was pushed over on her side. She was completely engulfed in water three or four times and then sank. Captain Joseph Vatcher of Burgeo fought the gale to the end and was heard by one of the two survivors saying, "If she goes down, I'll go down with her." Both survivors — Kenneth Bragg of Burgeo and George Bungay who resided in North Sydney — told how captain and crew had remained at their posts all day and battled the storm.

Built in 1911 and classed as a semi-knockabout, *Inez G*, once owned on the northeast coast and commanded by Captain George Gulliford, was sold to Burgeo. At sixty-six ton she was now at the mercy of Atlantic storms.

All through Friday morning and Friday night of September 25, 1925, the Burgeo schooner *Inez G* withstood a battering from nature's worst elements, but by Friday night Vatcher discovered she had begun to leak from the severe pounding. *Inez G* was riding out the storm at anchor with her two anchors holding firm, but water rising in the holds forced a run to North Sydney. Around nine pm a heavy squall turned her over on her side.

Captain And Four Of Crew Drown When Schooner Upsets

Weather Man Has Change Of Heart

THIS is a hard slap at the pessimist. He has been grouching ever since the Weather Man started to predict cooler weather. Now that "warm and showery" is forecast he will likely mutter about inconsistencies.

Inez G., of Newfoundland Meets With Disaster Three Miles Off Lingan, C. B.

SYDNEY, Sept. 26—"If she goes down, I'll go with her" were the last words spoken by Capt. Joseph Vatcher, of the 55 ton schooner Inez G., of Burgeo, Newfoundland, which sank three miles off Lingan, last Friday night. Capt. Vatcher

This is how *Halifax Herald* of September 26, 1925, headlined the loss of the Burgeo schooner *Inez G.*

Her crew hailed from Burgeo: Vatcher; Edward Harris; John Hiscock, originally from Codroy but living in Burgeo; Robert Strickland and another Robert Strickland (probably father and son). A sixth man James Wheeler, a passenger from North Sydney, was married with eight children. Vatcher left a wife and no children, both Sticklands were married with children. Harris and Hiscock were single.

Inez G left North Sydney several months previously, headed for Demerara and took on a cargo of liquor. Upon her return to American and Nova Scotian waters she lay off Cape Breton coast disposing of her cargo. Much of it had been off loaded when the September gale hit the Nova Scotia coast without warning.

While at anchor off Nova Scotia, George Bungay and Wheeler, two men employed as sword fishermen on another boat, had transferred to *Inez G* to get a passage to North Sydney from the fishing grounds.

When *Inez G* fell over on her side Bungay frantically tore a dory loose from its lashings and jumped into it. Bragg was

Author's collection

A small unidentified schooner lies at anchor somewhere near Newfoundland's south coast. Burgeo schooner Inez G would have been about this size, much too small to be caught battling a vicious September gale.

swept off the tilting deck by a heavy sea and was carried for some distance underwater by the sinking schooner. When he came to the surface he found himself by the side of the dory which had Bungay aboard. Bragg, weighted down with oilskins and wet clothes, grabbed the gunwales and with a superhuman effort Bungay pulled him in over the side.

They saw none of their comrades after the vessel fell over on her beam ends, although Bragg claimed to have heard someone shout frantically, "Oh my God, Oh my God!" Apart from that they neither heard nor saw any sign from any of their comrades.

Both men fought their way through high seas and wind and after an arduous struggle against the elements reached the shore at Lingan. Exhausted and suffering from exposure, they were taken into Menzies Forward's house and cared for.

Captain Vatcher, who had intended to leave *Inez G* at the end of her trip and retire from the sea, formerly commanded the little Burgeo steamer *Herbert Green*. He also owned the schooner *Julia F.C.* Six men — five from Burgeo, one from North Sydney — lost and two survivors.

But the sea was not finished with *Inez G*. About a month later the derelict and much of her cargo of liquor drifted in near shore between Bridgeport and Dominion, Nova Scotia, eventually grounded on a reef three quarters of a mile offshore and broke apart. Almost universally when wreckage comes near shore salvers attempt to secure whatever cargo or supplies they can.

People near Lingan Head had already salvaged fifty barrels of rum and then, in early November, a new rumour added frenzied interest in the wreck of *Inez G*. It was said that Captain Vatcher had seven thousand dollars stored in a chest aboard in the ill-fated schooner. For hundreds of people lining the shore, pieces of the wreck, like the deck of the schooner, meant nothing as they searched for more valuable goods.

Bernard MacIntyre, age forty-two, of Bridgeport had gone down to the beach with several other men to get casks which had drifted ashore. Five casks had already been successfully landed that day.

MacIntyre spotted a cask a short distance off shore and took off his shoes to wade out. When near the flotsam, he apparently stepped into deep water, but continued swimming, got hold of the cask and tried to get it to land. He gave a cry for help and immediately sank before any others working a short distance away on the shore could help.

MacIntyre, a miner by occupation, resided on MacIntyre's Lane, Bridgeport. He, his six brothers and a sister were well-known in the area. His brother Peter, a Glace Bay town councillor, and Michael were on the Glace Bay police force.

Three years previously another Burgeo schooner — *J.N. Rafuse* —had gone down with loss of three lives: Captain George Harvey, age 28 and single, of Fortune; mate Ambrose King, 25, Marystown; and cook Ephriam Billard, 33, of Burgeo.

On February 20, 1922, while on a journey from Cadiz laden with salt for St. John's, *J.N. Rafuse* owned by J.T. Moulton of Burgeo, was abandoned and the crew taken off by the S.S. *Terrier* headed for Liverpool, England. In the process of transferring the shipwrecked sailors to the steamer, the lifeboat capsized and the three were drowned as well as the first mate of *Terrier*, in charge of the lifeboat.

Three other of *J.N. Rafuse*'s crew — Bosun L. Janes and John Clothier, both of Burgeo and James Philpott of Jamestown, Bonavista Bay — survived. Captain Harvey had taken command of *Rafuse* a few months before and was on his first overseas voyage on her. He had previously commanded *General Byng* out of Grand Bank. He had a sister living in St. John's.

Chapter 62

Mission Boat Tragedy off West Point/Lapoile

Lapoile

Death from drowning off Newfoundland's rugged shores did not always come from shipwreck or missing dories nor was loss of life always those of fishermen. This was made evident when two clergy had a fatal mishap in the fall of 1937 while en route from West Point to La Poile, a small town situated about twenty kilometres eastward in La Poile Bay on the coast.

Reverend Oliver Jackson, the Newfoundland Superintendent of Missions for the United Church of Canada, and Reverend Wallace Harris, a student minister stationed at Petites, were headed for La Poile to hold missionary meetings. Jackson, in his capacity as superintendent and secretary of Christian education, visited most parishes in Newfoundland and Labrador. In northern Newfoundland trips were made by foot, train or dog sled, but on the South Coast most travel was by boat.

Local fishermen warned the clergy that seas were too rough, but Jackson and Harris knew that the people in the next parish were expecting them. At nine am on November 2, they left in the mission boat and were still in sight of land

Courtesy Rev. Vernon Cluett

In the days before roads and modern transportation, men, women and children often travelled the coast of Newfoundland in small boats such as St. Bernard (above). *St. Bernard*, with one mast and a bowsprit, was a small Fortune Bay trader owned by Arthur M. and Levi T. Cluett of Belleoram.

Often little boats like these were caught between ports in rough weather; many of them came to untimely ends.

when the boom on the small boat swung and knocked Jackson overboard. He was dressed in heavy clothes for the November weather and quickly disappeared. He was probably knocked unconscious.

Harris tried to reach for him, over-balanced and fell into the water. The men on the shore launched their small boats immediately and, although it was too late to save Rev. Harris, they recovered his body which was floating a half mile from the scene. It was three days later before Rev. Jackson's body was found.

A few hours after the men had fallen overboard, the Mission boat drifted onto White Island and was smashed to matchwood. Rev. Jackson, born in Wales, resided in St. John's; his funeral took place in the St. John's Gower Street United Church and was presided over by Rev. Jesse

Courtesy Robert Keeping

Schooner Antoine C. Santos frozen in ice at Harbour Le Cou, a town located a few miles west of Lapoile. To move a vessel farther into sheltered waters, a channel had to be cut in the ice and the vessel pulled through using all available manpower from the nearby settlements. At this time she was captained by Gabriel Fudge of Belleoram, who later went on to skipper the government trawler *Cape Agulhas* and *Malakoff*. For his years of dedicated service, Captain Fudge received the O.B.E. (Order of the British Empire) during King George VI's visit to Newfoundland in 1939.

Antoine C. Santos was lost on April 15, 1942, when she ran aground near Miquelon Head, St. Pierre Islands under Captain Jacob Thornhill.

Reynolds, who later served the Grand Bank congregation. Rev. Harris belonged to New Chelsea, Trinity Bay.

Chapter 63

Izetta's Wreck

McDougall's Gulch, Cape Ray

McDougall's Gulch, about seven miles east of Cape Ray, was the landfall of the shipwrecked schooner *Izetta*. Owned and commanded by George Lillington of Isle au Morts, *Izetta* was bound for Burnt Islands from North Sydney with a load of coal on August 10, 1915. She had been built in Ramea in 1900, but was sold to Bairds of St. John's twelve years later.

Lillington reported later that his schooner had been leaking badly all the way from North Sydney and the pumps had to be kept going constantly to keep her afloat. About twenty miles off Channel Head, the pumps clogged with coal dust. With the weight of coal and sea water, *Izetta* went under so suddenly, it barely gave the crew time to launch the dory over the side. Lillington and his crew stood by until the schooner sank and then set out for shore, twenty miles away.

Their landfall was McDougall's Gulch, a railway-siding community, about twenty kilometres northwest of Port aux Basques. Newfoundland *Census* records the town variously over the years as Wreck House, McDougall's Siding or Gulch with its highest population as thirty.

The town's name most likely originated with the McDougall family. After he married in the 1930s, Lauchie McDougall's homestead in the Gulch eventually became known as

Photo courtesy PANL

Schooner *Olive Evans,* at right with the Masonic symbol and words Grand Bank painted on stern, discharges dried cod at Barr's premises, St. John's. A railway spur line runs out onto the wharf.

Built in Mahone Bay, Nova Scotia, in 1905, she was brought as a coasting/trading vessel by Captain William P. Evans of Grand Bank (standing with an armful of fish, in centre, near weigh scale). According to family knowledge, *Olive Evans* had been a rum-runner before Evans owned her and had false bottoms built into the bunks. She was sold in 1921 to George T. Dixon's business of Fortune who put Captain William Ayres of Fortune in command.

Olive Evans went down on December 2, 1921, a short distance off shore north of Port aux Basques. Ayres and his crew stood by the schooner until she sank; then rowed ashore to the nearest land. At that point on the west coast the Newfoundland railway line ran near the shoreline; the shipwrecked crew walked up to the track and flagged down the next train.

McDougall's Gulch was the scene of another wreck when Dawe's of Cupids lost their schooner *Dora P. Lane* nearby. Skipper Bert LeDrew and crew abandoned ship off there on August 1, 1944.

Photo courtesy Jack Keeping

When the wooden ships of our grandfather's era became unfit or could not find work in the bank fishing industry, often they resurrected as coasting boats. When the coasting trade was supplanted by highways and modern technology, schooners were hauled upon a beach to rot.

Not so with the outmoded side draggers and stern trawlers. Some were sold to foreign countries; others, like *Alfred Booth* (above) were sent to the bottom. By July 1979 she had done yeoman service for Booth Fisheries, Fortune and was scuttled off Goblin Head, Baie d'Espoir where the water is reportedly 2500 feet deep.

Wreck House. High winds, sometimes reaching one hundred and forty kilometres per hour, funnelled down Table Mountains and occasionally lifted train cars off the tracks. Claiming he could smell or predict high winds, McDougall eventually earned the title, "Gale Sniffer Extraordinary to the Newfoundland Railway" and was hired to warn railway officials of potentially dangerous winds.

By 1915, the year of *Izetta*'s loss, McDougall's Gulch/Wreck House had four families. Its population never exceeded thirty and by 1975 the community was abandoned.

Appendix A

Crew List of S.S. *Beverley*

S.S. *Beverley* left Harbour Grace for Gibraltar on January 21, 1918 and was probably torpedoed on the voyage to Europe. There were no survivors. Her crew:

James Barrett, husband of Mary Barrett, 13 Holloway St., St. John's
Frank Barron, son of Kate Barron, Placentia
James Barron, husband of Julia Barron, 2 Bannerman St., St. John's
Thomas Carrigan, son of Catherine Carrigan, Logy Bay, St. John's E.
Richard Collins, son of Sarah F. Collins, 7 Mullock St., St. John's
John Dodd, son of John Dodd of 14 Boncloddy Street, St. John's
James Dooley, husband of Margaret Dooley, 13 Barron St. St. John's
Robert Green, husband of Priscilla Green, 85 King's Rd., St. John's
Fred Hann, 5 Spencer Street, St. John's
James Hearn, son of Jane Hearn, Caul's Lane, St. John's
Patrick Hearn, husband of Annie of Caul's Lane, St. John's
William Kenney, husband of Annie Kenney, Duckworth St., St. John's
Cebos Lewis, husband of Emma, Battery Road, St. John's
John Noftall, husband of Margaret Noftall, 22 Casey St., St. John's
Cornelius Pender, son of Ann Pender, 39 Plank Road, St. John's
John Power of Outer Cove
Albert Ryan, son of John Ryan, St. Joseph's, Salmonier
Peter Stewart, husband of Helen Stewart, 106 Water St., St. John's

Patrick Walsh, husband of Veronica Walsh, 36 Casey St., St. John's

Andrew Wilson, husband of Mary Wilson, 51 Carter's Hill, St. John's

Andrew Wilson, son of Mary Wilson, 51 Carter's Hill, St. John's

John Cunningham, residence uncertain

Eli Peddle, residence uncertain

Andrew Devereaux, residence uncertain

Appendix B

Crew List of Three Ships Sunk by Enemy Action WWI

Lake Simcoe, a barquentine owned by the St. John's business Baine Johnston, was sent to the bottom by a German submarine in the fall of 1915. There were no survivors:

Daniel Carew, son of Stephen Carew of Witless Bay
John Coady, son of Margaret Coady of 78 Lime Street, St. John's
William Eason, son of Isaac Eason of Manuels, C.B.
Richard Fleming, husband of Mary Ann Fleming, Spaniard's Bay
Silas M. Halfyard, husband of Jessie, 23 Carnell St., St. John's
Patrick Kirby, brother of James and John Kirby, St. John's
E. Newhook, son of Richard Newhook, Trinity
Noah Smith, husband of Martha Smith of Manuels, C.B.
Thomas White, husband of Annie White, 24 Casey St., St. John's
H.N. Peppas, residence uncertain
Duncan Briely, residence uncertain

Ethel, sunk by a German sub on January 15, 1918, while en route from St. John's to Seville, Spain carried the following crew:
James Carroll, husband of Mary Carroll, 57 Carter's Hill, St.John's
William Furneaux, son of Eliza Furneaux, 8 Monroe St., St. John's
James Ivey, son of Mary Ivey, 13 James St., St. John's
Edward Noseworthy, son of Jessie Noseworthy, Pennywell Rd., St. John's
Thomas Spracklin, 8 Monroe St., St. John's
John White, husband of Harriet White, Clifford St., St. John's

Watagua, sunk March 27, 1918, 450 miles W by N from Lisbon, en route from Burin to Gibraltar carried the following crew:

Andrew Driscoll, married, resident of Tor's Cove, Ferryland
Edward Fever, Rushoon, Placentia Bay
Eli Handcock, married of 39 Water Street West, St. John's
Richard Owen, married, 295 Hamilton Avenue, St. John's
John Brest, of Lunenburg, Nova Scotia

Appendix C

Folk Poem

The Loss of the Stanley Parsons, Dec. 12th, 1932

It was a fair November day
When the "Stanley Parsons" sailed away
And on her deck six brave men stood
In hope of returning with a cargo of food.

They sailed for the city of St. John's
All of them were Newfoundland sons
Residents of Long Island shore
With not a thought of taking one more.

A favourable time to St. John's they had
And left again with hearts so glad
Adding to their number a man brave and strong
And he also to Lush's Bight did belong.

These brave men thought of home once more
And returning to their native shore.
Loved ones at home were waiting too
For the "Stanley" to appear in view.

Soon after leaving St. John's harbour
For a while the wind was in their favour
But the wind soon changed and in a hurry
The last man who saw them was Capt. Burry.

The wind it blew a northeast gale
Maybe the "Stanley" lost a sail
But the gallant crew upon her deck
Did everything to save a wreck.

It's thought they ran ashore,
While others were thinking something more
But I myself thing they drove to sea
There are many others in favour with me.

The heartbroken families are waiting still
To see their loved ones return home well.
My hope returns and still I pray
That the missing ship will return some day.

If the "Stanley Parsons" never returns again
I'll wait no longer nor refrain
I'll extent my sympathy to the ones
Who lost husbands, lovers, brothers and sons.

Contributed by the Maye family, author unknown.

Appendix D

Crew list of S.S. *Tolsby*

S.S. *Tolsby*, wrecked January 13, 1908, near Drook, carried twenty-five crew who were rescued by people of the area. All the crew were citizens of the United States.

C.J. Payne, Captain
A. Boothroyd, Second Officer
Gregory Peter, Cook
Miguel Niclord, Able Seaman
Joseph Caboran, A.B.
Joseph Forres, A.B.
F.H. Osborne, Chief Engineer
J. McDonald, Third Engineer
W. Pike, Donkeyman
Toguro Longroad, Fireman
Albert Butz, Fireman
Andre Feodores, Fireman
David Osmond, Boy Apprentice

W.H. Phillips, Chief Officer
Alexander Windberg, Bosun
J. Searle, Steward
J. Jenkins, A.B.
J. Fergeraldo, A.B.
Hypolito Layian, A.B.
W.F. Robson, Second Engineer
J. Anthony, Fourth Engineer
S. Camerelina, Fireman
Joseph Romeo, Fireman
Louis Maryrim, Fireman
Stamp Scott, Boy Apprentice

Appendix E

Crew of *J.W. Wiscombe,* a five dory banker, who went to the Labrador fishing in 1962. On January 6, 1964, *J.W. Wiscombe* was wrecked at Point May. Information given by John Kelly, Marystown formerly of Mooring Cove.

Captain Albert Joyce, Burin Bay Arm
cook Jim Malloy, Marystown South
engineer Norman Hodder, Creston North
John Kelly, Mooring Cove
Arch Moore, Rushoon
George Norman, Rushoon
Dan Walsh, Marystown South
Len Fizzard, Creston North
Bernard Cheeseman, Shoal Point
Dick Kilfoy, Shoal Point
Michael Thomas Walsh, Marystown South
Kevin Brewer, Clattice Harbour
Cosimus "Cos" Farrell, Little Bay
Jim Barry, Spanish Room
Patrick Gaulton, Spanish Room

Author's collection

Not long after the hook and line fishery died out in the 1950-60s and the wooden schooners such as *J.W. Wiscombe* disappeared, vessels of another style, like the oil-drilling rig *Zapata Ugland*, appeared along Newfoundland's coast. *Zapata Ugland*, while undergoing re-fit and repair at the Marystown shipyard, is anchored off Mooring Cove, near Marystown, a town a generation previously saw sailing schooners moored in the harbour.

Sources of Major Sea Stories

S.S. *Sandbeach*	—	*Daily News*, December 7, 1932 and *Evening Telegram* December 23, 1932.
Ada Campbell	—	*Daily News* December 21, 1932.
Mindora	—	*Daily News* December 22, 1906
Francis Robie	—	Hackett, Joseph. *Heartbeat: Bay of Islands*. Corner Brook, 1992. *Evening Telegram* Nov. 14, 1946
W.E. Morrissey	—	*Daily News* February 26, 1911. *Evening Telegram* December 21, 1912.
Wimoda	—	*Daily News* April 27 and May 7, 1949.
Armistice	—	*Daily News* Jan. 1923; *Evening Telegram* June 1, 23
Stanley Parsons	—	*Daily News* December 13, 15, 21 and 22, 1932. *Evening Telegram* December 20, 1932. Personal conversation with Captain Michael Croke, St. John's (formerly of St. Brendan's) and with Ron Maye, Lewisporte (formerly of Lush's Bight). Guy, R.W. "One Hundred Years of Shipwrecks along the Straight Shore" in *Newfoundland Quarterly*, Vol. LXXIV, No. 2, Summer 1978.
Alma	—	*Outlook*, (Bay Roberts) week of December 3, 1907. and *Daily News* October 14 and 16, 1907.
Sydney Smith	—	Unidentified clipping in Newfoundland Historical Society Shipwreck files and from Southern Seamen's Museum (Herbert & Ruby).
Saucy Arethusa	—	*Daily News* November 13, 1929
Dorothy Baird	—	*Daily News* February 11 and March 8, 1930. *Clarenville Packet* December 4, 1980.
Francis P. Duke	—	*Evening Telegram* December 20, 1947. Personal conversation with George Combden, Fortune; Patrick Duke and Frank Bennett, St. John's.
Percy Wells	—	*Daily News* December 10, 1921 *Evening Telegram* December 12, 1921.
Rose M	—	*Evening Telegram*. September 1, 1922.
Mollie	—	Personal conversation with Abbott, Roland W., Musgrave Harbour, *Evening Telegram* December 22, 1944.
Mab	—	"Offbeat History" *Evening Telegram*, 1977.
Maxwell Corkum	—	*Evening Telegram* June 16, 1971. Personal conversation Capt. Ned Kean, St. John's.

Toukalou, Erema H	—	*Fisherman's Advocate* December 27, 1929. Personal conversation with Roland Abbott, Musgrave Harbour
Majestic	—	Unidentified clipping in shipwreck files, Newfoundland Historical Society (NHS).
Tishy, Athlete II	—	*Daily News* December 8 and 14, 1950.
Blue Blossom	—	*Daily News* and *Evening Telegram*, Nov. 15, 1920.
Nerette	—	*Daily News* November 10, 1919.
Cento	—	Unidentified clipping in shipwreck files, (NHS).
Albert J. Lutz	—	Unidentified clipping in shipwreck files, (NHS). Written correspondence from Harold Simms, Mass.
Effie M	—	Unidentified clipping in shipwreck files, (NHS).
Sperry	—	*Evening Telegram* May 29, 1907. *Cape Breton Post* May 27, 1907; Personal correspondence Rupert Morris, Trinity
Marion Rogers	—	*Evening Telegram* November 29, 1938. Personal conversation with Les Butler, Manuels
Edward VII	—	*Evening Telegram* December 22, 1933.
E.B. Phillips	—	*Evening Telegram* September 16 and 22, 1892.
C.A. Hubley	—	*Daily News* November 29, 1937. Written correspondence from Edith Burrage. Poem written by Mrs. William Hadden, 1898?
Catherine B	—	Janes, Ellis. "The Wreck of the *Catherine B*". In *Newfoundland Quarterly*, date undetermined. Personal correspondence with Mrs. Gertrude Pelley and Freeman Francis, Hant's Harbour. *Daily News* December 2, 1929.
Warren M. Colp	—	*Evening Telegram* December 16, 1930. *Daily News*, Dec. 16, 1930 and November 19, 1935. *Decks Awash* Vol. 10, No. 3, June 1981.
Maggie Bell	—	*Evening Telegram* September 12, 1966. Daily News November 10, 1913.
W.C. McKay	—	List of World War I Marine Casualties.
Czarina	—	*Daily News* December 31, 1923.
Freedom	—	*Daily News* December 4 and 12, 1924. *Decks Awash*, November 1982.
Maggie	—	Personal conversation Fred Handcock, Manuels. *Evening Telegram* November 7, 1896. Unidentified clipping in shipwreck files (NHS).
Phoebe	—	*Evening Telegram* November 13, 1909.

Red Gauntlet	—	*Evening Telegram* January 15, 1909.
Ruby W	—	Unidentified clipping in shipwreck files, (NHS). Letter by Captain Forward in *Daily News*, February 10, 1922.
Kinsman	—	*Daily News* January 4, 1922.
Evelyn(1924)	—	*Daily News* May 20, 1924. Horwood, Andrew *Newfoundland Ships and Men*. The Marine Researchers, St. John's, 1971.
Little Stephano & Cecil, Jr.	—	*Daily News* Jan.15, 1923; Ap. 21, 30; May 1, 1926. *Evening Telegram* "Offbeat History" Nov. 12, 1974. Personal conversation with Arch Stead, Catalina.
Cape Freels	—	Personal conversation with Les Buffett. *Daily News* March 12, 1976. *Evening Telegram* March 15, 1976.
Evelyn(1913)	—	*Evening Telegram* Jan. 9, 10, 11 and 13, 1913; May 20 and September 16, 1995. Personal conversation Bill Morry, Ferryland.
Gertie	—	*Evening Telegram* December 6, 1934
President Coaker	—	*Daily News* January 2, 1923; *Evening Advocate* Oct. 22, 1923; Feb. 1, 2, 4, 5, 1924; *Evening Telegram* Feb. 2, 4, 1924; *Weekly Advocate* Feb. 23, 1924.
A.B. Barteau	—	*Daily News* and *Evening Telegram* March 6, 1923.
Fond Return	—	*Evening Telegram* December ? and 24, 1910.
S.S. *Tolsby*		*Evening Telegram* January 18, 1908.
Jennie Barno	—	*Evening Telegram* August 18, 1960.
S.S. *Morien*	—	*Daily News* December 3, 1912 and October 2, 1922.
Clintonia	—	*Daily News* November 7, 1921. *Daily News* May 2, 1936 (*J.R. Rogers*)
Beatrice K	—	*Evening Telegram* November 4, 1921. Unidentified newspaper clipping of Dec. 17, 1924.
Joan Ellamae	—	*Halifax Chronicle Herald* May 3, 1957. *Daily News* September 21 and 23, 1955. (*Mont Murray*)
Minnie Pearl	—	*Evening Telegram* December 20, 1912. *Daily News* October 24, 1922 (Mariner).
Ontario	—	Unidentified clipping in shipwreck files (NHS).
Hubert Mack	—	Unidentified newspaper clipping headlined "Two Fishermen of Halifax".
Workman	—	Personal conversation with John Ben Anstey, Grand Bank and Eva (Anstey) Martin, St. John's. *Daily News* Feb. 8, 1923, and "Year End Report" December 31, 1923. Horwood, Andrew. "Some

		Ships and Men" in *The Book of Newfoundland.* Volume IV
Flirt	—	*Halifax Herald* March 16, 1937. Personal conversation with Gordon Weymouth, Grand Bank.
Wm S. McDonald	—	*New York Times* October 25, 1923.
Cape Bonnie	—	*Evening Telegram* February 22 and 23, 1967.
Iceland II, etc		*Cape Breton Post* February 24, 1967. *Halifax Chronicle Herald* February 27, 1967. Personal conversation Clayton Adams, Grand Bank.
Vogue	—	*Evening Telegram* December 3, 1921.
Florence Swyers	—	Unidentified clipping in shipwreck files (NHS).
Jean and Mona	—	*Post Record* (Cape Breton) September 14, 1951.
Inez G	—	*Halifax Herald* September 28, 1925. *Halifax Evening Mail* September 26, 1925. *Evening Telegram* October 13 and November 2, 1925
Mission Boat	—	Unidentified clipping dated Nov. 3, 1937. Written correspondence from Georgina Froats, Williamsburg, Ontario.
J.W. Wiscombe	—	Personal conversation with John Kelly, Marystown.

Index of Ships

A.B. Barteau 219
Ada E. Young 227
Adriatic 295
Albert J. Lutz 106
Alfred Booth 316
Alma 39
Amy B. Silver 188
Anna F & Mary P 246
Annie M. Parker 215
Antoinette 157
Antoine C. Santos 311
Ariceen 60
Armistice 25
Athlete II 33, 93
Beatrice K
(ex Bella G) 247
S.S. Bellaventure 206
Bernier 19
Betty & Molly 38
S.S. Beverley 317
Blue Blossom 97
C.A. Hubley 136
Camperdown 58
Cape Agulhas 34, 199, 311
Cape Bonavista
(ex A. Moulton) 295
Cape Bonnie 284
Cape Freels 199
Carranza 14
Catherine B 137
Catherine Mary Hann 260
Cecil, Jr. 193
Cento 101
Chesley R
(ex Maagan) 223
Clintonia (1921) 243
Clintonia (1923) 246
County of Richmond 62
Cora 117
Czarina 155
Daydream 30
Delawana II 263
Dolphin 40
Dora P. Lane 315
Dorothy Baird 51
Douglas H. Adams 59
D.P. Ingraham 231
Dunmore 248
E.B. Phillips 133
Edith Pardy 98
Erema H 81
Edmund B. Alexander 273
Edward VII 127
Effie M 111
Elizabeth Fearn 94, 171
S.S. Erna 177
S.S. Ethel 319
Ethel M. Petite 26, 245
S.S. Ethie 49
Eva U. Colp 280
Evelyn (1913) 205
Evelyn (1924) 189
Flirt 275
S.S. Florence 239
Florence Swyers 270, 295
S.S. Florizel 213
Fond Return 225
Francis P. Duke
(ex Alice Adams) 55
Francis Robie 13
Freda M 274
Freedom 159
General Byng 307
General Horne 62
George K 142
Gertie 209
Gladys P. Mosher 147
S.S. Glencoe 19, 94
Golden Hope 227
Gordon C 156
Grace Parsons 36
Harry and Ralph 36
Harry and Verna 191
Helen C. Morse 59
Henrietta 135
Henry L. Montague 106
Herbert and Ruby 48
Herbert L. Rawding 250
Herbert Warren 28
Hester Hankinson 163
S.S. Home 34
Hubert Mack 265
Hudson 203
Iceland II 284, 285
Ida Campbell 9
S.S. Illex 217
Inez G 303
Inger 257
Izetta 313
James Strong 32
Jean and Mary 61, 181
Jean and Mona 299
Jean Wakely 244
Jennie Barno 233
Jennie E. Ritcey 191
Jessie Beatrice 297
J.H. Blackmore 24
J.N. Rafuse 306
Joan Ellamae 251
John Millett
(ex General Jacobs) 131
John W. Miller 190
Josie and Phoebe 147
J.R. Rogers 245
Julia F 43
June 184
J.W. Wiscombe 324
S.S. Kyle 102
Kinsman 185
L.A. Dunton 300
Lake Simcoe 319
Landscape 57
Lillian M. Richard 29
Lilly 2
Little Princess 194
Little Stephano 193
Lloyd Jack 94
Mab 73
Maggie 165
Maggie Bell 149

Maggie G 72
Majestic 85
Maneco 33
Mark H. Gray 131
Marshall Frank 275, 302
Margaret K. Smith 297
Marguerite Ryan 115
Marie Yvonne 136
Mariner 257
Marion 98
Marion Rogers 121
Mary Ruth 161
Mary Ann Louis 261
Maureen and Michael 283
Maxwell R. Corkum 77
Metamora 280
Mindora 14
Minnie Pearl 255
Mintie 213
Miranda 19
Mission Boat 309
Misty Star 27
Mollie 69
Monica Hartery 131
Monica Walters 24, 126
Monitor 268
Mont Murray 253
S.S. Morien 237
Nedrill 175
Nerette 89
Neva Belle 69, 72, 183
Newfoundlander 21
Nina Beatrice 33
Nina Lee 269
Nina W. Corkum 30, 274
Nordica 248
Norma B. Strong 37
Norman W. Strong 37
Novelty 198
Olive Evans 314
Ontario 261
Palfrey
(ex Spencer II) 301
Pawnee 3
Passport 61, 91, 181
Pauline Lohnes 271
Percy Roy 179
Percy Wells 61
Pet 91
Phoebe 173
Polly and Robbie 283
Port Union 212
President Coaker 211
Progressive II 291
Raleigh 1
Red Gauntlet 177
Retraction 197
Revenue 105
S.S. Rosalind 130, 179
Rose M 65
Roy Bruce 249
Ruby W 181
Rupert Brand II 287
S.S. Sandbeach 3
Saucy Arethusa 48
Sidney Smith 45
Smuggler 109
S.S. Solway
(ex Meigle) 259
Sparkling Glance 27, 292
Spitfire 33
Sperry 115
St. Bernard 310
S.S. Stanhill 2
Stanley Parsons 31, 321
Stella 166
Teazer 24
Terra Nova 21, 24, 193
Theresa M. Gray 147
S.S. Tiber 166
Tishy
(ex Mollie Fearn) 93
S.S. Tolsby 229, 323
Toukalou 81
Trinity North 38
Vignette 15
S.S. Virginia Lake 117
Vogue 289
S.S. Walker 215
Walter G. Sweeney 58
Warren M. Colp 143
S.S. Watchful 97
Watagua 320
W.C. McKay 151
W.E. Morrissey 17
William Carson 252
William S. McDonald 279
Willing Lass 24
Wimoda 21
S.S. Wolfe 58
Workman 269
Zapata Ugland 325
Zaratoga 109
Zerda 254

Index of Towns

Argentia 252
Arnold's Cove 57
Badger's Quay 55, 77, 96
Bay de Nord 276
Barr'd Islands 57
Bay Bulls 226, 233
Bay of Islands 13, 17
Bear Cove, Witless Bay 135
Beaumont 29
Belleoram 38, 161 246, 292, 297, 310-311,
Bellburns 17
Big Barachoix 240
Bonavista 97, 101, 268
Boxey 279, 299
Bragg's Island 72
Brigus 97, 159, 126
British Harbour 58
Broad Cove 100
Brooklyn 165
Burdeaux Island 57
Burgeo 62, 107, 303
Burin 48, 191, 214, 215, 237, 248-249, 251, 239, 254, 255, 287
Burnt Point 144
Cabot Island 86
Calvert 209
Cape Broyle 107, 209
Cape Race 220, 223
Caplin Cove 61
Cappahayden 213
Carbonear 46, 91, 149, 155, 184, 189, 194, 198, 199, 205, 219
Carmanville 70, 82
Catalina 28, 101, 105, 197, 213, 270
Change Islands 47, 48, 107
Charlottetown 186, 295
Clattice Harbour 246
Coley's Point 58
Colinet 147
Colliers 3
Conche 40
Coomb's Cove 297, 300
Corner Brook 1, 3, 9
Crouse 149
Cupids 21, 147
Daniel's Cove 98
Deadman's Bay 36
Drook 229
Englee 25, 78, 98
English Harbour West 58, 189, 244, 161, 283, 289, 295, 300
Epworth 283
Fermeuse 217
Ferryland 205
Fischells 5
Flat Islands (B.B.) 183
Flower's Island 86, 193
Fogo 51, 55, 61
Forteau Bay 2
Fortune 57, 131, 159, 265, 269, 306
Freshwater 149
Garnish 14, 251, 253, 300
Gaultois 280
Grand Bank 40, 61, 62, 77, 77, 91, 98, 106, 117, 179, 223, 248, 269, 274, 280, 284, 315
Grate's Cove 69
Greenspond 55, 89, 142
Hant's Harbour 40, 133, 137
Harbour Breton 98, 271, 280, 283, 285, 289
Harbour Buffett 163, 188, 195, 244, 250
Harbour Grace 135, 155, 156, 317
Harbour Le Cou 311
Hare Bay 61
Harry's Harbour 30
Heart's Content 133
Heart's Delight 133
Heatherton 5
Herring Neck 143
Highlands 5, 13
Horwood 61
Horse Islands 58, 136
Ireland's Eye 213
Isle au Morts 313
Jamestown, B.B. 307
Jersey Harbour 271
Job's Cove 144
Keels 87
Kingwell 164
Lamaline 98, 257
Langdon's Cove 144
Lapoile 309
Lark Harbour 14
Lawn 261
Lethbridge 167
Little Bay Islands 31, 35, 59, 163
Little St. Lawrence 37
Lockston 116
Loo Cove 83
Lumsden 81
Lush's Bight 31, 321
Marystown 58, 95, 137, 245, 260, 324
McDougall's Gulch 313
McIvers 9
Merasheen 260
Molliers 276
Mooring Cove 325
Musgrave Harbour 72
New Bonaventure 123
New Chelsea 311
New Perlican 133, 136
Newtown 73
Norris Arm 27, 65
Old Perlican 92, 112
Parsons Harbour 276
Perry's Cove 149
Petley 126
Pilley's Island 94

Placentia 94, 171, 238, 301
Point Amour 1
Pool's Island 56, 94
Port Anson 38
Port aux Basques 178
Port Kerwan 217
Port Rexton 123, 213
Portugal Cove South 75, 229
Port Union 97, 106, 107, 211
Pushthrough 14
Ramea 62, 301, 256
Random 127
Random Island 173
Red Bay, Labrador 19
Red Island 248
Rencontre East 297
Renews 213
Round Harbour 143
Rushoon 203
Safe Harbour 33
Shambler's Cove 94
Ship Harbour 224
Shoe Cove 41
Silverdale 143
South East Bight 246
Spaniard's Bay 147
Spencer's Cove 56, 189
Springdale 24
St. Brendan's 94
St. Bride's 239-240
St. Fintan's 5
St. George's 5
St. John's 28, 95, 155, 165, 173, 175, 179, 181, 185, 189, 193, 196, 200, 219, 243, 245, 253, 269, 315, 317-320
St. Lawrence 233, 256, 264
St. Pierre 28, 66, 147, 233, 257, 311
St. Shott's 239
Three Arms 30, 43
Trepassey 209, 225, 233
Trinity, Bonavista Bay 22
Trinity, T. Bay 111, 115, 121, 230
Triton 42, 43
Trout River 20
Twillingate 45, 59, 60, 85, 153
Valleyfield 79, 96
Wesleyville 56, 85, 96, 189
West Point 309
Winterton 39, 133
Wood's Island 9, 18
Wreck House 313